Transcendence

Transcendence

On Self-Determination and Cosmopolitanism

Mitchell Aboulafia

Stanford University Press

Stanford, California

Stanford University Press
Stanford, California

© 2010 by the Board of Trustees of the Leland Stanford Junior University. All rights reserved.

No part of this book may be reproduced or transmitted in any form or by any means, electronic or mechanical, including photocopying and recording, or in any information storage or retrieval system without the prior written permission of Stanford University Press.

Printed in the United States of America on acid-free, archival-quality paper

Library of Congress Cataloging-in-Publication Data

Aboulafia, Mitchell.
 Transcendence : on self-determination and cosmopolitanism / Mitchell Aboulafia.
    p. cm.
 Includes bibliographical references and index.
 ISBN 978-0-8047-7019-4 (cloth : alk. paper) — ISBN 978-0-8047-7020-0 (pbk. : alk. paper)
  1. Autonomy (Philosophy) 2. Self (Philosophy) 3. Cosmopolitanism—Philosophy. 4. Transcendence (Philosophy) 5. Philosophy, Modern. I. Title.
 B808.67.A26 2010
 128—dc22
                            2010001787

Typeset by Bruce Lundquist in 10.9/13 Adobe Garamond

For Catherine Kemp

From so simple a beginning endless forms most beautiful and most wonderful have been, and are being, evolved.
—Charles Darwin

Contents

Acknowledgments ix

Introduction 1

PART ONE: TRANSCENDENCE AND SELF-DETERMINATION

1 Don't Fence Me In: Rorty and Sartre 13

2 On Freedom and Action: Dewey and Sartre 27

3 A (neo) American in Paris: Bourdieu and Mead 49

PART TWO: COSMOPOLITANISM AND TRANSCENDENCE

4 Mead on Cosmopolitanism, Sympathy, and War 71

5 W. E. B. Du Bois: Double-Consciousness, Jamesian Sympathy, and the Cosmopolitan 89

PART THREE: SOCIOLOGICAL AND PSYCHOLOGICAL CHALLENGES TO TRANSCENDENCE

6 Self-Concept in the New Sociology of Ideas: Reflections on Neil Gross's *Richard Rorty: The Making of an American Philosopher* 105

7 Eros and Self-Determination 124

8 What If Hegel's Master and Slave Were Women? 136

Notes	157
Bibliography	187
Index	193

Acknowledgments

Authors often find that it becomes more difficult to write an acknowledgment page the older they become. For an author's first book, the matter is rather straightforward. One typically thanks his or her parents, mentors, and perhaps a spouse or partner. But as the years roll on, one's history becomes deeper and carries with it an expanding network of debt, far too much to be repaid even modestly in the space of an acknowledgment page. Under these circumstances, the easiest route is to recognize those who are the "proximate causes" of one's latest work.

For support and encouragement, both intellectual and personal, I extend my gratitude to former colleagues in philosophy at Penn State, most of whom have moved on to other universities: Doug Anderson, Dan Conway, Véronique Fóti, Emily Grosholtz, Dale Jacquette, and Claire Katz. I would like to thank Joseph Esposito, Joseph Margolis, and Hilary Putnam for their advice and encouragement. Participants in my seminar "Mead on Sympathy and Cosmopolitanism" at the Society for the Advancement of American Philosophy's "Summer Institute (2008)" offered their insights and learning, for which I am grateful. For the past four years I have had the good fortune to be affiliated with The Juilliard School, which has not only surrounded me with incomparable art but made me a three-time winner: great colleagues, gifted students, and an administration and staff that have been extraordinarily supportive. In Juilliard's administration, I would like to single out for a word of thanks President Joseph W. Polisi, Provost Ara Guzelimian, Dean Karen Wagner, and Dean Emeritus Stephen Clapp. My colleagues in Interdivisional Liberal Arts have been enthusiastic partners as we have sought to reimagine and develop the liberal arts program at Juilliard. I would like to take this opportunity to acknowledge my gratitude to Lisa Andersen, Renée Marie Baron, Greta Berman, Anthony Lioi, Michael Maione, Anita Mercier, Roger W. Oliver, Ron Price, Gonzalo J. Sánchez, Jo Sarzotti, and Harold Slamovitz. My editor at Stanford, Emily-Jane Cohen, has been as insightful as she has been a pleasure to work with. Many thanks. At Stanford I also wish to thank Carolyn Brown and Cynthia Lindlof for their helpful suggestions. This book is dedicated to my wife, Catherine Kemp. I am blessed to have her as a companion (and comrade-in-arms). She means more to me than I can express.

Transcendence

Introduction

> As a matter of fact, the pragmatic theory of intelligence means that the function of mind is to project new and more complex ends—to free experience from routine and from caprice. . . . [T]he doctrine that intelligence develops within the sphere of action for the sake of possibilities not yet given is the opposite of a doctrine of mechanical efficiency. . . . [A]ction directed to ends to which the agent has not previously been attached inevitably carries with it a quickened and enlarged spirit. A pragmatic intelligence is a creative intelligence, not a routine mechanic.
> —John Dewey, "The Need for a Recovery of Philosophy"

In the modern world there has been an increasing expectation that individuals, in virtue of being persons, have a right to determine the course of their own lives. Indeed, one of the remarkable achievements of modernity is the widespread ideal that not only individuals but peoples, nations, and states have a "right" to self-determination. A pivotal figure here is Johann Gottfried von Herder, who managed to transfer Pietist beliefs regarding the sanctity of individuals to cultures.[1]

> In all the civil establishments from China to Rome, in all the varieties of their political constitutions, in every one of their inventions, whether of peace or war, and even in all the faults and barbarities that nations have committed, we discern the grand law of nature: let man be man; let him mould his condition according as to himself shall seem best. . . . Thus we every where find mankind possessing and exercising the right of forming themselves to a kind of humanity, as soon as they have discerned it.[2]

Transcendence: On Self-Determination and Cosmopolitanism accepts the modern ideal that individuals and peoples are entitled to define and develop themselves.[3] This is not to say that modern Westerners were the first to treat peoples of other lands with a degree of acceptance and respect, for of course they were not.[4] It is to say that the combination of ideas expressed by Herder in his less parochial moments—that peoples are fundamentally equal and worthy of respect, as are individuals, and are entitled to define and develop themselves as they think best—is not a combination that has found systematic and enduring expression before the modern world. Of course, this set of "entitlements" has met with resistance (apartheid and Jim Crow are not that far behind us), and various forms of Western imperialism belie these sentiments. Further, there are those who would argue that the notion of a "people" is itself problematic, and becoming more so daily as globalization increases. For the goals of this book, however, it is sufficient to acknowledge that different cultures and peoples exist, even if their compass and exact "natures" are contested.[5]

For several years I have been writing on two topics that may not seem to be related: the self-determination of individuals, which entails a capacity for existential choice, and cosmopolitanism, which entails an openness to transcultural social interaction. Individual self-determination deals with subjects insofar as they make choices that help shape who they are and how they define themselves. Cosmopolitanism appears to deal with individuals who have developed a sense of being "world citizens." However, as they stand, both of these delineations are inadequate. Subjects are not simply free to make any choices that they wish, and cosmopolitans are not necessarily rootless souls who have escaped their childhood cultures to dwell in the empyrean of a world community. A cosmopolitan may be someone who has developed a deep respect for the integrity and worth of different cultures while remaining attached to his or her own culture. Even as cosmopolitans we never entirely leave our "family" of origin as we find ways to accept, respect, and share the experiences of those with different roots.

In two earlier books, *The Mediating Self* and *The Cosmopolitan Self*, I developed a theory of *individual* self-determination and applied it to a form of cosmopolitanism that is primarily moral, psychological, and sociological, as opposed to economic.[6] Both of these works addressed the ideas of George Herbert Mead—in particular, his concepts of the social self, the significant symbol, the generalized other, spontaneity, emergence, novelty, and "sociality"[7]—in order to explain how the capacity for individual self-determination emerges, both ontogenetically and phylogenetically. I argued for a concept of freedom that does not appeal to inveterate notions of free will but instead relies on anticipatory experience, prereflective consciousness, and deliberation. In this book I build on these earlier works by drawing on a variety of philosophical orientations, for example, Scottish theories of sentiment, pragmatism, and existentialism. I defend an approach to self and society that shows how transcendence and self-formation are possible in spite of the weight of circumstance. "Transcendence" in this work denotes a supersession of the given, the accepted, the familiar, or the weight of circumstance. I offer a cosmopolitanism that makes room for both tradition and transcendence and that is once again primarily moral, psychological, and sociological.

Although the self-determination of individuals involves transcendence, as does a cosmopolitan sensibility, a people, no doubt, may prefer not to view their identity in terms of transcendence. Their identity as a people may require that they resist forms of "internal" transcendence as well as "external" interventions in their culture. The cosmopolitanism addressed in this book is sensitive to self-determination in this cultural sense. It respects cultural pluralism and distinguishes between individual and cultural self-determination. However, the conviction that individual self-determination is irreconcilably at odds with cultural self-determination is challenged. A developed capacity for personal self-determination can, for example, help generate support for the self-determination of other individuals and peoples. This is not to say that those committed to resisting the intrusion of cultures they view as alien will be satisfied with the model developed here. People, individually and collectively, will differ regarding just how much "transcendence" and self-determination are acceptable.

The goals of *Transcendence* are threefold: (1) to demonstrate the relevance of the concept of transcendence to credible notions of individual self-determination and cosmopolitanism; (2) to articulate a cosmopolitan sensibility that is attuned to cultural diversity and individual self-determination; and (3) to address conceptual affinities between philosophers from both sides of the Atlantic by examining the idea of transcendence.

Charles Taylor has contributed to our understanding of how cultural self-determination can be related to individual self-determination through his work on expressivism, which helps to bridge the apparent divide between a cosmopolitanism that is sensitive to cultural self-determination and the self-determination of individuals. For Taylor, expressivism supports the notion that individuals and cultures possess natures that are realized and defined only through their expression. Both cultures and individuals are seen as having a need and a "right" to express themselves. They can be treated as homologous by the expressivist because of the relationship between the viability of a culture and the capability of its members to have meaningful personal narratives.[8] They also bear comparison because a denial of "expression" limits self and cultural development. In terms of individual expression, which can be, mutatis mutandis, transferred to cultures, Taylor asserts,

> My claim is that the idea of nature as an intrinsic source goes along with an expressive view of human life. Fulfilling my nature means espousing the inner élan, the voice or impulse. And this makes what was hidden manifest for both myself and others. But this manifestation also helps to define what is to be realized. The direction of this élan wasn't and couldn't be clear prior to this manifestation. In realizing my nature, I have to define it in the sense of giving it some formulation; but this is also a definition in a stronger sense: I am realizing this formulation and thus giving my life a definitive shape. *A human life is seen as manifesting a potential which is also being shaped by this manifestation*; it is not just a matter of copying an external model or carrying out an already determinate formulation.[9]

Taylor's comments contain two important implications that are often conflated: we have inner natures that require expression; and in order to become ourselves, we must express ourselves. It is possible to subscribe to the latter statement without acceding to the former, and this is precisely the option that existentialists have been known to take, although it is not the one that Taylor selects in this passage. For the existentialist, we become who we are through our actions and choices, not because we have an inner nature that requires defining.[10] In other words, it is possible to be an expressivist without being an essentialist.

For Herder, on the other hand, the accent is placed on a people's unique nature or essence, which is realized as it expresses itself. A people, a *Volk*, should be allowed to develop at its own pace and in its own territory. Outside influences should not be allowed to taint a culture.[11] Herder's "cosmopolitan" would support the segregation of cultures, not their transcendence, in order to respect their unique identities. If one accepts Herder's assumption that self-determination is a matter of singular potentialities (personal or cultural) that are simply in need of expression, then a cosmopolitanism that entails transcendence will appear misguided.[12] I do not accept this assumption. The challenge in our times is to pursue a cosmopolitanism that is neither exclusionary (in respecting identity) nor crudely universal. If this challenge is met, although it may seem paradoxical, cosmopolitans will respect local cultures, the transcultural, and the "universal"; that is to say, they will recognize the importance of place and of transcendence.

However, the story presented in this book does not dismiss the notion of inherent potentialities. For example, it recognizes that differences in physiology, which may influence temperament, play a significant role in determining who we are and who we might become as individuals. We do not simply "transcend" such factors as if by magic. But what we have the capacity to do, which is woven into the "nature" of the self, is to transcend our given circumstances in various ways and thereby transform ourselves. One of the most obvious ways that we can accomplish this is related to our capacity to anticipate and deliberate about alternative courses of action and then to select a course. In so doing we not only transcend our circumstances but engage in a process of self-determination. I argue that the capacity for deliberation and choice are not mysterious. They are in fact features of the social development of the self.

One of the underlying assumptions of *Transcendence* is that Hegel's urtext on recognition, the master-slave dialectic in *The Phenomenology of Spirit*, sets the stage for demonstrating the extent to which selves are social and how they depend on others and social arrangements for their development. But Hegel's account is embedded in a set of claims about Spirit's self-development, and the pre-Darwinian framework of his system limits the extent to which social-psychological insights generated by pragmatism and later schools of thought can be brought to bear on questions of transcendence. So in spite of the fact that Hegel's dialectic can be read as a mode of thought that capitalizes on the mind's capacity for transcendence, and that Taylor reads him as perhaps the most influential expressivist, Hegel's dialectic of recognition will need considerable updating if it is going to be of assistance in linking individual self-determination with cultural or group self-determination. George Herbert Mead's thought—specifically, his account of the social development of the self—provides just such an updating. Mead should be read as a neo-Hegelian, and if he is read in this light, the relationship between individual self-determination, cultural self-determination, and cosmopolitanism becomes reasonably transparent. Mead demonstrates how individuals develop cognitive selves through learned behaviors and through action—first and foremost, through communicative action. It is through communication, especially through the development of language, that cognitive selves first arise, and they continue to change through ongoing interaction.

In *Transcendence* I offer an alternative to the ways that Herder and Hegel think about self-determination. Herder's expressivism involves an essentializing of social roles and peoples in an uncritical fashion. And neither Hegel nor Herder supplies a sufficiently genetic account of how symbolic expression helps to develop the self in a manner that makes individual and cultural self-determination possible. I address these deficiencies not only by engaging Mead but by examining thinkers from both Europe and the United States for whom there is a set of concerns that revolves around notions of transcendence. I draw primarily, but by no means exclusively, on two traditions, pragmatism and existentialism. These traditions are uniquely positioned to help demonstrate how transcendence is a feature of individual and cultural self-determination, as well as cosmopolitanism. However, given that I am drawing on a range of thinkers, the term "transcendence" does not have a univocal meaning in this book, although there is a family resemblance among its uses. In light of this variety, a few words are called for about avenues for addressing transcendence.

When we think of transcendence in a philosophical context, one notion that readily comes to mind was made famous by Jean-Paul Sartre in the middle of the last century. "Transcendence" is a term that he uses to describe the way in which human beings are not confined to the given, to the *en-soi* (in-itself), to facticity. As a matter of fact, Sartre at times refers to the *pour-soi* (for-itself), the human being, simply as a "transcendence." We are not confined to the past, to what we have been, because of the spontaneity of consciousness and the manner in which our projects are directed toward future activity. In an early work, *The Transcendence of the Ego*, Sartre tells us,

> Transcendental consciousness is an impersonal spontaneity. It determines its existence at each moment, without anything *before* it being conceivable. Thus each moment of our conscious life reveals to us a creation *ex nihilo*. Not a new *arrangement*, but a new existence. There is something anguishing for each of us, to experience directly this tireless creation of an existence of which *we* are not the creators. At this level man has the impression of ceaselessly escaping

from himself, of overflowing himself, of an abundance always unexpected taking him by surprise. And he saddles the unconscious with the task of accounting for this transcending of the Me by consciousness. The Me cannot in fact cope with this spontaneity, for *the will is an object which itself is constituted for and by this spontaneity*.[13]

This level of existential freedom proves to be indefensible, as Sartre himself acknowledges in later works (although he never abandons the notion of the project and a commitment to forms of transcendence). The fact is that as members of social groups and cultures we do seem to be "confined" in various ways to the given, to cultural assumptions and roles that we inherit, which appear to determine how we behave and think. These roles not only define who we are within a culture but also are the spectacles through which we observe and comment on cultures that are not our own.

In *Radical Hope*, Jonathan Lear addresses the power of socialization and succinctly summarizes the ways in which we define ourselves in terms of roles and cultural ideals when we live in a flourishing culture. The backdrop for Lear's comments is the devastation experienced by the Crow when activities central to their culture, for example, the use of the coupstick in battle to mark territory, were no longer possible.

If we consider a vibrant culture, it is possible to distinguish:

1. *Established social roles.* These will include socially sanctioned forms of marriage, sexual reproduction, family, and clan; standard social positions such as warrior, squaw, medicine man, and chief; ceremonial rituals; and so on.
2. *Standards of excellence associated with these roles.* These give us a sense of a culture's own ideals: what it would be, say, to be really outstanding *as a chief, as a squaw, as a warrior, as a medicine man.*
3. *The possibility of constituting oneself as a certain sort of person—namely, one who embodies those ideals.* I shall call such a person a *Crow Subject.* This is what young Plenty Coups aspired to: to be a chief, to be outstanding as chief, and thus to be a living embodiment of what it was to be a Crow.[14]

Lear's categorization of social roles in Crow culture helps raise a question that is central to this book, namely, if the axial nature of roles and ideals in societies is provisionally accepted, then how are we to understand possibilities for transcendence?[15] More specifically, in what ways have a variety of modern, primarily twentieth-century, philosophers—in spite of the obvious plausibility of Lear's portrayal of roles and standards that are important in flourishing cultures—sought to address the transcendence of roles within a culture and the boundaries between cultures? How do these thinkers understand possibilities for transcendence that undermine the central importance of Lear's third point regarding specific cultural ideals, which appear to be parochial? One of the goals of this book is to show how it is possible to respect the reality of acculturation and processes of socialization *and* maintain a commitment to existential choice, which involves a form of transcendence.[16]

It's worth noting that the culture Lear is describing would be viewed by Max Weber as a traditional one, that is, a culture *not* characterized by bureaucratic, technological, and goal-based rationality but one in which timeless values and long-standing customs are fundamental. Yet even members of such traditional societies have traveled and experienced cultural differences. If exposure to different cultures, and an appreciation for the horizons of one's own, is all that is meant by cosmopolitanism, it would be safe to say that forms of cosmopolitanism have existed throughout recorded history.[17] But the specific form of cosmopolitanism that I explore in this work entails a basic respect for peoples and cultures that are not one's own and a receptivity to the experiences of different peoples. In other words, this form of cosmopolitanism involves transcendence of the familiar. Again, I take this constellation of attitudes to be a relatively recent historical phenomenon, not more than a few centuries old at best.[18] However, I do not discuss the *historical* development and impact of expressivism and cosmopolitanism. The same is true regarding notions of existential choice and self-determination. My goal is to clarify how individual self-determination is possible through articulating the role(s) of transcendence in this process. To say this is not to deny the weight of habit, custom, temperament, and circumstance. It is to claim that individuals are capable of helping to define their own narratives and select courses of action that are dependent on their deliberations and choices.

The book is organized into three main sections. Part 1 offers an approach to individual self-determination that weighs the influence of community and habit, setting the stage for a discussion of cultural self-determination and cosmopolitanism in Part 2, which in turn lays the groundwork for challenges to notions of self-determination and cosmopolitanism in Part 3. Although the earlier chapters prepare the way for later ones, *Transcendence* does not offer a seamless argument that moves from self-determination to cosmopolitanism and then to constructive criticism. Rather, the central themes of the book are interwoven within and among the chapters, with each part offering a series of perspectives on aspects of self and society.

Chapter 1 sketches two approaches to existential freedom and transcendence, one emphasizing consciousness (Sartre) and the other, language (Rorty). This is the most unalloyed statement of the existentialist position on freedom and transcendence in the book. The limitations of equating "existential freedom" with individual self-determination are addressed in Chapter 2 by delving into how "freedom" should be understood if habit, reflection, and deliberation are given their due. This chapter complements Sartre's existentialism with Dewey's pragmatism. Chapter 3 continues to address pragmatism's contribution to our understanding of individual self-determination—this time with the assistance of Mead—through demonstrating the dangers of conceding too much to the sociological. This chapter also discusses concepts—for example, novelty, role-taking, the generalized other, and sociality—that play an important role in the model of cosmopolitanism developed in Part 2.

Part 2 addresses the relationship between individual and cultural self-determination. Specifically, Chapter 4 develops a model of cosmopolitanism that respects sympathetic attachments to kin and countrymen while sustaining the possibility of being a world citizen. The ideas articulated in this chapter draw on insights regarding self-development and self-determination that were addressed in Part 1 and augments them with insights from Mead's later work. Chapter 5 extends the discussion of cosmopolitanism by using Du Bois's reflections on culture, race, and double-consciousness to support and to raise difficulties for the model developed in Chapter 4, in part by drawing on the Scottish Enlightenment and Hegel. These difficulties are by no means insuperable but must be addressed, and they are highlighted by the trials of the "Color Line."

Part 3 further explores cosmopolitan sensibilities and self-determination through insights and challenges stemming from (1) the sociology of ideas and sociological determinism, (2) the relationship of the instinctual to psychological development, and (3) the psychology and sociology of gender. Chapter 6 discusses the strengths and weakness of Neil Gross's new sociology of ideas and his approach to strategic action and the concept of self. In developing his sociology of ideas, Gross uses Richard Rorty as a case study to support his theory, and this brings Rorty back into the discussion both as an object of study and as a potential critic of an overly socialized conception of human beings. In the last two chapters, Hegel—whose account of recognition stands behind many of the insights of *Transcendence* but who has thus far remained mostly offstage—comes explicitly to the fore. Chapter 7 addresses Herbert Marcuse's struggle not to let the instinctual undermine possibilities for self-determination and a "free civilization." It clarifies and augments Marcuse's argument by appealing to Hegel's dialectic of limit, the concept of determinate choice, as well as to a version of Sartre's notion of "the project." Chapter 8 turns to Hegel's urtext on the master and slave. It discusses gender inequities and their impact on self-determination, differences between Hegel's dialectic of recognition and Mead's concept of the social self, and how the "biological," in certain circumstances, can serve as a mode of transcendence. A discussion of self-determination and cosmopolitanism in the context of recent American politics, focusing on Barack Obama as a philosophical pragmatist, can be found in an Afterword to *Transcendence* on the Stanford University Press website, www.sup.org.

Part I
Transcendence and Self-Determination

§1 Don't Fence Me In
Rorty and Sartre

> The notion of an unclouded Mirror of Nature is the notion of a mirror which would be indistinguishable from what was mirrored, and thus would not be a mirror at all. The notion of a human being whose mind is such an unclouded mirror, and who *knows* this, is the image, as Sartre says, of God. Such a being does *not* confront something alien which makes it necessary for him to choose an attitude toward, or a description of, it. He would have no need and no ability to choose actions or descriptions.
>
> —Richard Rorty, *Philosophy and the Mirror of Nature*

If we accept Jürgen Habermas's contrast between philosophies of consciousness and those that arose after the linguistic turn, then Sartre's work must be viewed as mired in the nineteenth and early twentieth centuries. As a philosopher committed to the centrality of language, Rorty would appear to have little in common with Sartre, the quintessential philosopher of consciousness. However, if we follow an insight attributed to Hannah Arendt, that what a philosopher fears most reveals something fundamental about the philosopher's thought, then Sartre and Rorty have more in common than one might expect. Both fear that our capacity for transcendence—for going beyond the given, the accepted, the posited, or the familiar (without appealing to a deity)—can be thwarted by misplaced beliefs and convictions. This shared fear would be of little consequence if it remained at this level of generality, but as we will see, both Sartre and Rorty are committed to versions of existential choice that address their shared concern. Through highlighting similarities between these thinkers, this chapter sketches an "existentialist" account of transcendence that, as noted in the Introduction, sets the stage for a more developed account of self-determination in the chapters ahead. This is, of course, not to say that there aren't substantial differences between Sartre and Rorty, and an important one will be addressed near the end of this chapter.

Rorty illuminates his affinities to the early Sartre near the close of *Philosophy and the Mirror of Nature* (hereafter cited as *PMN*). In the book's introduction Rorty notes that he will be using "some ideas drawn from Gadamer and Sartre to develop a contrast between 'systematic' and 'edifying' philosophy, and to show how 'abnormal' philosophy which does not conform to the traditional Cartesian-Kantian matrix is related to 'normal' philosophy" (*PMN*, 11). For Rorty, Sartre is an "edifying" philosopher, and he defends philosophers of this stripe against those who view philosophy systemically or through the narrow lens of analytic epistemology. In the third part of *Mirror of Nature*, which is the focus of this chapter, Rorty discusses ideas and themes that he develops in his later writings, especially the notion of philosophy as a conversation. And he addresses these ideas in a manner that binds them to his interpretation of existentialism. Rorty cites Heidegger and Sartre multiple times in the closing pages of *Mirror of Nature*, and he invokes Sartre's distinction between the *pour-soi* and the *en-soi* at key junctures.

Given the wide number of claims associated with the early Sartre, for the purpose of comparing him to Rorty, I will simply assert that Sartre's existentialism entails the following ten claims: (1) existence precedes essence; (2) human beings do not have a fixed essence or nature; (3) the *en-soi* and the *pour-soi* are fundamental dimensions of our being-in-the-world; (4) there is no transcendental ego; (5) consciousness is spontaneous and free; (6) the self/consciousness can be objectified and reified; (7) we can deceive ourselves about freedom, so bad faith remains a permanent possibility; (8) philosophical and scientific determinisms mislead us about the human condition; (9) others can and do seek to define and limit us; and (10) the individual has projects, and these projects help "define" the self.[1]

The list could go on, but these points will serve the ends of this chapter, which seeks to sketch similarities between these thinkers, ones that have often been overlooked, from the vantage point of Rorty's claims in *Mirror of Nature*. From this perspective, it is clear that Rorty would only completely reject number 5. He would accept the others as they stand or with modifications that reframe them in a manner congenial with his linguistic turn. If we bear in mind that each philosopher endorses transcendence in ways related to these points, their (limited) kinship will become apparent.

A caveat is in order. I appeal to Rorty's interpretation of Sartre even though his gloss on Sartre's ideas is bound to make scholars of the latter's work wince. There are few specialists who have not disputed Rorty's "strong" readings of figures in the tradition. He appears to pick and choose what he finds appealing in philosophers and, even while distorting their views, insists that his interpretations are legitimate. It's important to bear in mind that Rorty is well aware of what he is up to. Crispin Sartwell tells the following story about this facet of Rorty's self-understanding.

> Richard Rorty was my teacher and dissertation supervisor at the University of Virginia in the 1980s. One semester he taught a course that was focused around the classic book *Truth and Method* by Hans-Georg Gadamer. Rorty and Gadamer were friends, though Gadamer was a very old man at that point. At any rate, late in the semester Gadamer appeared in our seminar. Rorty introduced him by recapitulating the interpretation of *Truth and Method* that had been mounted in the previous weeks. As Rorty spoke, Gadamer just shook his big, eminent, bereted head. When the introduction was over, Gadamer said, in German-accented English, "But Dick, you've got me all wrong." Rorty gave the grin and shrug and said "yes, Hans. But that's what you should have said."[2]

Rorty took delight in being a provocateur, and this delight was related to Rorty's personal and philosophical distaste for fixed categories that trump one's potential for redescription and self-transformation. I mention his enjoyment of playing the gadfly not to reduce Rorty's work to his psychology but to highlight how the person and his philosophy were more in tune than many have suspected. As we shall see, Rorty is quite explicit in *Mirror of Nature* about how the *pour-soi* must not be reduced to the *en-soi*.[3] This turns out to be a thread that runs throughout his later thinking, although its Sartrean version is most explicitly developed at the close of *Mirror of Nature*. (I would even venture to suggest, but will not defend here, that his "strong" readings of others can be interpreted in part as a way of avoiding "the look" of the other, that is, the circumscription of the self by the other. Rorty sought to look through Sartre's famous keyhole and shrug off—by literally giving the well-known Rortyan grin and shrug—anyone seeking to define him in his act of defining the other.) In spite of his seeming irresponsibility regarding the work of other thinkers, he was consistent about his desire to remain in conversation with them, even as he distorted their words. It is telling that he managed to remain good friends with so many of those whom he criticized or got wrong, for example, Hilary Putnam, Hans-Georg Gadamer, and Jürgen Habermas. So I am giving Rorty the benefit of the doubt. He doesn't have to get Sartre (exactly) right to be involved in an interesting conversation with him.

Before beginning the conversation, I want to relate an exchange that I had with Rorty. It may provide modest insight into the philosopher's development and reveal why a comparison with Sartre is worth pursuing. In the mid-1990s I invited Rorty to lecture at campuses of the University of Colorado. At dinner with several colleagues, we talked about the philosophical works that had first inspired us. Given his background in analytic philosophy, and the commonly held assumption that he came to continental philosophy only after his analytic training, Rorty's answer proved surprising.[4] Rorty noted that as a teenager his first philosophical passions were Hegel and Nietzsche, specifically, Hegel's *Phenomenology of Spirit*. (I don't recall him mentioning a particular text by Nietzsche.)

Considering the appeal that Dewey's left-Hegelianism would eventually have for Rorty, Hegel certainly makes sense as an early source of inspiration. Further, the Hegel of the *Phenomenology* is especially appropriate as a source of inspiration in terms of the notion of self-transformation through redescription that looms so large in Rorty's corpus. What the mature Rorty most admired about Hegel is his extraordinary ability to interpret and redefine the ways in which people have viewed themselves. In this sense, the *Phenomenology* is a work of continual transcendence, a transcendence in immanence, from one form of consciousness to the next, within the confines of human history. Of course, Rorty does not talk about "forms of consciousness." He speaks of language games or different types of discourse. But these are sources of transcendence for him, as we shall see. In Sartre's terms, they allow us to generate new stories about the self, new objectifications that can in turn be transcended. Although one needs to be cautious in speculating about whether youthful interests remain consequential, there is little doubt that Hegel remained a sustaining presence. One can also make the argument, although I won't develop it here, that Rorty found ways to use tools he drew from the analytic tradition to realize Nietzschean insights about the importance of "grammar" and language in defining ourselves. Further, Nietzsche's notion of self-overcoming, sans the metaphysics of the "will to power," is present in Rorty's mature thought, if only in the form of the strong poet as an agent of self- and social transformation.[5]

What then is the connection between these anecdotal remarks and Rorty's relationship to Sartre, specifically, the early Sartre whom he addresses in *Mirror of Nature*? Both Nietzsche and Sartre are invoked as exemplars of the edifying approach toward philosophy that Rorty endorses.[6]

> There are great philosophers who dread the thought that their vocabulary should ever be institutionalized, or that their writing might be seen as commensurable with the tradition. . . . The later Wittgenstein and the later Heidegger (like Kierkegaard and Nietzsche) are of the latter sort. . . . Great edifying philosophers are reactive and offer satires, parodies, aphorisms. They know their work loses its point when the period they were reacting against is over. They are *intentionally* peripheral. Great systematic philosophers, like great scientists, build for eternity. Great edifying philosophers destroy for the sake of their own generation. . . . Edifying philosophers want to keep space open for the sense of wonder . . . wonder that there is something new under the sun. (*PMN*, 369)

As opposed to those who build systems for eternity, those who engage in edification are involved in a form of *Bildung*. "Since 'education' sounds a bit too flat, and *Bildung* a bit too foreign, I shall use 'edification' to stand for this project of finding new, better, more interesting, more fruitful ways of speaking" (*PMN*, 360). Although some thinkers may seek to have their discourse normalized, that is, become the prevailing discourse, "edifying discourse is *supposed* to be abnormal, to take us out of our old selves by the power of strangeness, to aid us in becoming new beings" (360). Rorty is referring here to the distinction between normal and abnormal discourse, "a distinction which generalizes Kuhn's distinction between 'normal' and 'revolutionary' science" (320). Rorty develops this parallel by noting that *consensus*, which is typically found in "normal science," is also found in other types of discourse, including philosophy. He cautions us that the distinction between normal and revolutionary philosophers is not identical to the one between systematic and edifying philosophers; it is possible to be a revolutionary systematic philosopher, who remains committed to objective truth and accurate representations, or a revolutionary edifying philosopher. The revolutionary systematic philosopher ultimately seeks to establish a new school and to have his or her thought institutionalized (369–370). The edifying philosopher is committed to a creative abnormal discourse that breaks entrenched patterns and disciplines, that allows us to describe ourselves in new, and hopefully, more interesting ways. Rorty views existentialism, which falls for him within the "tradition" of edifying discourse, as "reactive." "To adopt the 'existentialist' attitude toward objectivity and rationality common to Sartre, Heidegger, and Gadamer, makes sense only if we do so in a conscious departure from a well-understood norm. 'Existentialism' is an *intrinsically reactive* movement of thought, one which has point only in opposition to the tradition" (366).

For the sake of argument, let's assume that one of the primary motives behind Rorty's work is to help prevent people from believing that they are limited to normal discourse, for this belief circumscribes the scope of human achievement by casting the net of ahistoricism and essentialism over human actors. For Rorty, it should be noted, abnormal discourse is parasitic on normal discourse. The "new" arises in reaction to the accepted, the given, the habitual. This is a relatively old theme in pragmatism. The notion of novelty is central to all of the major classical pragmatists—Charles Peirce, William James, George Herbert Mead, and John Dewey—and the stability of the habitual is viewed as the condition for the possibility of novel responses.[7] If one wanted to place a gloss on the relationship between these terms, one might be inclined to say that normal discourse is Rorty's linguistic nomenclature for what the pragmatists would have labeled the habitual, whereas abnormal discourse corresponds to the novel. For Rorty, however, there is no metaphysical reason why we must have both normal and abnormal discourses, but this has in fact been the case in recorded human history. Yet whether one views novelty in metaphysical terms or not, Rorty and pragmatists typically prize it.[8]

Rorty treats Sartre's *en-soi* as the given of normal discourse. The *pour-soi* is aligned with abnormal discourse, and Rorty claims that we have a "sense of ourselves as *pour-soi*, as capable of reflection, as choosers of alternative vocabularies" (*PMN*, 379).[9] The comparison between the *pour-soi* and the chooser of alternative vocabularies is not an accident. At minimum, both are ways of describing actors who are capable of transcendence. Further,

Sartre's contrast between the *pour-soi* and the *en-soi* can be used to illuminate Rorty's view that the discursive is a necessary condition for choice and responsibility: "If we could convert knowledge from something discursive, something attained by continual adjustments of ideas or words, into something as ineluctable as being shoved about, or being transfixed by a sight which leaves us speechless, then we should no longer have the responsibility for choice among competing ideas and words, theories and vocabularies. This attempt to slough off responsibility is what Sartre describes as the attempt to turn oneself into a thing—into an *êntre-en-soi*" (375–376). Here we have an explicit connection between Sartre's notion of responsibility, the *en-soi*, and Rorty's commitment to language as a source of transcendence. There can be no responsibility (for defining oneself, for example) if knowledge is ineluctable and the "adjustments of ideas or words" are stillborn. Discursive knowledge allows one to avoid being transformed into an in-itself, which is incapable of responsibility. As long as discursive knowledge exists, transcendence is possible.

Rorty's commitment to transcendence is also found in one of his most well-known distinctions, that between philosophers who aim at truth through *inquiry* and those who engage in *conversation*. This distinction parallels the one between systematic and edifying philosophy, that is, philosophies that claim to be objective and transhistorical and philosophies that acknowledge their historicity and contingency. "The difference between conversation and inquiry parallels Sartre's distinction between thinking of oneself as *pour-soi* and as *en-soi*, and thus that the cultural role of the edifying philosopher is to help us avoid the self-deception which comes from believing that we know ourselves by knowing a set of objective facts" (*PMN*, 373).

Rorty will go on to criticize Sartre, at least indirectly, for suggesting that there may be a metaphysical difference between the *en-soi* and the *pour-soi*. Nonetheless, both Rorty and Sartre find the notion of a self that possesses an essence unacceptable. (A complement to this claim is their criticism of transcendental approaches that argue that the ego should be viewed as a priori.) The objectification of the self in terms of a set of fixed deterministic categories is a form of self-deception for both Sartre and Rorty. There is no privileged description of the self that is not subject to revision for both thinkers. Nor is there one right way of describing "reality" for the early Sartre and Rorty. In Sartre's terms, our descriptions are inevitably linked to the values that we hold, and the values that we hold are not fixed. In

Rorty's interpretation of Sartre, "The notion of 'one right way of describing and explaining reality' supposedly contained in our 'intuition' about the meaning of 'true' is, for Sartre, just the notion of having a way of describing and explaining *imposed* on us in that brute way in which stones impinge on our feet.... From Sartre's point of view, the urge to find such necessities [logical or physical] is the urge to be rid of one's freedom to erect yet another alternative theory or vocabulary" (*PMN*, 375–376).

One could argue that the linguistically tainted interpretation of Sartre that Rorty offers does a disservice to Sartre's phenomenological method in *Being and Nothingness*. Perhaps. But let's avoid the temptation to catalogue their differences and continue to focus on the similarities, specifically, Rorty's views regarding existentialism's appreciation of the limits of the fact-value distinction.

> This "existentialist" attempt to place objectivity, rationality, and normal inquiry within the larger picture of our need to be educated and edified is often countered by the "positivistic" attempt to distinguish learning facts from acquiring values.... But from the viewpoints of Gadamer, Heidegger, and Sartre, the trouble with the fact-value distinction is that it is contrived precisely to blur the fact that alternative descriptions are possible in addition to those offered by the results of normal inquiries. It suggests that once "all the facts are in" nothing remains except "noncognitive" adoption of an attitude—a choice which is not rationally discussable. It disguises the fact that to use one set of true sentences to describe ourselves is already to choose an attitude toward ourselves, whereas to use another set of true sentences is to adopt a contrary attitude. (*PMN*, 363–364)

What Rorty offers is a form of linguistic existentialism, a philosophy that is nonessentialist, that agrees with Sartre that there is no transcendental ego and that existence precedes "essence," and that avoids limiting human beings to the *en-soi*. But Rorty does not defend these claims through arguing for a consciousness that is spontaneous, a "nothing" that is separated from itself by nothing, as Sartre famously does. Instead he turns to language, and he claims that if we pay attention to how languages are used in practice—to the importance of conversation and to the differences between normal and abnormal discourse—we will be able to avoid the mistake of viewing human beings as only existing *en-soi* and not *pour-soi*.

> To see keeping a conversation going as a sufficient aim of philosophy ... is to see human beings as generators of new descriptions rather than beings

one hopes to be able to describe accurately. To see the aim of philosophy as truth—namely, the truth about the terms which provide ultimate commensuration for all human inquiries and activities—is to see human beings as objects rather than subjects, as existing *en-soi* rather than as both *pour-soi* and *en-soi*, as both described objects and describing subjects. . . . For only if we had such a notion of a universal description could we identify human beings-under-a-given-description with man's "essence." (*PMN*, 378)

Sartre famously argues in "Existentialism Is a Humanism" that there can be no human nature because there is no God to have an idea of human nature.[10] Sartre was later critical of this essay, but the claim about human nature, namely, that there is no human nature, no human essence, was a cornerstone of his early thought. Rorty is sympathetic, and he provides a way of supporting Sartre's "intuition" without invoking the Deity and without metaphysical commitments. He argues that we cannot identify a human essence because this would require that "all possible descriptions can be rendered commensurable with the aid of a single descriptive vocabulary" (*PMN*, 378). If such a vocabulary is impossible, then the delineation of a universal human essence is unachievable.[11] For Rorty, such a vocabulary is indeed impossible, and "human nature" must remain a chimera. Further, Rorty is well aware of the trap that some may fall into by converting the *pour-soi* into a human nature. This is a trap that he believes that existentialism in its better moments avoids.

> So not even by saying that man is subject as well as object, *pour-soi* as well as *en-soi*, are we grasping our essence. We do not escape Platonism by saying that "our essence is to have no essence" if we then try to use this insight as the basis for a constructive and systematic attempt to find out further truths about human beings. That is why "existentialism"—and, more generally, edifying philosophy—can be *only* reactive, why it falls into self-deception whenever it tries to do more than send the conversation off in new directions. (*PMN*, 378)

Another way of falling into error regarding human nature is to seek to establish a universal pragmatics (Habermas) or a transcendental hermeneutics. Rorty will have none of it, and in explaining why, he articulates how he thinks Sartre avoids this trap: "For it seems to promise just what Sartre tells us we are not going to have—a way of seeing freedom as nature (or, less cryptically, a way of seeing our creation of, and choice between, vocabularies in the same 'normal' way as we see ourselves *within* one of those vocabularies)" (*PMN*, 380).

This is an interesting move on Rorty's part. He is arguing that it is self-deceptive to view choice between vocabularies as part of a "normalized" vocabulary. In Sartre's terms this would be a version of trying to be God, an in-itself that is also simultaneously a for-itself. We are either free, which involves movement between vocabularies, or we find ourselves within a given vocabulary, which carries with it a type of facticity. For Rorty, conflating the creation of a new vocabulary with the facticity of normal discourse is a form of bad faith. However, Sartre would not agree with Rorty about the manner and extent to which we are "constrained" by a given "normal" vocabulary.

I will avoid the temptation of entering into a discussion here about whether, and to what extent, the early Sartre's phenomenological ontology is susceptible to Rorty's criticism of philosophies that seek to discover unchanging truths. Certainly Sartre did not want to see his claims about freedom serve as the ground for a new form of Platonism. (No doubt Sartre was aware that people might misread his claims about freedom as claims about human nature.) Instead, I want to address the relationship of "objective" knowledge to responsibility and self-transformation. I then want to focus on a major difference between Rorty and Sartre, namely, the degree to which they would be willing to accept a form of determinism that Rorty refers to as "physicalism."

Although Rorty rarely appeals to the Sartrean notion of the project, he does so in one rather striking passage in *Mirror of Nature*, in which he also addresses responsibility and objective knowledge.

> *Sartre . . . sees the attempt to gain an objective knowledge of the world, and thus of oneself, as an attempt to avoid the responsibility for choosing one's project.* For Sartre, to say this is not to say that the desire for objective knowledge of nature, history, or anything else is bound to be unsuccessful, or even bound to be self-deceptive. . . . To sum up this "existentialist" view of objectivity, then: objectivity should be seen as conformity to the norms of justification (for assertions and for actions) we find about us. Such conformity becomes dubious and self-deceptive only when seen as something more than this—namely, as a way of obtaining access to something which "grounds" current practices of justification in something else. . . . Agreeing with the naturalists that redescription is not "change of essence" needs to be followed by abandoning the notion of "essence" altogether. (361, emphasis added)

For Rorty, objective knowledge can be equated with normal discourse, which certainly has a fundamental role to play in our lives. But acceptance of this "objective realm" can become a way of avoiding the freedom to choose one's projects. This occurs if one converts a respectable activity, engaging the world according to accepted norms and practices, into a quest for certainty, that is, into a quest for "something which 'grounds' current practices of justification in something else." Clearly, for Sartre, as for Kierkegaard, objective knowledge that does not understand its limitations can be used to seduce us from our freedom. However, while Rorty worries, as does Sartre, about the substitution of the *en-soi* for the *pour-soi*, and the forms of bad faith that may be involved, *unlike* Sartre he views "freedom" as contingent on "the objective." Here is how Rorty explains the relationship between the objective and the *pour-soi*.

> Education has to start from acculturation. So the search for objectivity and the self-conscious awareness of the social practices in which objectivity consists are necessary first steps in becoming *gebildet*. *We must first see ourselves as* en-soi—*as described by those statements which are objectively true in the judgment of our peers*—before there is any point in seeing ourselves *pour-soi*. . . . Later perhaps, we may put less value on "being in touch with reality" but we can afford that only after having passed through stages of implicit, and then explicit and self-conscious, conformity to the norms of the discourses going on around us. (*PMN*, 365, emphasis added)

Abnormal discourse can be said to be parasitic on normal discourse, as edifying philosophy can be said to be parasitic on systematic philosophy. Rorty remains true here to the developmental orientation of leading pragmatists, which extends back at least to James's *Principles of Psychology*. The empirical self is seen as emerging in interaction with others and through learned behaviors. Specifically, the reference to the judgment of one's peers can be traced back to James's use of Scottish philosophy in *The Principles of Psychology*, as well as to Mead and Dewey.[12] It is precisely this sort of genetic approach that Sartre seeks to avoid in *Being and Nothingness*. Consciousness and (self-)consciousness do not develop from the *en-soi*. Freedom is not dependent on learning or learned behaviors. And this is one reason why I claimed earlier that Rorty would totally reject the notion of the spontaneity of consciousness.

Rorty is not in fact adverse to accepting a form of determinism that Sartre would find completely inimical to his position, that is, physicalism.

In the penultimate chapter of *Mirror of Nature*, Rorty asserts the following about physicalism and freedom.

> Physicalism is probably right in saying that we shall someday be able, "in principle," to predict every movement of a person's body (including those of his larynx and his writing hand) by reference to microstructures within his body. The danger to human freedom of such success is minimal, since the "in principle" clause allows for the probability that the determination of the initial conditions (the antecedent states of microstructures) will be too difficult to carry out except as an occasional pedagogical exercise. (354)

It appears that ignorance of the antecedents of microstructures allows us to be free. On one level, this is to say no more than Spinoza would have said. I have the feeling of being free because I am not an Infinite Mind and therefore cannot comprehend all of the causes that determine my actions and thoughts. In other words, I can say that I am free from the control of other people because in practice it is too difficult to ascertain "the initial conditions (the antecedent states of microstructures)" that allow for accurate prediction of my body's movements.[13] This said, Rorty isn't quite finished with the topic, for one's freedom doesn't appear to rest solely on the inability of others to ascertain these initial conditions. Even if it were possible to predict the noises that would come from another person's mouth—for example, by tracking them back to the antecedent states of microstructures—this doesn't mean that we would be in a position to engage the person in a conversation. Prediction of sounds cannot be equated with understanding. Meaningful statements about people, for example, cannot be equated with meaningful statements about microstructures, even if both types of "noises" are in principle predictable. For Rorty, this provides a degree of freedom since microstructures (and their antecedents) do not confine us to one type of description or language.

> The fact that we can predict a noise without knowing what it means is just the fact that the necessary and sufficient microstructural conditions for the production of a noise will rarely be paralleled by a material equivalence between a statement in the language used for describing microstructures and the statement expressed by the noise. This is not because anything is in principle unpredictable, much less because of an ontological divide between nature and spirit, but simply because of the difference between a language suitable for coping with neurons and one suitable for coping with people. (*PMN*, 355)

Leaving aside the question of why Rorty believes that physicalism will win the day, it is quite clear that a firewall between freedom and transcendence on the one hand, and determinism on the other, is the multiplicity of language games and our capacity for redescription. As we have seen, the *pour-soi* is to be understood as a redescription "machine." The vastly different sorts of vocabularies that we have for describing ourselves and the world rescue us from determinism.

Sartre, of course, would reject this whole line of argumentation. Physicalism of the sort that Rorty appears to be defending is a nonstarter. It embeds us in a causal matrix. "It is essential therefore that the questioner have the permanent possibility of dissociating himself from the causal series which constitutes being and which can produce only being."[14]

This dissociation, for Sartre, is not a matter of moving from one language game to another. There is a "rift" between the *pour-soi*, the nothing that is consciousness, and the being of the *en-soi*. For Rorty, claims of this sort reflect an outdated form of metaphysics. Of course, physicalism can be viewed as metaphysical, although Rorty could offer it as the best hypothesis that science currently has available for coping, and "coping" is all that Rorty needs to scratch misplaced metaphysical itches. Classical pragmatists such as Peirce, James, Dewey, and Mead would find unacceptable the proposition that "movement" is in principle predictable. From Peirce's tychism to Mead's notion of the novel event, these thinkers defend a robust realism in their view of novelty (this pertains even to James, who is often thought of as a nominalist). As we will see in the next two chapters, Dewey and Mead ventured away from Hegel in part via Darwin, that is, via the antiessentialism that comes with the (*unpredictable* in principle) transformation of species. (Rorty's interpretation, all the way down, of Dewey as an antirealist and a historicist is one of the reasons that pragmatists have rejected Rorty's claim that he is a Deweyan. Rorty's response has been to insist that Dewey would have been better off excising the segments of *Experience and Nature* that are metaphysical and therefore ahistorical.)[15]

Sartre and Rorty appear to inhabit different (metaphysical) universes. Yet any universe that closes off the possibility of transcendence, which denies us the opportunity to redefine ourselves and have alternative projects, would be an anathema to them. Rorty appears to believe that he shares a good deal with Sartre and the existentialists. Although it may not be an existentialism that Sartre would endorse, Rorty's sensibilities are indeed closer to those of (certain) existentialists than many may have imagined.

In support of this claim, I close with a quotation from Rorty that I believe Sartre would find (mostly) congenial and that also provides an interesting transition to the next chapter on Dewey and Sartre. As we shall see, many of their similarities as thinkers relate to Rorty's assertions in this passage.

> [Kant] created new forms of philosophical bad faith—substituting "transcendental" attempts to find one's true self for "metaphysical" attempts to find a world elsewhere. By tacitly identifying the moral agent with the constituting transcendental self, he left the road open to ever more complicated post-Kantian attempts to reduce freedom to nature, choice to knowledge, the *pour-soi* to the *en-soi*. This is the road I have been trying to block by recasting ahistorical and permanent distinctions . . . in terms of historical and temporary distinctions between the familiar and the unfamiliar, the normal and the abnormal. (*PMN*, 383–384)

§2 On Freedom and Action
Dewey and Sartre

John Dewey had little to say about existentialism in his correspondence, but in November 1947 he wrote to Robert Daniels.

> I have to confess—or perhaps boast—that I haven't read either Toynbee or Existentialism. . . . The reviews of Nouy, spite of his being a best seller closed him off entirely for me. And much the same for existentialism. I think they are the reactions of people who are scared and haven't got the guts to face life. . . . De Sartre [*sic*], I take it, is typical or symbolic of the present state of Europe; has to have some refuge from its terrible state—a kind of new-stoicism in which existence reduces pretty well to what the individual, giving up everything else as hopeless, can make out of it on his own hook. As I haven't read a word of him, you don't need to bother with what I say.[1]

Even though Dewey claims that he had not been reading existentialism, he feels little compunction about dismissing it and castigating the cowardice of those who find this sort of work appealing. This would seemingly include Sartre, who had been making an art out of reproaching the cowardly on his side of the Atlantic, especially those who dared to flee their freedom and deny contingency. Although perhaps not as direct on the topic of cowardice as Sartre, Dewey certainly wasn't shy about criticizing those he thought unwilling to confront the uncertainties of life. Perhaps it is fair to say that Sartre, and to a lesser extent Dewey, had in their own inimitable ways over the years perfected a subgenus of the argument *ad hominem, ad hominem propter ignaviam*. (Although Dewey had the good grace to suggest that Daniels not take what he says about Sartre seriously, since he hadn't read a word of him.)

In terms of Dewey's comments, note that this is the same John Dewey who had chided William James in 1891 about his lack of perspective on Hegel in a letter that addressed James's *Principles of Psychology*. In Dewey's view, James simply hadn't been generous or careful enough in his remarks on Hegel.

> I am not going to burden you with my reflections or criticisms, but I cannot suppress my own secret longing that you had at least worked out the suggestion you throw out on page 304 of vol I. If I understand at all what Hegel is driving at, that is a much better statement of the real core of Hegel than what you criticize later on as Hegelianism. Take out your "*postulated*" 'matter' & 'thinker,' let 'matter' (i.e. the physical world) be the organization of the *content* of sciousness up to a certain point, & the thinker be a still further unified organization [*not* a uni*fy-ing* organ as per Green] and that is good enough Hegel for me.... I surrender Green to your tender mercies, but the unity of Hegel's Self (& what Caird is driving at) is not a unity in the stream as such, but of the *function* of this stream—the unity of the world (content) which it bears or reports.[2]

There are two points immediately worthy of note in comparing these letters. The first is the obvious point that Dewey's generosity toward Hegel is not extended many years later toward Sartre and existentialism. Dewey was writing late in life, as a man approaching his nineties, set in his ways, when he heard about the postwar wave of existentialism. Hegel, on the other hand, was formative for Dewey. But what is also noteworthy about this correspondence is the specific passage that Dewey cites from the *Principles* when he is telling James that his own work is closer to Hegel than James realizes. This passage can be read as a precursor of Sartre's account of consciousness in *The Transcendence of the Ego* and *Being and Nothingness*. Here is an excerpt from the passage to which Dewey refers. James is discussing the relationship of the self to the not-self in terms of the stream of consciousness.

> Over and above these parts there *is* nothing save the fact that they are known, the fact of the stream of thought being there as the indispensable subjective condition of their being experienced at all. But this *condition* of the experience is not one of the *things experienced* at the moment; this knowing is not immediately *known*. It is only known in subsequent reflection. Instead, then, of the stream of thought being one of *con*-sciousness, "thinking its own existence along with whatever else it thinks," (as Ferrier says) it might be better

called a stream of *Sciousness* pure and simple, thinking objects of some of which it makes what it calls a 'Me,' and only aware of its 'pure' Self in an abstract, hypothetic or conceptual way. Each 'section' of the stream would then be a bit of sciousness or knowledge of this sort, including and contemplating its 'me' and its 'not-me' as objects which work out their drama together, but not yet including or contemplating its own subjective being. The sciousness in question would be the *Thinker*, and the existence of this thinker would be given to us rather as a logical postulate than as that direct inner perception of spiritual activity which we naturally believe ourselves to have.[3]

James is clear that he is being speculative in this passage, but it is not only a harbinger of his future analyses of the nature of conscious experience.[4] It is cited by Dewey's intellectual soul mate, George Herbert Mead, in one of his most important articles, "The Social Self."[5] In other words, James's speculations in the *Principles* were engaged and developed by the later James, as well as by Mead, although the latter reinterpreted James's insights to include a social dimension. Yet what is so striking about this passage is its proximity to Sartre's *Transcendence of the Ego* and *Being and Nothingness*. James appears to be trying to account for what in Sartrean terms would be understood as a nonthetic, nonpositional, prereflective consciousness, which Sartre, like James, contrasts with an (impure) reflective consciousness that has the self as an "object." Both are eliminating any vestiges of a transcendental ego.[6] Dewey—well before he fully appropriated naturalism and functionalism—did not see the self as a metaphysical substance. James A. Good makes this point by quoting Dewey: "As early as his 1897 *Psychology*, Dewey claimed that 'Self is, as we have so often seen, *activity*. It is not something *which* acts; it is activity.' This definition of the self demonstrates that he never believed in a substantial self."[7]

In light of just these few passages, it is somewhat surprising that so little has been written on the relationship of Dewey and Sartre.[8] And it is even more surprising given the degree to which they share insights and assumptions central to their respective philosophies. This shared terrain should be more adequately explored. The goal of this chapter is to further this exploration by highlighting similarities between these thinkers, fully acknowledging that there are striking differences. This exploration will provide basic elements of the model of individual self-determination—for example, prereflective awareness, reflection, anticipatory experience, deliberation, mediation, and spontaneity—that is further developed in Chapter 3. In this chapter I appeal to Sartre's popular essay "Existentialism Is a

Humanism," in addition to more sophisticated works such as *The Transcendence of the Ego* and *Being and Nothingness*. I cite several of Dewey's works, although I focus primarily on one section from his *Ethics* in order to clarify how Dewey's understanding of action, choice, and responsibility is comparable to the early Sartre's position on these notions.

Freedom as Practical and Ontological

Many commentators are hesitant to cite "Existentialism Is a Humanism" in a scholarly work. It was meant to be a popular lecture, given to address current criticisms of existentialism, especially among Marxists. We know that Sartre had serious reservations about it and thought it contained ideas that needed clearer formulation.[9] Two points here. First, the lecture was given without notes,[10] lending spontaneity to many of its most memorable turns of phrase, which often parallel insights in his more sophisticated early works. Second, in a new edition of Sartre's essay one can find a post-lecture discussion with the audience in which Sartre defends "popularization." And the manner in which he does so is quite in line with the way in which Dewey thought about his more popular work. For example, Dewey's (and Tufts's) *Ethics* was meant to appeal to a relatively wide audience, and for years American students in colleges and universities used it as a textbook. Although it was certainly not a spontaneous lecture, neither was it a work meant solely for professional philosophers. The point here is that Dewey and Sartre shared a commitment to communication with "the public," and this is a central feature not only of the men but of their philosophies. For both thinkers communication is a form of praxis. In this regard it's worth looking at Sartre's response to the issue of "popularization" in the post-lecture discussion. It occurs in the context of a question from the audience about an earlier article in *Action*.

> In all sincerity, it is possible that the article in *Action* did somewhat dilute my arguments. Many of the people who interview me are not qualified to do so. This leaves me with two alternatives: refuse to answer their questions, or agree to allow discussion to take place on a simplified level. I chose the second because, when all is said and done, whenever we present our theories in the classroom, we agree to dilute our thinking in order to make it understood, and that doesn't seem like such a bad thing. If we have a theory of commitment, we must be committed to the very end. *If existentialist philosophy is, first and foremost, a philosophy that says "existence precedes essence," it must be*

experienced if it is to be sincere. To live as an existentialist means to accept the consequences of this doctrine and not merely to impose it on others in books. If you truly want this philosophy to be a commitment, you have an obligation to make it comprehensible to those who are discussing it on a political or moral plane.[11]

Notice that Sartre reasserts a central claim of "Existentialism Is a Humanism," namely, that "existence precedes essence," in response to the question, and he frames his willingness to publish simplified versions of his work in terms of his commitment to engagement. He specifically mentions that if we are committed, we must be committed to making our ideas clear to audiences so they can respond. In answer to a question on the relationship of morality to existentialism, Sartre makes the following assertions.

We are dealing with a freedom-based philosophy. If there is no contradiction between our morality and our philosophy, we cannot wish for anything more. The types of commitment differ in accordance with the times. In an era when an act of commitment was perceived as revolutionary, writing the *Manifesto* was a necessity. In an era such as ours, when various parties are each calling for revolution, making a commitment does not mean joining one of them, but trying to clarify concepts in order to both identify respective positions and attempt to influence the various revolutionary parties.[12]

In addition to the importance Sartre attaches to clarifying concepts (for political ends), I call the reader's attention to the memorable claim Sartre makes here that if we are dealing with a philosophy that is focused on freedom, we cannot wish for anything more than that there be no contradiction between our morality and our philosophy. This position is consistent with Sartre's view of freedom as the highest value, the condition for the possibility of choosing other values.[13] But interpreting the assertion that freedom is the highest value requires a reasonably nuanced view of what Sartre means by freedom, and this in turn requires, as David Detmer has argued, that freedom should be understood as ontological and practical for Sartre.[14] And when freedom is understood in terms of the practical, Sartre and Dewey represent, as we shall see, kindred spirits.[15]

However, the project of comparing Dewey and Sartre may seem to falter on an obvious and seemingly intractable disagreement. Choice appears for Dewey to be a function of the reflections that ensue when we encounter problematic situations. Following in the footsteps of Hegel, Dewey brings the dialectic down to earth by reinterpreting mediation in terms of the overcoming of obstacles, that is, in terms of solutions to problems through a process of inquiry that involves reflection. The early Sartre, on the other hand, appears to argue for a radical notion of freedom that emphasizes spontaneity, and a phenomenological orientation to experience that suspends the need for a neo-Hegelian approach to mediation. *Being and Nothingness* is to be understood as a phenomenological ontology, and Sartre's discussions of "being's" relationship to what he calls our original project would not prove congenial to Dewey.[16]

Critics have claimed that the early Sartre offers an impossible notion of an omnivorously omnipresent freedom. In order to answer these critics, David Detmer argues in *Freedom as a Value* that that one must distinguish between Sartre's understanding of freedom as ontological and as practical. This distinction will help avoid an apparent inconsistency in Sartre's work. On the one hand, from the vantage of ontology, freedom appears to be absolute because of consciousness's capacity to choose. On the other hand, there are facticity, the coefficient of adversity, the situation, and the human condition.[17] All of the latter limit the scope of possible action. They help us understand that when Sartre is speaking of freedom as ontological, he is not claiming that the freedom to choose should be understood in terms of the success of our choices; that is, it should not be confused with practical freedom. He observes in *Being and Nothingness*, "In addition it is necessary to point out to 'common sense' that the formula 'to be free' does not mean 'to obtain what one has wished' but rather 'by oneself to determine oneself to wish' (in the broad sense of choosing). In other words success is not important to [ontological] freedom."[18] Our choices always confront specific conditions, for example, the crag that the mountaineer seeks to climb. And these conditions relate to our projects, which make certain "obstacles" appear as obstacles. The mountain climber has a project that entails viewing the crag as an obstacle to be overcome, whereas the individual who never seeks to climb a mountain does not experience the crag as an obstacle, as a challenge to his or her practical freedom.

Distinguishing between freedom of choice and the freedom of obtaining is an alternative way of differentiating ontological freedom and practical freedom. According to Detmer,

> The slave, the unemployed worker, and the prisoner are free in one sense of the word, that designated by such expressions as "freedom of choice" and "ontological freedom," but relatively unfree in another sense, that designated

by "freedom of obtaining" and "practical freedom." Moreover, according to Sartre, it is precisely *because* the slave, the unemployed worker, and the prisoner are free in the first sense, that it is possible to (1) describe them as being unfree in the second sense, (2) condemn those who render them unfree in this sense, (3) encourage them to become free in this sense, and (4) help them to do so.[19]

Although Dewey would not be comfortable with an approach that treats freedom as ontological, at least not in a Sartrean fashion, he would be quite comfortable discussing practical freedom. Yet, as we shall see, *Dewey presupposes the possibility of freedom, in a quasi-ontological sense, as an ingredient in the "freedom of obtaining" or "practical freedom."* To defend this assertion will require addressing Dewey's understanding of the relationship of the past to the future, which parallels in important ways Sartre's understanding of it, sans the latter's ontological aspirations. But before turning to the relationship of past to future, we should address the relationship of "the will" to "choice" for Sartre. Doing so will help clarify further the ontological "nature" of consciousness and freedom for Sartre, exhibit basic similarities between Dewey and Sartre on choice, and set the stage for the discussion of the past, the future, and anticipatory experience in the next section.

One of the great confusions that attend discussions of Sartre's understanding of choice is that he is read as if he is referring to reflective, self-conscious choice. In spite of the virtues of "Existentialism Is a Humanism," his account of choice in this lecture is seriously problematic, especially in some of its most memorable passages, for precisely this reason. For a readership that is unfamiliar with Sartre's use of the distinction between prereflective and reflective consciousness, the lecture leaves the impression that he supports a view of choice as a primarily reflective or deliberative phenomenon. This is especially true if we underscore several passages that refer to "willing" and his famous example of the student who must decide whether to stay at home with his mother or go off to war, in spite of Sartre's claim that the student must heed his feelings.[20] However, as we know from Sartre's early philosophical works, *The Transcendence of the Ego* and *Being and Nothingness*, consciousness is spontaneous, and its very spontaneity is such that choices are prereflective and nonthetic, that is, prior to a (self-)conscious "free will." It is, nevertheless, possible that (impure) reflection or deliberation can play a role in our decisions.[21] I return to this point later, for freedom in practice often does appear to include reflective activity for Sartre, although we will have to distinguish reflection as ontologically understood from ways that reflection can take place in practice. (Here is one place where "Existentialism Is a Humanism" will prove less misleading than it may appear to be at first.)

In *The Transcendence of the Ego* Sartre is quite clear about the fact that the will should be understood as "produced" by a spontaneous consciousness. So we have Sartre claiming, in a relatively well-known passage, the following:

> Transcendental consciousness is an impersonal spontaneity. It determines its existence at each moment, without anything *before* it being conceivable. Thus each moment of our conscious life reveals to us a creation *ex nihilo*. Not a new *arrangement*, but a new existence. There is something anguishing for each of us, to experience directly this tireless creation of an existence of which *we* are not the creators. At this level man has the impression of ceaselessly escaping from himself, of overflowing himself, of an abundance always unexpected taking him by surprise. And he saddles the unconscious with the task of accounting for this transcending of the Me by consciousness. The Me cannot in fact cope with this spontaneity, for *the will is an object which itself is constituted for and by this spontaneity.*[22]

In *Being and Nothingness* Sartre modifies his claims regarding the impersonality of consciousness, and significant portions of his presentation defend the position that there is a personal quality to prereflective consciousness. This does not change the fundamental point that Sartre is making, that is, we choose before we reflect on our choices. Notice that this seems to put to him at odds with Dewey. From the latter's perspective, problem-solving activity and choice require reflection. Here we clearly see the influence of a Hegelian sensibility regarding mediation and how the latter is necessary in order to overcome contradiction or conflict. For Dewey, Hegel's "conflict" is transformed into "the problem," and in the moral sphere resolution entails a synthetic activity that leads to a functionally unified self.

Nevertheless, as inclined as Dewey is to emphasize the overcoming of problems, the pre- or nonreflective does play an important role in his philosophy insofar as our actions involve nonreflective habitual "choices," that is, preferences and practices. Much of our life is lived nonreflectively.[23] As a matter of fact, in the very first section of the chapter in his

Ethics on the moral self, "The Self and Choice," Dewey declares, "Prior to anything which may be called choice in the sense of deliberate decision come spontaneous selections or *preferences*."[24] For Dewey, human beings are continually making nonreflective choices, that is, spontaneous selections. If it is kept in mind that Dewey appears to be reserving the term "choice" for what Sartre refers to as "deliberation," and that by "choice" Sartre seems to be referring to what Dewey means by "preference," the parallelism between their positions is more apparent.

But aren't choices free, truly spontaneous, for Sartre, whereas preferences for Dewey are determined? This objection appears credible, yet it will prove deceptive. Once again, I am not claiming that Sartre and Dewey have identical positions, only that there is a degree of similarity that has implications for our practices as agents. How and in what manner are their views of choice and freedom commensurate? To answer this question, we must first discuss the manner in which Dewey and Sartre address the relationship of the past to the future.

Past, Future, and the Anticipatory

From Sartre's vantage point, the fundamental duality of the in-itself and the for-itself should be understood in terms of the in-itself's facticity and the for-itself's relationship to the future. The for-itself is the nihilation or negation of the in-itself, and of its own past as an in-itself. In having a negative relation to the in-itself, consciousness "knows" that it is not-the-object-of-which-it-is-aware, for example, it has an immediate prereflective awareness of not being the inkwell sitting on the desk. As a prereflective, nonpositional, nonthetic consciousness, it is indirectly aware of itself as a "personal" consciousness, and it can have this awareness because of its relationship to what it lacks. We all have projects, and these projects, and our "original" project, define who we are nonessentialistically. They can do so because projects are by definition anticipatory and entail being aware of what we have not yet accomplished. Sartre declares, "I can assume consciousness of myself only as a particular man engaged in this or that enterprise, anticipating this or that success, fearing this or that result, and by means of the ensemble of these anticipations, outlining his whole *figure*."[25] One's past is interpreted in relationship to one's future, to what one lacks, to what one has yet to accomplish. In other words prereflective (self-)consciousness and projects involve an awareness of unaccomplished ends, which are *my* ends. But this awareness should not be understood as reflective. We move through the world with a prereflective (self-)awareness of that which we lack. These claims are elucidated by Sartre in *Being and Nothingness*.

> We have seen that human reality as for-itself is a lack and that what it lacks is a certain coincidence with itself. Concretely, each particular for-itself (*Erlebnis*) lacks a certain particular and concrete reality, which if the for-itself were synthetically assimilated with it, would transform the for-itself into *itself*. It lacks *something for something else*—as the broken disk of the moon lacks that which would be necessary to complete it and transform it into a full moon. Thus the lacking arises in the process of transcendence and is determined by a return toward the existing in terms of the lacked.[26]

> We are now in a position to elucidate the mode of being of the possible. The possible is *the something* which the For-itself lacks *in order to* be itself. . . . The Possible . . . outlines the limits of the non-thetic self-consciousness as a non-thetic consciousness. The non-reflective consciousness (of) thirst is apprehended *by means* of the glass of water as desirable, without putting the Self in the centripetal position as the end of the desire.[27]

For Dewey, while there's no question that habit and the past are fundamentally important, his notion of intelligence as a creative activity is bound up with future possibilities and anticipatory experience. Of course, he is not going to describe consciousness in terms of "nothingness," as we find in Sartre, but in practice their positions resonate in interesting ways.[28] The following passages are from Dewey's "The Need for a Recovery of Philosophy" and *Logic: The Theory of Inquiry*.

> The preoccupation of experience with things which are coming (are now coming, not just to come) is obvious to anyone whose interest in experience is empirical. Since we live forward; since we live in a world where changes are going on whose issue means our weal or woe; since every act of ours modifies these changes and hence is fraught with promise, or charged with hostile energies—what should experience be but a future implicated in a present! . . . Anticipation is therefore more primary than recollection; projection than summoning of the past; the prospective than the retrospective. Given a world like that in which we live, a world in which environing changes are partly favorable and partly callously indifferent, and experience is bound to be prospective in import; for any control attainable by the living creature depends upon what is done to alter the state of things.[29]

The idea that negation is connected with change, with becoming other or different, is at least as old as Plato. But in Plato change, altering or othering, has a direct ontological status. . . . But in modern science, correlations or correspondences of change are the chief object of determination. It is no longer possible to treat the relation of the negative proposition to change and alteration as declarative of defective being. On the contrary, the negative proposition as such formulates a change *to be* effected in existing conditions by operations which the negative proposition sets forth.[30]

The "trick" to addressing the similarity between Dewey and Sartre is to see that they both assume that experience entails prereflective and reflective relationships to the future. Dewey often emphasizes the moment of reflection and its relationship to problem-solving activity, but this does not undermine the fact that pre- or nonreflective habitual activities can be understood as involving the anticipatory. This is clear at least as far back as Dewey's analysis of stimulus and response in his famous article "The Reflex Arc Concept in Psychology."[31] Non- or prereflective anticipatory experience is in fact a condition for the possibility of habit functioning in the manner in which Dewey typically describes it. Sartre clearly thinks that projects are situated in the mode of prereflective consciousness, but he also speaks as if we can be aware of our projects when we reflect, especially when we confront dilemmas.

One must be careful not to overplay the similarities. Dewey has a naturalistic and functionalist bent that would surely be problematic for Sartre. But notice in the passages just cited the degree to which Dewey views the future and the anticipatory as fundamental features of human experience, and the existential context in which he sets these claims in the first quotation. The world is one of challenge and adversity, and any organism that is going to flourish in this sort of world requires an orientation toward the future. For Sartre, the orientation to the future is basic to the ontology of consciousness, but he is also attuned to adversity as an inescapable feature of the human condition and of freedom. As Sartre notes, there can be a free for-itself only as engaged in a resisting world. "Outside of this engagement the notions of freedom, of determinism, of necessity lose all meaning."[32] If we stress the nature of practical freedom, Sartre's and Dewey's shared sensibilities become apparent. Even though Sartre's account of how the anticipatory is possible is different from Dewey's more naturalistic account, their theories of action both depend on a practical orientation toward the future. For both, human beings actively anticipate possibilities, and this is directly linked to Sartre's and Dewey's understanding of freedom. This is not only explicit in Sartre but also explicit in Dewey, as the following passage from "The Need for a Recovery of Philosophy" shows.

> As a matter of fact, the pragmatic theory of intelligence means that the function of mind is to project new and more complex ends—to free experience from routine and from caprice. Not the use of thought to accomplish purposes already given either in the mechanism of the body or in that of the existing state of society, but the use of intelligence to liberate and liberalize action, is the pragmatic lesson. . . . [T]he doctrine that intelligence develops within the sphere of action for the sake of possibilities not yet given is the opposite of a doctrine of mechanical efficiency. Intelligence *as* intelligence is inherently forward-looking; only by ignoring its primary function does it become a mere means for an end already given. The latter *is* servile, even when the end is labeled moral, religious, or esthetic. But action directed to ends to which the agent has not previously been attached inevitably carries with it a quickened and enlarged spirit. A pragmatic intelligence is a creative intelligence, not a routine mechanic.[33]

I suggest that we interpret Dewey's critique of the mechanical as corresponding to basic features of Sartre's claims regarding the in-itself. One of Sartre's primary concerns is that deterministic models assume a set of causal connections that make freedom impossible. The mechanical, that which is simply an expression of efficient causality, is by definition the in-itself. The process of questioning, for Sartre, has affinities to Dewey's understanding of the necessary conditions for resolving a problematic situation through detaching oneself from ingrained habits. Both thinkers dismiss determinism. Here is Sartre from *Being and Nothingness*.

> It is essential therefore that the questioner have the permanent possibility of disassociating himself from the causal series which constitutes being and which can produce only being. If we admitted that the question is determined in the questioner by universal determinism, the question would thereby become unintelligible and even inconceivable. A real cause, in fact, produces a real effect and the caused being is wholly engaged by the cause in positivity; to the extent that its being depends on the cause, it can not have within itself the tiniest germ of nothingness.[34]

If we bracket the language of being, Sartre can be seen as saying something that Dewey would find quite congenial, that is, if we look merely to the past, creative responses to situations become impossible. And this is for reasons that both Dewey and Sartre would share, namely, that human beings are by definition agents who have projects that continually transform the given. For Dewey, it is best to refer to an awareness of the consequences of possible actions in order to avoid the morass of living in the past. Certainly this makes Dewey more comfortable than the early Sartre with science as a source of transformation. But an interesting question arises here. If science were interpreted in the way that Dewey understands it—as a practice that doesn't make wide-ranging deterministic claims about the world—would Sartre be less at odds with Dewey's orientation toward science? One can argue that it is not science per se that disturbs Sartre. What troubles him is the interpretation of the activities of scientists that understands them as discovering efficient causes that deny human freedom.

I had promised to address Dewey's and Sartre's views on choice after a discussion of the past and the future, but since questions have been raised about the transformation of the given and determinism, a brief exchange between Dewey and Sartre on action will prove useful. After this discussion, I turn to choice and responsibility in the final section.

Action and Self

Dewey and Sartre can be viewed as theorists of action. In what ways are their approaches similar? Toward the end of "Freedom: The First Condition of Action," in part 4 of *Being and Nothingness*, Sartre summarizes the section in eight points. The first two are especially germane to a comparison of Sartre and Dewey on action. First, Sartre discusses psychologists of the nineteenth century, and the position that he outlines bears a marked similarity to those of James and Dewey.

> The psychologists of the nineteenth century who pointed out the "motor" structures of drives, of the attention, of perception, *etc.* were right. But motion itself is an act. Thus we find no *given* in human reality in the sense that temperament, character, passions, principles of reason would be acquired or innate *data* existing in the manner of things. The empirical consideration of the human being shows him as an organized unity of conduct patterns or of "behaviors." To be ambitious, cowardly, or irritable is simply to conduct oneself in this or that matter in this or that circumstance. The Behaviorists were right in considering that the sole positive psychological study ought to

be of conduct in strictly defined situations. . . . Thus human reality does not exist first in order to act later; but for human reality, to be is to act, and to cease to act is to cease to be.[35]

Sartre is on target. This is an adequate summary of the position that Dewey presents in his *Ethics*, especially in the chapter on the moral self. For example, Dewey states,

> If a man says he is interested in pictures, he asserts that he *cares* for them; if he does not go near them, if he takes no pains to create opportunities for viewing and studying them, his actions so belie his words that we know his interest is merely nominal. Interest *is* regard, concern, solicitude, for an object; if it is not manifested in action it is unreal. . . . Benevolence or cruelty is not something which a man *has*, as he may have dollars in his pocket-book; it is something which he *is*; and since his being is active, these qualities are *modes of activity*, not forces which produce action.[36]

If Sartre agrees that conduct is as important as Dewey takes it to be, then what is Sartre's problem with "behaviorism"? Sartre outlines his major disagreement with it in the second point of his summary.

> But if human reality is action, this means evidently that its determination to action is itself action. If we reject this principle, and if we admit that human reality can be determined to action by a prior state of the world or of itself, this amounts to putting a *given* at the beginning of the series. Then these *acts* disappear as acts in order to give place to a series of *movements*. Thus the notion of conduct is itself destroyed with Janet and with the Behaviorists. The existence of the act implies its autonomy.[37]

Dewey would reply that one does not have to assume the either/or position that Sartre defends with regard to the freedom of the act, that is, we do not have to assume that we are either completely autonomous or determined. For Dewey, Sartre's dualism is an artifact of an outdated set of philosophical problems that leads to unnecessary disputes about the ontology of freedom. Yet he too refuses to accept that freedom is undermined by "causality." Here is Dewey.

> No argument about causation can affect the fact, verified constantly in experience, that we can and do learn, and that the learning is not limited to acquisition of additional information but extends to remaking old tendencies. As far as a person becomes a different self or character he develops different desires

and choices. Freedom in the practical sense develops when one is aware of this possibility and takes an interest in converting it into a reality. Potentiality of freedom is a native gift or part of our constitution in that we have *capacity* for growth and for being actively concerned in the process and the direction it takes. Actual or positive freedom is not a native gift or endowment but is acquired.[38]

The Sartrean response would be that in spite of Dewey's invocation of "freedom," he is still working with a neo-Hegelian model of the self adjusted to suit the language of habit and conduct. Hence, mediation and determinism reign. But this would be to simplify what is in fact a more complex position (on both sides of the equation). For Dewey, the self is not a fixed being-in-itself that changes solely due to forces that impinge on it. There are multiple selves, including old, fixed, and somewhat retrograde selves, and new selves that address new possibilities. Dewey notes that "a self changes its structure and its value according to the kind of object which it desires and seeks; according, that is, to the different kinds of objects in which active interest is taken."[39] Is this not another way of saying that a self can be "defined" by its projects (or that it can become self-determining)? For Dewey, what fosters active interest is not only prior experiences and given habits but an orientation to the world that is open to new possibilities.

> At each point there is a distinction between an old, an accomplished self, and a new and moving self, between the static and the dynamic self. . . . The growing, enlarging, liberated self . . . goes forth to meet new demands and occasions, and readapts and remakes itself in the process. It welcomes untried situations. The necessity for choice between the interests of the old and of the forming, moving, self is recurrent. It is found at every stage of civilization and every period of life. . . . For everywhere there is an opportunity and a need to go beyond what one has been, beyond "himself," if the self is identified with the body of desires, affections, and habits which has been potent in the past.[40]

It is unlikely that Dewey's account of the transformation of the self, or of transcendence, would persuade Sartre that Dewey has overcome treating the self as a bundle of habits, an object of reflection, an in-itself, and this in turn would suggest that Dewey can't appreciate the fundamental spontaneity of prereflective consciousness. But even in *Being and Nothingness* Sartre is well aware that what we call character traits, dispositions, are linked to the for-itself in a fashion that is more "intimate" than that of the in-itself of, say, an inkwell. In discussing Leibniz's treatment of Adam, in which he is attempting to show that Adam does not have an essence, Sartre makes the following comment.

> For us, on the contrary, Adam is not defined by an essence since for human reality essence comes after existence. Adam is defined by the choice of his ends; that is, by the upsurge of an ekstatic temporalization which has nothing in common with the logical order. Thus Adam's contingency expresses the finite choice which he has made of himself. But henceforth what makes his *person* known to him is the future and not the past; he chooses to learn what he is by means of ends toward which he projects himself—that is, by the totality of his tastes, his likes, his hates, etc. inasmuch as there is a thematic organization and inherent *meaning* in this totality.[41]

Notice that Sartre is not denying that one can learn about oneself. To do so, one must look to the ends toward which one projects oneself in the context of one's original project.[42] Insofar as one does, it is possible to relate to oneself as thematically organized, that is, as someone who has certain tastes, likes, hates, and so on. However, these can change depending on one's orientation to the future. They are not fixed essences. Sartre affirms in *Being and Nothingness*, as he does in "Existentialism Is a Humanism," that existence precedes essence. And for Sartre, "My essence is what I have been."[43] But what I have been is subject to reinterpretation depending on changes in my orientation toward the future, the projects that I undertake. How different is Sartre's position in practice from Dewey's, which involves the possibility of transforming one's habits in light of new interests?

Dewey insists that his position embraces free acts, and his insistence is in large measure related to the future directedness of human beings. We are not fixed by the past because we can anticipate multiple courses of action and the consequences of these actions.[44] For Dewey, our openness toward alternative courses of action is a way of speaking about choice without the ontological assumptions entailed by Sartre's description of consciousness as nothing. Dewey's position is in fact congenial with that of the later Sartre, in which the project remains a central motif, but social conditions are more internalized than is suggested by his treatment of facticity in *Being and Nothingness*.[45] What I am arguing is that even though the language of character that Dewey invokes in his *Ethics* would be unacceptable to Sartre, in practice there is an affinity between their approaches. And this can be seen in how they discuss the practical implications of choice.

Choice, Deliberation, Responsibility

From a Sartrean perspective values are subjective and must be understood in light of the lack that "inhabits" consciousness. As Detmer argues, "The point to be noticed is that what I am calling 'the subjectivity of values' is an ontological thesis, that is, a thesis about what exists and the manner in which it exists. Sartre is arguing that values do *not* exist, or, more precisely, that they owe such existence as they have to human consciousness which bring them into being—they have, in other words, only a 'subjective' existence."[46] Interestingly, Detmer goes on to argue that there may be a tension in Sartre's position, for there are places in which he seems to be claiming that there are objective values. This would place him closer to Dewey's position in which values, as social values, become part and parcel of one's funded experience. Dewey thinks of this experience as potentially retrograde, because old values, which we "intuit," do not help address new and different situations. "There is a permanent limit to the value of even the best of the intuitive appraisals of which we have been speaking. These are dependable in the degree in which conditions and objects of esteem are fairly uniform and recurrent. They do not work with equal sureness in the cases in which the new and unfamiliar enters in. 'New occasions teach new duties.' . . . Extreme intuitionalism and extreme conservatism often go together."[47]

We know that for Sartre choice must be seen as prior to the will—or better, as coeval but ontologically prior to the will[48]—and prior to reflection, although, as we shall see, in practice reflective consciousness can play a role in our decisions. How, then, does Dewey understand choice? He tells us, "Prior to anything which may be called choice in the sense of deliberate decision come spontaneous selections or *preferences*."[49] So even if Dewey does not supply the same sort of ontology for understanding these preferences, he recognizes that there are "choices," preferences, which appear to arise spontaneously, that is, without deliberation. He thinks of these preferences as "organic rather than conscious."[50] We move toward some objects rather than others because of temperament and habit. Another way of stating this is to say that human beings have unrealized interests, for even habits typically involve ends. And once put in these terms, our future directedness can be viewed as a significant factor in our preferences.

Sartre wants to argue that at every moment consciousness is "separated" from its past by "nothing." Therefore, at each moment we are free; we are free from our past, and we are free in relationship to a future that entails what we lack. Now this is the ontological story. However, when Sartre actually talks about a moral decision in "Existentialism Is a Humanism," he provides us with the example of his student. What is challenging about the situation, from a Sartrean vantage point, is that the student cannot rely on prior principles or religious beliefs to make his decision. He is presented with alternatives that conflict—stay at home to care for his mother or go to war—and he must make a choice because the alternatives are at odds. The very recognition of the alternatives, of the moral dilemma, appears to require reflection, that is, *a positing of oneself as the actor who can take alternative paths*. Now framing choice in this manner is actually congenial with Dewey's position. Dewey assumes that there are preferences, which for our purposes we can relate to the spontaneity of consciousness, but these preferences will not help us when confronted by new situations, specifically, situations in which there is a conflict. Dewey states in his *Ethics*,

> We are so constructed that both by original temperament and by acquired habit we move toward some objects rather than others. Such preference antecedes judgment of comparative values; it is organic rather than conscious. Afterwards there arise situations in which wants compete; we are drawn spontaneously in opposite directions. Incompatible preferences hold each other in check. We hesitate, and then hesitation becomes deliberation: that weighing of values in comparison with each other of which we have already spoken. At last, a preference emerges which is intentional and which is based on consciousness of the values which deliberation has brought into view. We have to make up our minds, when we want two conflicting things, which of them we *really* want. That is choice. We prefer spontaneously, we choose deliberately, knowingly.[51]

Sartre does not dismiss deliberation, which is a mode of reflection, in *Being and Nothingness*. Instead, he argues that one can choose to deliberate in a manner consistent with his ontology.

> Actually causes and motives have only the weight which my project—i.e., the free production of the end and of the known act to be realized—confers upon them. When I deliberate, the chips are down. And if I am brought to the

point of deliberating, this is simply because it is a part of my original project to realize motives by means of *deliberation* rather than by some other form of discovery (by passion, for example, or simply by action, which reveals to me the organized ensemble of causes and of ends as my language informs me of my thought). There is therefore a choice of deliberation as a procedure which will make known to me what I project and consequently what I am. And *the choice* of deliberation is organized with the ensemble motives-causes and end by free spontaneity.[52]

It may seem that we now have a clear-cut way of bringing Sartre and Dewey together. Both seem to accept the importance of deliberation. Sartre might say to Dewey that he has chosen a project or an original project—for example, to engage life as an educator—that includes deliberation. Dewey's mistake would not involve a commitment to deliberation but believing that he didn't need an ontology to describe freedom as the necessary condition for choosing deliberation. But in terms of action, is there a substantial difference between deliberating because of an original project and deliberating in order to address a significant, perhaps lifelong, concern? This doesn't appear to be a difference that makes a difference.

Unfortunately the situation is more complicated than it might first appear. Sartre's passage on deliberation occurs in the context of his attempt to show how causes, motives, and the will can be used to undermine the spontaneity of consciousness. We employ them to try to gain control of this spontaneity. By our grasping them through reflection, they appear to supply a capacity for voluntary choice. However, employing them in this fashion in effect turns the for-itself into an in-itself. (The individual seeks to utilize them in order to satisfy the desire to be a for-itself-in-itself simultaneously, that is, God.) Read in this light, the passage is not talking about deliberative choice but a kind of self-revealing that is a quality of deliberation. "And if I am brought to the point of deliberating, this is simply because it is a part of my original project to realize motives by means of *deliberation* rather than by some other form of discovery."[53] Sartre also states, "The result is that a voluntary deliberation is always a deception. How can I evaluate causes and motives on which I myself confer their value before all deliberation and by the very choice which I make of myself?"[54]

Sartre's ontological commitments here are questionable. It is hard to see how one's original project or projects are going to avoid encountering situations in which reflection on one's past, perhaps through a consideration of causes and motives, is not a feature of the overcoming of obstacles and "voluntarily" choosing new projects. And interestingly enough, in the very same section of *Being and Nothingness* as the passages just cited, Sartre notes,

> The recovery of former motives—or the rejection or new appreciation of them—is not distinct from the project by which I assign new ends to myself and by which in the light of these ends I apprehend myself as discovering a supporting cause in the world. Past motives, past causes, present motives and causes, future ends, all are organized in an indissoluble unity by the very upsurge of a freedom which is beyond causes, motives, and ends.[55]

So in spite of insisting on a "freedom which is beyond causes, motives, and ends," Sartre also acknowledges that seeing former motives "is not distinct from the project by which I assign new ends to myself." Although one shouldn't interpret this passage as implying that deliberation initiates new projects for Sartre, it appears that our past, which surfaces in deliberation, does at times become intertwined with new projects.[56] These claims suggest that the ontological is intertwined with the empirical in a manner that undermines Sartre's exorbitant claims for ontological freedom. His ontology is in fact often a philosophical anthropology, but proving this is beyond the scope of this chapter.[57] However, if the latter claim about the ontological and the empirical is correct, then it may prove prudent to expend our energies looking to empirical and practical "expressions" of human freedom, which for both Sartre and Dewey entail guiding interests and projects that involve anticipatory experience. And this brings us to the question of responsibility. Sartre asserts in "Existentialism Is a Humanism,"

> Thus, the first effect of existentialism is to make every man conscious of what he is, and to make him solely responsible for his own existence. And when we say that man is responsible for himself, we do not mean that he is responsible only for his own individuality, but that he is responsible for all men. . . . When we say that man chooses himself, not only do we mean that each of us must choose himself, but also that in choosing himself, he is choosing for all men. . . . I am therefore responsible for myself and for everyone else, and I am fashioning a certain image of man as I choose him to be. In choosing myself, I choose man.[58]

Sartre is committed to fashioning a "better" world, and this is not an inconsequential aspect of his philosophy. When we choose, we should choose with regard to the world that we are shaping. If one were to ask him what is more basic, taking responsibility for one's (past) failings or ridding oneself of one's failings, in his more purely philosophical moments he might not wish to choose. He might say, ontologically speaking, they are both choices. But they aren't equal choices in practical terms. In fact, ridding oneself of one's failings must take priority. Sartre, we assume, is an existentialist, not a Kantian. If he were to emphasize the confessional aspect of responsibility, he would betray his own notion of committed action. The only reason to dwell on what one has done is to stop doing it, that is, to act differently. And acting differently is not only more important in the sense of "making a better world" or fashioning myself in a "better" way. It is more important because it entails at least an indirect acknowledgment of the original failing; whereas the acknowledgment of the failing is in itself no guarantee that change will ensue. One is left wondering how different in practice Sartre's position is from Dewey's regarding responsibility. Here is Dewey on the topic of responsibility.

> Now the commonest mistake in connection with the idea of responsibility consists in supposing that approval and reprobation have a retrospective instead of prospective bearing. The possibility of a desirable *modification* of character and the selection of the course of action which will make that possibility a reality is the central fact in responsibility. . . . A human being is held accountable in order that he may learn; in order that he may learn not theoretically and academically but in such a way as to modify and—to some extent—remake his prior self. The question of whether he might when he acted have acted differently from the way in which he did act is irrelevant. The question is whether he is capable of acting differently *next* time; the practical importance of effecting changes in human character is what makes responsibility important.[59]

If Sartre were to focus his efforts on taking individuals to task for not recognizing that their choices are their own, I submit that he would be less of a (committed) existentialist in (Sartre's own terms) than is Dewey. If Sartre were to get trapped in a rhetoric of responsibility that is not future directed, he would betray the projective character of his own project and the heart of his philosophical project in *Being and Nothingness*. Although at times he appears to be tempted to "scold" others (or characters in his fiction) for their failings, especially their cowardice, of course he doesn't simply do this. He is quite clear that we have a responsibility to view our actions in terms of their impact and to see them in light of the larger world. This becomes ever more apparent in his later works, but it is right there in "Existentialism Is a Humanism."

Sartre clearly endorses maximizing freedom, which means that ontological freedom is inseparable from practical freedom. That the latter is crucial is clear in *Being and Nothingness*, as well as in "Existentialism Is a Humanism." And when we talk about practical freedom, responsibility entails giving priority to consequences—moving from transcendence alone to a thoughtful process of deliberation, which requires a consideration of consequences—that is, if you are a pragmatist or an existentialist of a certain stripe. As different as Dewey and Sartre may be—and one could very well write a book on the differences—if the practical orientation of their philosophies doesn't make them siblings, it at least makes them philosophical cousins, which is also true for Bourdieu and Mead, to whom we now turn.

§3 A (neo) American in Paris
Bourdieu and Mead

Pierre Bourdieu and George Herbert Mead, separated by several generations, an ocean, national and local traditions, and fields (in Bourdieu's sense of the term),[1] are without a doubt intellectual soul mates. Of course, even soul mates are not given to a complete sharing of interests, and there are indeed important differences in this pair's views. Although differences would be expected, the affinities—which have not passed unnoticed by Bourdieu—require explanation. Queried about two recent studies that have suggested connections between his thought and Dewey's—the latter, Mead's lifelong compatriot—Bourdieu responds,[2]

> I came across these studies very recently and they stimulated me to take a closer look at Dewey's philosophy, of which I had only very partial and superficial knowledge. Indeed, the affinities and convergences are quite striking, and I believe I understand what their basis is: my effort to react against the deep-seated intellectualism characteristic of all European philosophies (with the rare exceptions of Wittgenstein, Heidegger, and Merleau-Ponty) determined me, unwittingly, to move very close to philosophical currents that the European tradition of "depth" and obscurity is inclined to treat as foils, negative reference points.[3]

Bourdieu notes that among the commonalties he finds is a drive to overcome dualisms, for instance, those of subject/object and internal/external. This is surely on the mark with regard to Dewey and Mead, but there is a good deal more to report. Mead and Bourdieu share, for example, a social conception of mind and agency; a penchant for nonpositivistic approaches to the empirical sciences; a dedication to the interdisciplinary;

views that link certain kinds of problem-solving behavior to reflection; a commitment to giving the bodily and dispositional their due; a concern with lived, nonscientized time; recurrent appeals to "open" systems, improvisation, and the role of conflict in change; a pluralistic vision; a preference for analyzing language in terms of use; an emphasis on reasonableness as opposed to a transcendental notion of reason; a willingness to speak the language of interest and a healthy suspicion regarding views from nowhere; and even similar uses of sports metaphors and analogies. And the list could go on.

The goals of this chapter are fourfold. First, given the limited understanding and the even more limited acceptance of pragmatism in Europe, it is of some importance that one of the Continent's premier intellectuals has echoed themes and ideas addressed some ninety years ago by American thinkers. This confluence is clearly worthy of illustration.[4] Second, there is more at work here than historical or antiquarian impulses. For all of their similarities, there are indeed important differences between Mead and Bourdieu, and one of them centers on the degree to which Mead's model supports notions of transcendence and self-determination that Bourdieu's social theory does not. Third, an examination of Mead's more notable insights—for example, on language, roles, the generalized other, novelty, sociality, the "I" and "me," and social systems—will help to clarify elements of the model of individual self-determination that is being developed in this book. And finally, this chapter provides the groundwork for the application of Mead's ideas to the development of a theory of cosmopolitanism in Chapters 4 and 5, which in turn will further illuminate possibilities for self-determination in both individuals and groups.[5] I begin with a brief introductory overview of possible avenues for comparing Mead and Bourdieu and then discuss in some detail key similarities and important differences.

∽

While there are a number of ways one could approach the theoretical underpinnings of Bourdieu's work, the tension that he sets up in *The Logic of Practice* between so-called objective and subjective orientations is a natural place to begin a comparison to Mead, for in many ways the latter's project can be understood as an attempt to find a path between just such a Scylla and Charybdis. Bourdieu addresses the tension as one between the subjectivism or finalism (that is, the projectism) of a Sartre and the determinism or mechanism of structuralism. Both of these approaches fail to grasp the dynamics of an agent engaged in a social world, of habitus to field, and they fall into myths of self-creation or reductive mechanism. "There is an economy of practices, a reason immanent in practices, whose 'origin' lies neither in the 'decisions' of reason understood as rational calculation nor in the determinations of mechanisms external to and superior to the agents."[6]

As long as we divide the world into subjects and objects, the one confronting the other in an external relationship, we will not be able to avoid falling into mechanism or subjectivism. The way out of this dualism is through an understanding of habitus (and fields). Bourdieu tells us in "A Lecture on the Lecture" that

> the source of historical action . . . is not an active subject confronting society as if that society were an object constituted externally. This source resides neither in consciousness nor in things but in the relation between two states of the social, that is, between the history objectified in things, in the form of institutions, and the history incarnated in bodies, in the form of that system of enduring dispositions which I call habitus. The body is in the social world but the social world is also in the body.[7]

All of this is, of course, well known to readers of Bourdieu, but what is intriguing here is the extent to which these sentiments would be seconded by Mead and in response to just the sort of unacceptable dichotomy that Bourdieu is attempting to overcome. Mead's penchant for using the terms "subject" and "object" can be quite misleading in this regard, for it may give the impression that he succumbs to a type of dualism that Bourdieu insists on castigating. But when one actually examines Mead's texts in any detail, it is clear that he is in large measure modifying the traditional uses of these terms, using them as shorthand for his own innovations, which are in line with Bourdieu's. In fact, Mead was something of a social ecologist for whom traditional Cartesian dualities made little sense and who thought that one's bodily dispositions—attitudes in his language—shape and are shaped by their immersion in various environments.

In order to elucidate just how closely aligned Bourdieu's and Mead's views of the social world are, one might step back a bit to the underpinnings of Mead's ideas, specifically to the work of William James. If there was one question that tormented James, it was the issue of freedom versus determinism, a variant of Bourdieu's subjectivism versus mechanism. Unlike Mead or Dewey, James never developed a social theory that might have allowed him to address this issue in a fashion that Bourdieu would find compelling. But many of Mead's insights hark back to James's psychology, specifically to his notion of habit and his model of the stream of consciousness. James writes, "Habit is thus the enormous fly-wheel of society, its most precious conservative agent. It alone is what keeps us all within the bounds of ordinance, and saves the children of fortune from the envious uprisings of the poor. It alone prevents the hardest and most repulsive walks of life from being deserted by those brought up to tread therein."[8] Bourdieu sees the habitus as basically just such a conservative force, yet one that doesn't leave agents mired in the way things were because dispositions can be transferred and utilized in different contexts. James, too, did not view his notion of habit in strictly deterministic terms. For both James and Bourdieu we can learn to improve our lives by reflecting on the kinds of habits or dispositions that we possess and by making a concerted effort to reinforce or extinguish specific ones through our practices.

Mead can be viewed as developing James's notion of habit in the direction of a social behaviorism, in which repertoires of socially generated behaviors and dispositions crystallize into what he calls the "me," his shorthand for a constellation of attitudes that we associate with particular agents or selves, and which emerges in relationship to specific social contexts. Mead's "me" is comparable to Bourdieu's habitus, a connection that we will examine later. Suffice it to say at this juncture that Mead's view of socialization never led him to a mechanistic determinism and that both Bourdieu and Mead agree that reflection and self-awareness can at times help modify unwanted behaviors. There is, however, an additional point of comparison between James, Bourdieu, and Mead that should be noted. Habits can be thought of as allies in achieving the good life precisely because they *do not* require reflection for their success. James tells us that

> the more details of our daily life we can hand over to the effortless custody of automatism, the more our higher powers of mind will be set free for their own proper work. There is no more miserable human being than one in whom nothing is habitual but indecision, and for whom the lighting of every cigar, the drinking of every cup, the time of rising and going to bed every day, and the beginning of every bit of work, are subjects of express volitional deliberation.[9]

Bourdieu shares with many a pragmatist a desire to sing the praises of the nonreflective activities that fill so much of our waking lives and that so much of the Western philosophical tradition has belittled. Note in this regard Mead's language in the following passage, which addresses the relationship between scientific endeavors, a type of reflective activity, and what he labels the "biologic individual." For Mead, the latter lives in *the world that is there*, that is, a settled environment that serves as the background for reflective and critical endeavors.

> This immediate experience which is reality, and which is the final test of the reality of scientific hypotheses as well as the test of the truth of all our ideas and suppositions, is the experience of what I have called the "biologic individual." . . . [This] term lays emphasis on the living reality which may be distinguished from reflection. . . . [T]he actual experience did not take place in this form [i.e., reflection] but in the form of unsophisticated reality.[10]

The appeal to the social construction of reality takes a turn to the bodily with Mead, as it does with Bourdieu; and both exhibit a marked sensitivity to understanding action in terms of bodily dispositions and interests. Yet there are a number of important differences between their approaches. For example, both can be viewed as having an Aristotelian strain in their thought that gives habit its due, and both avoid spectator theories of knowledge because they view knowledge as interest laden, but they differ on the degree to which disinterestedness is possible. Mead is influenced by Scottish theorists of sentiment and supports a version of Adam Smith's impartial spectator, whereas Bourdieu is in Nietzsche's camp with regard to the impossibility of disinterestedness. Mead can be viewed as falling between Habermas and Bourdieu here. On the one hand, for Mead, Habermas's neo-Kantian views on impartiality are still too dependent on the transcendental, but, on the other, Bourdieu's Nietzschean orientation toward interest and power would strike Mead as too relativistic (and as uncharitable to boot). Mead remained something of a secularized Christian in his expectations regarding the possibilities of overcoming and broadening one's interests and in his belief in mutuality. In discussing the ideal of democracy, he writes rather late in his career, "The most grandiose of these community ideals is that which lies behind the structure of what was called Christendom, and found its historic expression in the Sermon on the Mount, in the parable of the Good Samaritan, and in the Golden Rule. These affirm that the interests of all men are so identical, that the man who acts in the interest of his neighbors will act in his own interest."[11] Many of the differences between Mead and Bourdieu turn on the Nietzschean aspects of the latter's thought, those that allow Bourdieu to develop tools to analyze power relations that Mead did not possess but that may prevent him from seeing possibilities for mutuality and reciprocity that Mead could envision.[12]

~

Bourdieu seeks to avoid choosing between mechanism and subjectivism, determinism and freedom, by appealing to habitus and fields. Mead's approach to the dilemma is to offer the "I" and the "me" facets of the individual, which he views in functional terms. The "I" is the "source" of innovations that modify the socially constituted "me." But to understand just what Mead hopes to accomplish with these distinctions, we must back up a bit and address, however briefly, his model of language acquisition and his account of roles.

Mead followed Wilhelm Wundt in emphasizing the birth of human language in gestures between animals, which Mead had a penchant for explaining by appealing to a dogfight. In such a struggle, one dog may growl and a second may react by baring its fangs or growling back. Such behaviors can be viewed as gestures, as parts of a social act that initiate responses. Mead refers to an exchange of gestures, in which there is a response by a second organism and a counterresponse by the first, as a "conversation of gestures." Meaning in this circumstance is defined in terms of the responses of the organisms; for example, a growl means the baring of fangs. This is not to say that animals are (self-)consciously aware of the meanings of their gestures, that is, of the responses that they or other animals will make to their gestures.[13] They are not able to say to themselves, if I do x, y will follow. A (self-)conscious awareness of meaning awaits the presence of human beings who possess language.

Human beings often engage in non-(self-)conscious conversations of gestures of the sort just described, which Mead illustrates in terms of boxers and fencers who must learn how to read cues, gestures, in order to avoid injury. And, interestingly enough, it is in reference to this example that Bourdieu refers, approvingly, to Mead.[14] Here are Mead's words describing this type of exchange, which occur right after he presents an account of a dogfight:

> We find a similar situation in boxing and in fencing, as in the feint and the parry that is initiated on the part of the other. And then the first one

of the two in turn changes his attack; there may be considerable play back and forth before actually a stroke results. This is the same situation as in the dog-fight. If the individual is successful a great deal of his attack and defense must not be considered, it must take place immediately. He must adjust "instinctively" to the attitude of the other individual. He may, of course, think it out. He may deliberately feint in order to open up a place of attack. But a great deal has to be without deliberation.[15]

This passage not only reveals Bourdieu's affinities to Mead but also sets the stage for points of contention. What Bourdieu finds congenial about Mead's approach is that it avoids the false distance from practice that occurs when one is (theoretically) analyzing someone else's practice, for example, by viewing the person mechanistically. This distancing can lead to faulty conclusions regarding the nature of the agent's relationship to his or her practices. Theory about action is quite different from actual encounters, and too often theoreticians forget just how different they are precisely because they are analyzing someone else's practices. This is a luxury that boxers cannot afford. In Bourdieu's words,

> As for the anthropologists, they would have been less inclined to use the language of the mechanical model if, when considering exchange, they had thought not only of *potlatch* or *kula*, but also of the games they themselves play in social life, which are expressed in the language of tact, skill, dexterity, delicacy or *savoir-faire*, all names for practical sense.... When one discovers the theoretical error that consists in presenting the theoretical view of practice as the practical relation to practice... then simultaneously one sees that at the root of this error is the antinomy between the time of science and time of action, which tends to destroy practice by imposing on it the intemporal time of science.[16]

For Mead, as for Bourdieu, much of our lives takes place on a nonthetic level of awareness, one in which we are not self-consciously positing alternative futures. For both, reflection occurs when problems arise that may require reasoned decisions or strategic planning, which is quite different from the non-self-conscious reasonableness that guides our daily unproblematic practices. Bourdieu tells us that

> there is an economy of practices, a reason immanent in practices, whose "origin" lies neither in the "decisions" of reason as understood as rational calculation nor in the determinations of mechanisms external to and superior to the agents.... In other words, if one fails to recognize any form of action other than rational action or mechanical reaction, it is impossible to understand the

logic of all the actions that are reasonable without being the product of a reasoned design, still less of rational calculation; informed by a kind of objective finality without being consciously organized in relation to an explicitly constituted end; intelligible and coherent without springing from an intention of coherence and a deliberate decision; adjusted to the future without being the product of a project or a plan.[17]

Mead also assumes that there is, or can be, a reasonableness to activities that are not undergoing critical evaluation; they take place in *the world that is there*. However, differences between Mead and Bourdieu begin to surface when we consider the place of significant symbols—that is, gestures that entail (self-)conscious cognition and help lead to reflection—in Mead's model.

For Mead, gestures become significant symbols when those using them are capable of becoming aware of their meanings. The key here is the vocal gesture. If I say, "Look out!" as you are about to slip on an icy street, I hear the gesture as you do, and I can respond to my own gesture as you do, for example, by slowing my pace. "Gestures become significant symbols when they implicitly arouse in an individual making them the same responses which they explicitly arouse, or are supposed to arouse, in other individuals, the individuals to whom they are addressed."[18] Vocal gestures allow human beings to (self-)consciously respond as others do to a symbol, which means that they can anticipate what another's reaction to a significant symbol might be.[19] They can even talk to themselves in the absence of others by taking the linguistic role of the other. The bottom line here for Mead is that this capacity allows one to turn experience back on itself, that is, to reflexively respond to stimuli. This reflexivity is at the heart of what he calls "mind."

> It is by means of reflexiveness—the turning back of the experience of the individual upon himself—that the whole social process is thus brought into the experience of the individuals involved in it; it is by such means, which enable the individual to take the attitude of the other toward himself, that the individual is able consciously to adjust himself to that process, and to modify the resultant of that process in any given social act in terms of his adjustment to it. Reflexiveness, then, is the essential condition, within the social process, for the development of mind.[20]

It is the vocal gesture that allows "mind" to develop, and with "mind" human beings have the capacity to become reflexively aware of increasingly complex social interactions, for example, social roles, and to produce solutions to problems through reflection. Although Mead clearly distinguishes the reflective from the nonreflective, he insists that we typically move rather naturally between them in our daily rounds. A notion of reflexivity is also important to Bourdieu's position, for the social scientist depends on it to become aware of his or her own biases. In this regard, reflexion is a methodological tool for producing better social science. But Bourdieu also raises the question of the place of reflexivity in daily life, and here, while bowing to the possibility of requiring it in times of trouble, his rhetorical task is to downplay its importance.

For Mead, roles can be understood as constellations of behaviors that are accessible to a reflexive apprehension, and they become available by utilizing mechanisms similar to those found in the vocal gesture. In order to take the role of a doctor, I must (to some degree) be able view my actions from the perspective of the patient. I must have built into my repertoire of behaviors both sides of an exchange in order to play my side, as I do when I anticipate a response to my vocal gesture. Given how commonplace the notion of role-taking has become, this should all appear straightforward enough, but there is actually a pitfall lurking. Mead uses the expression "taking the role of the other" to describe a number of different kinds of exchanges, and many of them are not self-conscious ones, nor do they necessarily involve behaviors as complex as those of roles portrayed in the theater. For instance, in caressing a doll, a very young child may take the role of certain behaviors of a parent without actually playing at being a parent. As counterintuitive as it at first may seem, Mead's role theory does not lead to all the world being a stage. Gary Cook provides some rather helpful advice here: "We can avoid some of the misleading connotations of the phrase 'taking the role of the other' by using in its stead the alternative phrase Mead himself often employs, namely, 'taking the attitude of the other.' An attitude, he says, consists of a behavioral disposition, a tendency to respond in a certain manner to certain sorts of stimuli, or the beginnings of an action that seek an occasion for full release or expression."[21]

This is actually a rather significant clarification, for Bourdieu is quite critical of traditions in sociology that would establish themselves along lines that Wilhelm Dilthey would suggest, that is, through a notion of "psychic participation," or in terms of Edmund Husserl's "intentional transposition into the Other," which are "sophisticated versions of the spontaneous theory of understanding as 'putting oneself in somebody else's place.'"²² Given that Bourdieu aggregates phenomenologists and interactionists, and that Mead is often viewed as the grandfather of symbolic interactionism, Bourdieu or his followers might very well be misled by Mead's language. No doubt complex and self-conscious role-taking is a basic feature of Mead's approach, but by no means does every use of the phrase "taking the role of the other" suggest an empathy born of ideational understanding or an exchange of ideas and feelings entailed in complex social roles. To put this in other terms, this clarification is important because it will allow us to more easily see just how similar Mead's "me" is to Bourdieu's habitus in its appeal to the attitudinal. It is worth noting one additional point: Mead's model builds in a notion of reciprocity at a very basic level. One must be able to anticipate and take the attitude of the other in order to speak and play one's part. To what degree this activity should be viewed in strategic or manipulative terms is debatable and represents a potential bone of contention between Mead and Bourdieu. But what is clear is that if one emphasizes the reciprocity involved in Mead's model—as opposed to novelty, the dispositional, and systemic entanglements—then the step to Habermas's ideal of a communication community is not a long one.²³

There are varying degrees of complexity possible in the process of taking the attitude of the other, so that the child learning to take specific attitudes—for example, the relatively isolated behavior of caressing a doll—should be viewed differently from the medical intern who is "playing" at being a doctor, which might more properly be called role-playing. The latter requires an internalization of two sets or constellations of "exchangeable" attitudes, that is, doctor and patient. However, even though role-playing of this type necessitates considerably more complex sets of behaviors than caressing a doll, Mead is careful (at times) to distinguish it from the presentation of a self, or a "me."²⁴ The terms "self" and "me" are reserved for yet more complicated sets of behaviors that Mead tries to explain in terms of his neologism, the *generalized other*. If we think of roles as being played in relationship to *specific others*, then selves can be said to arise in relationship to complex networks of interactions with the assistance of generalized others, and these networks or systems bear comparison with Bourdieu's fields.

> The organized community or social group which gives to the individual his unity of self may be called "the generalized other." The attitude of the gener-

alized other is the attitude of the whole community. Thus, for example, in the case of such a social group as a ball team, the team is the generalized other in so far as it enters—*as an organized process or social activity*—into the experience of any one of the individual members of it.[25]

What is important here is not so much the example of a ball team but the phrase "organized process." We can think of various "systems," such as families or even corporations, as giving rise to generalized others, which in turn produce "me's." While not identical to Bourdieu's fields, which are "zones" of social interaction marked by rivalry, such systems are clearly homologous to them.[26] The following groups can be said to have generalized others: "Some of them are concrete social classes or subgroups, such as political parties, clubs, corporations, which are all actually functional social units, in terms of which their individual members are directly related to one another. The others are abstract social classes or subgroups, such as the class of debtors and the class of creditors, in terms of which their individual members are related to one another only more or less indirectly."[27]

Such groups give rise to generalized others, and the consciously apprehended "me" arises as one turns back—reflects, so to speak—on one's own behaviors and views them from the perspective of a generalized other. The group, then, is both the source of behaviors and the "place" from which we can "view" our behaviors, in a manner analogous to the way in which we become aware of the meaning of a gesture by viewing it in terms of the other person's response. Various communities give rise to different "me's," and some communities may be thought of as more inclusive than others—for example, political parties or religious orders—because their attitudes permeate other "me's"; hence, they can be thought of as giving rise to metaselves. Further, even the same communities do not generate identical "me's" because of the different positions that each individual has in a group. We are, so to speak, Leibnizian monads of particular social worlds. And this parallels Bourdieu's view that "each individual system of dispositions is a structural variant of the others, expressing the singularity of its position within the class and its trajectory."[28] However, Mead and Bourdieu part company over the importance of self-consciousness for the realization of the "singularity" of an agent. Mead insists that the "me," or the self, and self-consciousness go hand in hand. The self is an "object" of cognition, framed by the generalized other, and only by having this object before one's eyes can one properly speaking be said to have a self, as opposed to a bundle of nonsystemic behaviors. Here Mead distances himself from Bourdieu in emphasizing the importance of reflection. While both wish to overcome the Cartesian subject, and both have a sophisticated view of the individual as a social agent, Mead remains committed to the category of self-consciousness as a key factor in agency and "singularity."

For Mead, to be aware of a "me" requires what he calls the "I." We can think of the "I" and "me" as phases of experience that are the *functional* equivalents of a transcendental ego and an empirical self. One cannot be aware of the "me" unless there is a subject, an "I," present to provide the "consciousness of" the empirical object, that is, the "me." Not only does the "I" allow us to be aware of the "me"; it also serves as the "source" of responses. "The 'I' is the response of the organism to the attitudes of the others; the 'me' is the organized set of attitudes of others which one himself assumes."[29] The "I's" responses are (in varying degrees) novel, and by definition they cannot be self-consciously appropriated (immediately) as they take place. Appealing to the example of a ball game once again, we can say that a play initiated by an "I" is never identical with a past play. Every response is somewhat unique, and it is self-consciously "known" only retrospectively. "If you ask, then, where directly in your own experience the 'I' comes in, the answer is that it comes in as a historical figure. It is what you were a second ago that is the 'I' of the 'me.'"[30] As a historical figure the "I" has become a "me," a response that is now "included" in some systemic "me."

If we think of the "me" as homologous to Bourdieu's habitus, and social groups or communities as comparable to fields, then we are left wondering if there is a category that parallels the "I" in Bourdieu's approach. At first glance it may appear that the "I" is too spontaneous for inclusion in Bourdieu's model, but even though the "I" is the source of novel responses, we cannot presume that the "I" exists unmarked by previous experience, for its responses typically draw on learned behaviors. It is also worth noting in this regard that in Mead's model of systemic transformation, a new ("me") system could not arise if events—the "I's" responses, for instance—were so novel that they could not couple with a prior system in order to transform it. (This would also be true, for example, in the case of a biological mutation that is so novel that it fails to survive long enough to transform its environment.) So one should not confuse

Mead's approach with the extreme self-creationism of Sartre's account of consciousness as nothing in *Being and Nothingness*.³¹ Finally, since much of the way we respond to the world is nonreflexive, the "I"—which responds before the individual is self-consciously aware of what he or she has done—can be said to be the home of our nonreflexive engagement with the world, which Bourdieu places in the realm of the habitus. All of this suggests that a good deal of what Mead describes as the "I" is covered in Bourdieu's notion of the habitus, and Bourdieu it seems is even willing to speak of habitus in terms of spontaneity. "The *habitus* is a spontaneity without consciousness or will, opposed as much to the mechanical necessity of things without history in mechanistic theories as it is to the reflexive freedom of subjects 'without inertia' in rationalistic theories."³²

Because the "I" is not reflexively aware of its actions as it produces them, and because it does so in a rather spontaneous fashion, it can be compared to features of the habitus. Yet there are differences. Bourdieu would be uncomfortable with the "I's" penchant for novelty and the way in which Mead appears to assume that the "I" and "me" can work together to set up a situation in which novelty and reflexivity are available to an agent, suggesting just the kind of subjectivism that Bourdieu wants to avoid.³³ And the novelty that Mead locates in the responses of the "I" is not merely an artifact of human activity, for novel events are embedded in the fabric of nature, the warp in nature's woof. They are the ultimate source of change for Mead and are responsible for the flow of time itself; without them we would be living in a Parmenidian universe.³⁴ If Mead, for example, were asked to explain the dynamism and ongoing modifications of Bourdieu's fields, he would not focus on exchanges of various types of capital that produce and are produced by fluctuations in power relations but on the presence of novel events. Although Bourdieu and Mead view the agent in terms of constellations of dispositions, for Mead agents are conceived of as sources of novel behaviors that quite often modify these constellations. Bourdieu, on the other hand, tends to emphasize how the habitus of an agent manages to place a damper on insurgent novelty.

> Early experiences have particular weight because the *habitus* tends to ensure its own constancy and its defence against change through the selection it makes within new information by rejecting information capable of calling into question its accumulated information, if exposed to it accidentally or by

force, and especially by avoiding exposure to such information. . . . Through the systematic "choices" it makes among the places, events and people that might be frequented, the *habitus* tends to protect itself from crises and critical challenges by providing itself with a milieu to which it is as pre-adapted as possible.[35]

While a habitus that is inclined to welcome novelty with (at least) somewhat open arms would be a rather strange beast for Bourdieu, this doesn't mean that he takes himself to be a determinist, and he has on a number of occasions sought to address the issue. When asked about innovation and agency in the face of the seeming durability of the habitus in an interview, Bourdieu turns first to flagellating those who are as enraptured with the notion of themselves as creators as they are obsessively preoccupied with their singularity.[36] He then goes on to tell us that "habitus is not the fate that some people read into it. Being the product of history, it is an *open system of dispositions* that is constantly subjected to experiences, and therefore constantly affected by them in a way that either reinforces or modifies its structures. It is durable but not eternal!"[37] Bourdieu also assures us that a habitus can undergo modification in the face of different fields or even as a result of an "awakening of consciousness and social analysis."[38]

Yet, in spite of Bourdieu's protestations (perhaps he doth protest a bit too much here), there is something rather Spinozist about his work, not so much the hard determinism of Spinoza but the latter's appeal to *conatus*, to each "thing's" striving to persevere in its own existence, with the understanding that every "thing" is intimately conjoined in a series of relationships (causes) that permit it to be what it is. While Bourdieu may not directly appeal to Spinoza's concept, a comparable notion of the inertial looms rather large in his pluri-verse, a world in which a habitus can be thought of as preserving itself because it follows a given trajectory. It may very well be that those who charge Bourdieu with determinism are in fact detecting recurring invocations of determinism's kissing cousin, the inertial.

When Bourdieu speaks about transformations of the social world, he tends to emphasize how given dispositions and schemes can be transposed to different contexts. Novelty seemingly has little or nothing to do with the process. "Because the *habitus* is an infinite capacity for generating products—thoughts, perceptions, expressions and actions—whose limits are set by the historically and socially situated conditions of its production, the conditioned and conditional freedom it provides is as remote from creation of unpredictable novelty as it is from simple mechanical reproduction of the original conditioning."[39]

Mead, on the other hand, emphasizes the role that the upsurge of genuinely novel (unpredictable in principle) events plays in the transformation of the social world. Here he is more influenced by biological models of evolutionary development than is Bourdieu, ones in which mutations or new forms of life manage to introduce themselves into a given ecosystem or organism and create a realignment of prior relationships. In fact Mead develops an analysis of the process of the transformation of systems based on the introduction of a novel event (or organism) into an existing system. His analysis emphasizes a stage between an old system and a new one, a phase of transformation and emergence, which he refers to as "sociality."

> When the new [life] form has established its citizenship the botanist can exhibit the mutual adjustments that have taken place. The world has become a different world because of the advent, but to identify sociality with this result is to identify it with system merely. It is rather the stage betwixt and between the old system and the new that I am referring to. If emergence is a feature of reality this phase of adjustment, which comes between the ordered universe before the emergent has arisen and that after it has come to terms with the newcomer, must be a feature also of reality.[40]

That Mead refers to this state as one of sociality is no accident. Social interaction requires a continual grappling with the new, which can be spoken of as either relative to us—for example, when we deal with cues, situations, fields that we have not previously experienced—or as a change in "objective" conditions—for example, when a novel event is introduced into an existing system. The reality of novelty often confronts us with the need to select alternative courses of action for ourselves. Mead would want to emphasize that human beings can utilize the limbolike state of sociality to weigh and choose options, which Bourdieu would no doubt view as falling into the mandibles of subjectivism or finalism. But for Mead, this weighing of options, which is a form of deliberation, makes *self-determination* possible. We are not restricted to prereflective actions and reactions, that is, habits. Mead would agree with Dewey that we can choose ends and trajectories for ourselves because we can look to the future and anticipate alternative courses of action. (Of course, there are no guarantees that we will anticipate accurately.) While reflection is made possible by language, it is reinforced by problematic situations, which often arise because of novel events. And the betwixt and between of sociality can buy us time, so to speak, to reflect on alternatives and determine how we wish to proceed.[41]

Differences between Mead and Bourdieu can be viewed as stemming from how they view reflective activity. Mead sees it as intimately bound up with our daily nonreflective rounds, as part and parcel of who and what we are, so much so that self-consciously derived initiatives appear as readily available options, which are often smoothly integrated with the nonreflective. Bourdieu tends to view reflection rather negatively, with the exception of its proper use by social scientists, because it serves to distance us from prereflective experience. So, for example, we find Bourdieu remarking,

> And there is every reason to think that as soon as he reflects on his practice, adopting a quasi-theoretical posture, the agent loses any chance of expressing the truth of his practice, and especially the truth of the practical relation to the practice. . . . In contrast to logic, a mode of thought that works by making explicit the work of thought, practice excludes all formal concerns. Reflexive attention to action itself, when it occurs (almost invariably only when the automatisms have broken down), remains subordinate to the pursuit of the result and to the search (not necessarily perceived in this way) for the maximum effectiveness of the effort expended.[42]

Passages such as this one tend to suggest that Bourdieu is not beyond bifurcating experience into reflective and nonreflective domains in his quest to invoke the pragmatic. This bifurcation is especially troubling because so much of his work centers on overcoming such dualisms, an overcoming that would do away with the need to valorize one side over another. This is not to say that such a division cannot provide a useful shorthand for a range of experiences. But this is quite different from setting the terms at odds for the purpose of valorizing one of them, and it appears that under the guise of helping to counterbalance misplaced appetites for theory, Bourdieu has succumbed to just such a temptation. The nonreflective actions of the boxer in the ring or the athlete on the field are seen as having a grace—no, a power—that reflective activities do not have, at least those that are not performed by sociologists setting their biases in order. Here it appears that Nietzsche is at work, or to blame, in leading Bourdieu in the direction of a hyper-aestheticized notion of excellence grounded in some sort of animal naturalness. As the following remark suggests, Bourdieu appears rather comfortable residing in Nietzsche's shadow, echoing as he does the latter's suspicions regarding the "thinker's" contributions to the demise of virtue:[43] "Excellence (that is, practical mastery in its accomplished form) has ceased to exist once people start asking whether it can be taught, as soon as they seek to base 'correct' practice on rules extracted, for the purposes of transmission, as in all academicisms, from the practices of earlier periods or their products."[44] Although Bourdieu has claimed that he "never really got into the existentialist mood," it appears that he hasn't remained immune from the spell of one of existentialism's most problematic progeny: the jargon of authenticity.[45]

On the one hand, it could be argued that Mead has an advantage over Bourdieu with regard to this dichotomy, for while both tend to bifurcate the reflective and nonreflective, Mead doesn't view reflective activities as somehow opposed to—and less authentic than—nonreflective ones but as intertwined with them in our daily affairs. For Mead, reflection is a fundamental type of problem-solving behavior, and problems, in his broad definition of the term, continuously confront us. On the other hand, Bourdieu has been through the fires of Husserl, Heidegger, and especially Merleau-Ponty, and hence insists that the habitus entails a nonreflective capacity for intelligent behavior and anticipatory experience, which Mead may *appear* to reserve for the reflective sphere given the importance of problem-solving behavior in his philosophy. But to place anticipatory experience solely in a reflective sphere would be to misread Mead, because the habitual also contains nonreflective anticipatory moments for him.[46] The difference between Mead and Bourdieu here does not turn on whether there can be nonreflective anticipatory experience; it turns on the manner and the degree to which reflection can be integrated with the nonreflective.

Yet as different as they may be with regard to reflection, there is clearly a sense in which they share a similar understanding of transformation. If *novelty* is defined as the displacement and mapping of one set of dispositions or schemas onto another, then both agree that novelty can be a major source of change. Although for both Bourdieu and Mead novelty may arise due to the transpositions of schemas and habits into different contexts, for Mead it also emerges due to the unpredictably idiosyncratic, which has its locus in the individual. Individuals can introduce *change* into social systems due to their unpredictable (in principle) novel responses, according to Mead. But this is not all. Individual human beings actually have something of an obligation to do so, and this calls for self-assertion.

> The "I" is the response of the individual to the attitude of the community as this appears in his own experience. His response to that organized attitude in turn changes it. . . . But if the response to it is a response which is of the nature of the conversation of gestures, if it creates a situation which is in some sense novel, if one puts up his side of the case, asserts himself over against others and insists that they take a different attitude toward himself, then there is something important occurring that is not previously present in experience.[47]

Note that one asserts oneself not only for one's own interest, but because by so doing something important occurs "that is not previously present in experience." Mead reveals his attachment here to a tradition that foregrounds creativity and transcendence of the given; and individuals, as originators of novel responses, are viewed in a favorable light when they promote novelty in conversation with others. Although Mead would not have spoken in Martin Buber's language regarding the spark of the divine in the other, there is a sense in which individuals are a source of continuing wonder to him because of their capacity to say and do novel things, because they can exceed our expectations. And, of course, this sensibility, shared to a degree by Buber and Mead, is quite in line with Judaic and Christian teachings that link creation and irreducible individuality. So, in spite of the apparent lack of Christian humbleness in Mead's insistence on self-assertion, it would be misleading to read Nietzsche into his comments. Notwithstanding Mead's secular turn, his liberal, midwestern, progressive Christian roots continued to influence him.[48]

There are additional connections to this tradition in Mead's thought that are worth highlighting. Conversations of gestures—whether reflective or nonreflective—not only help sustain novel responses but can also nurture mutuality. For Mead, a conspicuous feature of our everyday social and linguistic exchanges is that we continually take the perspective of others, and by doing so, we enhance our capacity for empathy, sympathy, and impartiality. Bourdieu would want to place some distance between himself and models that emphasize empathy and impartiality, not only because they do not seem sufficiently sensitive to objective conditions but also because they appear insufficiently attuned to the nature of interests, or *illusio*. According to Bourdieu, we can never escape our interests and must even ask what interests universalism serves. To be a social actor is to have a stake in a certain game.

> To understand the notion of interest, it is necessary to see that it is opposed not only to that of disinterestedness or gratuitousness but also to that of *indifference*. To be indifferent is to be unmoved by the game: like Buridan's donkey, this game makes no difference to me. Indifference is an axiological state, an ethical state of nonpreference as well as a state of knowledge in which I am not capable of differentiating the stakes proposed. Such was the goal of the Stoics: to reach a state of ataraxy (*ataraxia* means the fact of not being troubled). *Illusio* is the very opposite of ataraxy: it is to be invested, taken in and by the game. . . . Each field calls forth and gives life to a specific form of interest, a specific *illusio*, as tacit recognition of the value of the stakes of the game as practical mastery of its rules.[49]

Since it is hard to imagine how one could exist for Bourdieu without at each moment being immersed in a field, it is also hard to imagine how one could ever escape from "interestedness." Mead, following William James's lead, is also quite convinced that a transhistorical rationality that would allow us to escape our interests is simply not in the cards for social and historical beings such as ourselves. That we are perspectively bound creatures should alone give us pause when we hear claims to disinterested observations from the mount. Nevertheless, there is considerable difference between Mead and Bourdieu here, as the following statement by Mead makes patently clear.

> We are definitely identified with our own interests. One is constituted out of his own interests; and when those interests are frustrated, what is called for then is in some sense a sacrifice of this narrow self. This should lead to the development of a larger self which can be identified with the interests of others. I think all of us feel that one must be ready to recognize the interests of others even when they run counter to our own, but that the person who does that does not really sacrifice himself, but becomes a larger self.[50]

No doubt the skills involved in the sharing of attitudes and interests can be used in a manipulative or strategic fashion, and not just for the "enlargement" of the self. And Bourdieu is quite skillful in attuning us to the ways in which human beings have sought to accumulate various forms of "capital," which they then employ to support their preferred interests. For Bourdieu, Mead would have been something of a babe in the woods. Mead believed that the modern world might very well see the rise of so-called abstract groups that would be increasingly open to participation by those removed in time and place.[51] He believed in his own pragmatized version of Kant's enlarged mentality, one that did not seek to deny interests but to expand them through shared (or potentially shareable) experiences. He continued to believe in the merits of a secularized version of the Christian commonwealth of his youthful dreams, where all human beings would be brothers and sisters who would be able to see their interests (at times) as the interests of their neighbors. And, in a rather Jamesian fashion, he continued to believe that our belief in this ideal was part and parcel of the practice that could help to realize it. Bourdieu, of course, would find all of this as unconvincing as it is quaintly American and provincial. Ideas and practices cannot avoid being tainted by (unspecified) interests, and he would be moved to unmask any pretensions to the contrary. In Part 2 we will see how Mead's ideas regarding the self, abstract groups, sociality, impartiality, and mutuality relate to an "enlarged mentality" and a cosmopolitanism that challenges Bourdieu's assumptions. And in Chapter 6 we will address the limitations of a recent model of the self that borrows from Bourdieu.

Part II
Cosmopolitanism and Transcendence

§ 4 Mead on Cosmopolitanism, Sympathy, and War

> As man advances in civilisation, and small tribes are united into larger communities, the simplest reason would tell each individual that he ought to extend his social instincts and sympathies to all the members of the same nation, though personally unknown to him. This point being once reached, there is only an artificial barrier to prevent his sympathies extending to the men of all nations and races. If, indeed, such men are separated from him by great differences in appearance or habits, experience unfortunately shews us how long it is, before we look at them as our fellow-creatures. Sympathy beyond the confines of man, that is, humanity to the lower animals, seems to be one of the latest moral acquisitions.
> —Charles Darwin, *The Descent of Man*

When we say of someone who lives in our community that she is a good neighbor, we not only mean that she does us no harm. We imply that this person is willing to assist those in her community when they are in distress. And when we speak of the good Samaritan, we speak of a person who is willing to assist those in need, even if they are not members of her local community. The charitableness of this individual extends to those in distress, whether near or far. How are we to understand the moral psychology of persons whose benevolence transcends the provincial and extends to strangers? What leads individuals to a cosmopolitan perspective on the needs of others, while others remain solely committed to kith and kin? These questions can be addressed from a variety of vantage points: psychological, economic, cultural, and sociological. In this chapter I offer the outlines of a moral psychology that is indebted to George Herbert Mead.

In doing so, I will discuss the relationship between sympathetic feelings, empathy (which involves taking the perspectives of others), cosmopolitanism, and a sense of obligation that is a condition for successfully alleviating distress. Mead's views on war will also be examined, for they shed light on the relationship between nationalism, national self-determination, and cosmopolitanism, topics that will also be addressed in the next chapter.

∼

George Herbert Mead should be viewed as a social constructionist or, perhaps better, as a social reconstructionist. As a political progressive in the heyday of the progressive movement in the United States, Mead was clearly committed to relieving the undeserved suffering of those in his own and in other lands.[1] Mead endorses a version of cosmopolitanism that speaks to our obligations to those who suffer. Although this issue obviously does not exhaust the field of ethics, it does say a good deal about Mead as an ethicist and as a moral psychologist. Mead's most sustained contributions were to social theory and social psychology. Although he was keenly interested in ethics, and he wrote and acted on these interests, those looking to Mead for a refined ethical system will be disappointed. Nevertheless, his insights are promising and worth developing.

If we are to follow Mead, and also those who are in Habermas's camp, in addressing our obligations to those who suffer undeservedly, we will need to appeal to notions of reciprocity and perspectivism to assist us. For Mead, as we have seen in Chapter 3, taking the perspectives or roles of others is basic to the development of the self, and individuals can have multiple selves. As an object of cognition the self depends on the internalization of roles, which can be viewed as perspectives. It also depends on reflexivity and a capacity for self-consciousness, which are grounded for Mead in the pragmatics of language development and the exchange of roles.[2] If we find ourselves in circumstances that generate the taking of alternate perspectives in a sustained fashion, we can develop an "enlarged mentality," to borrow and modify Kant's phrase along Arendtian lines. In Arendt's words, "In the *Critique of Judgement* . . . Kant insisted upon a different way of thinking, for which it would not be enough to be in agreement with one's own self, but which consisted of being able to 'think in the place of everybody else' and which he therefore called an 'enlarged mentality' (*eine erweiterte Denkungsart*)."[3]

According to Mead, we do not simply share perspectives that are always already given. We continually encounter perspectives that are different and in varying degrees novel. When certain social conditions are present—for example, the absence of threats by others—these past and present perspectives aren't dismissed but engaged, and the engagement helps to foster inclusiveness and an ability to step outside the local. I will refer to the ability to take the roles of others as "empathy."[4] On the one hand, Mead is convinced that the greater the number of perspectives that we share, the greater will become our sensitivity to others. Solidarity and inclusiveness will result. On the other hand, if we find ourselves mired in an unwillingness to grapple with new and different perspectives, we will grow less tolerant and more insensitive. We will become ever more exclusionary and parochial. By remaining open to the novel lives of others, we avoid effacing them with our own forms of life. As noted earlier, Buber reminds us that one of the characteristics of the person, the Thou, is his or her ability to surprise us, to present us with the new. So, remaining open to novel perspectives can be viewed as a way of seeking to avoid reducing others to our categories or to circumscribed narratives; that is, it can be seen as a form of respect. For Mead, as for Herder, this respect extends to other peoples.

Mead has a story to tell here. He thinks that the modern Western world has set the stage for an increased sensitivity to others, those both near and far. He locates an aspect of this sensibility in the romantic temper. He does not, and cannot, argue that a sensitivity to others is confined to the modern self. A claim of this sort would run contrary to his account of the ontogenesis of the self. As long as human beings have lived in nonmonolithic communities that possessed language, selves have existed and been dependent on others for their genesis. But historical conditions, which of course include material conditions, transform how selves are realized. In his *Movements of Thought in the Nineteenth Century*, Mead argues that romanticism revealed a fundamental shift in our relationship to the past, and this shift in turn was responsible for a transformation in the way in which the self came to be experienced.

> What the Romantic period revealed, then, was not simply a past, but a past as the point of view from which to come back at the self. One has to grow into the attitude of the other, come back at the self, to realize the self; and we are discussing the means by which this was done. Here, then, we have the makings of a new philosophy, the Romantic philosophy.[5]

> It was because people in Europe, at this time, put themselves back in the earlier attitude that they could come back upon themselves. . . . As a characteristic of the romantic attitude we find this assumption of rôles.[6]

For Mead, the romantic temper was uniquely suited to the development or the "expansion" of the self because it nurtured our capacity to see ourselves, "to come back at the self," from the perspective of others. As the past became enlivened through the experience of taking the perspective of historical or fictional characters, new ways of relating to the self arose, which in turn generated new relationships to the past (and one's own past). In other words, people organized or reorganized the past in relation to their current emerging selves and their selves in relation to emerging pasts.[7] Selves are by nature reflexive, but romanticism made something of a fetish of this reflexivity, this "coming back at the self," and exemplary romantics delighted in their ability to take the roles of others, both past and present.[8] The upshot was that new narratives appeared that entailed taking the perspective of others in ways that "broadened" the self.[9] This is, of course, not to say that selves did not exist before romanticism. And it is definitely not to claim that cosmopolitanism was a product of romanticism. (Mead certainly knew too much about history, literature, and philosophy to make a naïve claim of this sort.) Rather, it is to claim that the character of selves was altered by the ways in which people came to experience a multitude of others, those both living and dead.[10]

In short, romanticism generated inventive ways of engaging others through role-taking, which in turn led to the generation of "enlarged" selves. For Mead, the formation of selves that have an enhanced capacity for "growth" is crucial to moral development. When the self encounters problematic situations—for example, those of a moral nature—the way in which the self responds results in either its stagnation or its transformation and growth. There is an old self that maintains accepted values or a new one that integrates different values, but to integrate these values, it must move beyond both selfishness and self-sacrifice, which prove to be two sides of the same coin.

> To leave the field to the values represented by the old self is exactly what we term selfishness. The justification for the term is found in the habitual character of conduct with reference to these values. Attention is not claimed by the object and shifts to the subjective field where the affective responses are identified with the old self. The result is that we state the other conflict-

ing ends in subjective terms of other selves and the moral problem seems to take on the form of the sacrifice of the self or the others. Where, however, the problem is objectively considered, although the conflict is a social one, it should not resolve itself into a struggle between selves, but into such reconstruction of the situation that different and *enlarged and more adequate personalities may emerge.*[11]

Old selves must be willing to give way to new selves to avoid what he terms "selfishness." This will lead to an enlargement of the self, that is, a more cosmopolitan self, which is attuned to inclusion.

Mead thinks that one of the advantages of modernity is that it makes available a larger repertoire of potential selves. He is a cosmopolitan who sees the expansion of communication and contact with others as sources of growth, including moral growth, which in turn has the potential to help give birth to a more democratized world order less given to strife. With regard to the relationship of communication to cosmopolitanism, Mead's position is akin to Arendt's, as the following passage from her lectures on Kant's political philosophy suggests (although Mead would take exception to the phrase "sheer fact of being human").

> One can communicate only if one is able to think from the other person's standpoint; otherwise one will never meet him, never speak in such a way that he understands. . . . Finally, the larger the scope of those to whom one can communicate, the greater is the worth of the object. . . . One judges always as a member of a community, guided by one's community sense, one's *sensus communis*. But in the last analysis, one is a member of a world community by the sheer fact of being human; this is one's "cosmopolitan existence."[12]

For the sake of argument, let us suppose that Mead's account is accurate, that is, following on the heels of romanticism, and the growing complexity of modern society, the tendency to take alternative perspectives in the modern Western world increased.[13] But why should we assume that taking alternative perspectives, understood as empathetic responses, leads to *sympathy*, that is, to compassion for others? Quantitative change does not necessarily produce qualitative transformation, or at least qualitative transformation worthy of endorsement. Perhaps engaging in perspective-taking is best understood as a form of entertainment, so that we do not arrive at a morally informed or enlarged self but at something more akin to a theatrical self or perhaps the aesthete in Kierkegaard's *Either/Or*. What is it about taking alternative perspectives, as well as a willingness to accept novelty, that leads to compassion and moral growth as opposed to, say, some sort of hedonistic self-indulgence or the manipulation of others for selfish ends?

There is, however, a reason why Mead believes that moral development—at least in terms of compassion, that is, a sensitization to the suffering and needs of others—is a likely, although by no means a necessary, outcome of the expansion of perspectives. Mead is led to this conclusion in part because of the influence of the Scottish sympathy theorists, and this can be seen, for example, in his basic assumption about a biological predisposition to compassion. Mead claims, "Back of the obligation of the donor lies the human impulse to help those in distress. It is an impulse which we can trace back to animals lower than man. . . . The kindliness that expresses itself in charity is as fundamental an element in human nature as are any in our original endowment. The man without a generous impulse is abnormal and abhorrent."[14]

Mead seeks to combine a natural disposition for sympathy, compassion, with the capacity for taking the perspective of others, to yield a morally informed, enlarged or cosmopolitan mentality. In this regard Mead and Adam Smith can be seen as fellow travelers. However, in spite of their similarities, Mead would find Smith and other theorists of moral sentiment limited in their understanding of how role-taking and empathy develop; for example, there is no self-and-other dialectic in this tradition, at least not one that would satisfy the neo-Hegelian in Mead. In synthesizing a sentiment for sympathy with a dialectic of self and other that entails empathy, Mead provides a plausible route for avoiding the reduction of perspective-taking to the merely strategic or aesthetic, one that I want to explore further by addressing his notion of obligation, which will in turn help to illuminate the place of sympathy in his cosmopolitanism.

As important as sympathy and empathy are for Mead's account of cosmopolitan benevolence, they cannot in themselves generate an adequate ethical response to the suffering of others. They are but two legs of the proverbial three-legged stool. To adequately respond to others, we must also possess a sense of *obligation*.

> The sympathetic identification with the individual in distress . . . calls out in us the incipient reactions of warding off, of defense, which the distress arouses in the sufferer, and these reactions become dominant in the response of the one who assists. He places himself in the service of the other. We speak of this

attitude as that of unselfishness or self-effacement of the charitable individual. But even this attitude of devotion to the interest of the other is *not* that of obligation. . . . *The earliest appearance of the feel of obligation is found in the appraisal of the relief to the distressed person in terms of the donor's effort and expenditure.*[15]

Mead is too sophisticated a social theorist not to be sensitive to the social and historical dimensions of the experience of sympathy, yet as we have seen, he argues that there is a biological impulse to compassion. Mead even suggests that the social component of the self stands to impulses as form does to matter for Aristotle.[16] However, obligation is not located in the sympathetic feeling itself, nor even in visceral urges and reactions to assist, as important as these may be as necessary conditions for obligation, but in reflection on the circumstances of the distress and in a commitment to alleviate it, that is, in the "effort and expenditure" we are prepared to make in response to our sympathetic feelings. As a pragmatist he can no more be satisfied with sympathetic feelings than he can be with good intentions. The "effort and expenditure" (especially if successful) will typically involve reflecting on various courses of action and anticipating their consequences, capacities that were addressed earlier.

For a pragmatist the point is to transform the conditions that create distress, and here is where the notion of obligation comes into its own for Mead. The latter occurs when we recognize that a concerted effort on our part is required to alleviate suffering. But why after an initial reaction to and an acknowledgment of distress are some individuals motivated to move beyond their feelings of sympathy or compassion to a sense of obligation? Before answering this question, I want to interject a caveat. I have not been speaking of justice or injustice when discussing Mead's position, not because he does not address justice but because for Mead justice involves a form of identification with others in terms of rights, as opposed to kindly and charitable impulses, and it entails a form of self-assertion. Although he speaks of rights, Mead's understanding of cosmopolitanism is best approached through moral categories such as benevolence, which are more readily linked to his social psychology.

To answer why some individuals develop a greater sense of obligation than others, we might take an easy path and say that the normative content of generalized others, or the systemic organizations of attitudes of particular groups or communities, directs individuals to act in specific circumstances. People simply follow internalized group norms, and some group norms focus on addressing the needs of others. But as important as group norms may be, surely in themselves they cannot totally explain why some individuals are more motivated than others to move beyond feelings of sympathy to a sense of obligation, for those who are members of the same group or community may respond quite differently to suffering.[17]

An alternative, yet complementary, explanation begins with a truism based on experience, namely, there are differences between individuals regarding the intensity of their responses to the suffering of others. Some people are more prepared to sympathize with others, either because of individual constitution or developmental factors. In traditional empiricist terms we can say that these individuals experience distress and suffering with greater force and vivacity than others, which in this case means that they experience the suffering of others as in some sense their own. As Adam Smith remarks, "For as to be in pain or distress of any kind excites the most excessive sorrow, so to conceive or to imagine that we are in it, excites some degree of the same emotion, in proportion to the vivacity or dulness [sic] of the conception."[18]

When individuals experience the distress of others in a lively manner, they are more prepared to stand or remain standing in the others' shoes (that is, perspective) because of the intensity of their own experience. This in turn can lead to a desire and a willingness to act to alleviate the distress, because the experience of the other—or better, the character and intensity of the other's experience—is in some sense their own experience. There are no guarantees here, for of course we can imagine sadistic or masochistic types who refrain from acting, and do so for opposing reasons. And at times fear or selfish ends get the better of us. Nevertheless, it is a reasonable hypothesis that those who are deeply attuned to the distress of others are more inclined to act to remove the distress, and there is empirical evidence to support this claim.[19]

However, the relationship between sympathy, empathy, and obligation is more complex than was just suggested. We do not necessarily move directly from the intensity of sympathy through increased empathy to obligation. For example, how readily we can empathize with others, take their perspectives, may be a factor in whether we are capable of sustaining for a stretch of time an initial (prereflective) sympathetic response. Further, if we have learned how to move in and out of perspectives with relative ease, we are more likely to transform an initial sympathetic feeling into a sense of obligation. How so? Through engaging alternative points of view, perspectives, we develop our capacity to evaluate courses of action that may help alleviate suffering. In other words, knowledge of what may be possible makes us more likely agents of change, ready to see the world in terms of obligations, because we gain a purchase on how we may be able to make a difference. And here it is worth emphasizing that a *developed* capacity for taking new and different perspectives is not determined by biological impulses but is the result of practice and habit. The taking of perspectives tends to build on itself, both for individuals and collectives. It is a form of praxis. We become habituated to experiencing the experience of the other.[20] And this in turn enhances our capacity for envisioning alternative courses of action.

Yet isn't there a danger in linking sympathy and obligation? If the force and vivacity of feelings play a significant role in motivating us, wouldn't sympathy incline us to be moved by those who are closest to us, kin and countrymen, to the exclusion of strangers, to be good (local) neighbors but not good Samaritans? Has Mead simply succumbed to the seduction of venerating sentiments? Doesn't an appeal to feelings simply return us to a pre-Critical vantage point that can't comprehend the need for duty and the moral law? Where are we to locate the impartial spectator, who prompts us to transcend the parochial, who calls on us to consider the stranger, who moves us to become more cosmopolitan?[21]

Impartiality is related to the facts that individuals are members of different types of communities and communities operate at different levels of abstraction. For Mead, we take the perspective not only of singular others but of generalized others. Groups and communities have generalized others—that is, systemic organizations of attitudes—and these generalized others function at different levels of abstraction. So, for Mead, "concrete social classes or subgroups, such as political parties, clubs, corporations, which are all actually functional social units," can be said to have generalized others, as can a family. And so can "abstract social classes or subgroups, such as the class of debtors and the class of creditors," whose members are related indirectly.[22] According to Mead, selves as objects of cognition arise that correspond to these more abstract communities. But the process does not stop here. Through the practice of taking different perspectives and utilizing symbols that are more abstract, we develop a capacity to extend our horizons to communities that are tied together by increasingly abstract commitments, for example, a commitment to certain kinds of rights (which I mention only in passing since we are not examining rights).[23] "The very universality and impersonality of thought and reason [are] from the behavioristic standpoint the result of the given individual taking the attitudes of others toward himself, and of his finally crystallizing all these particular attitudes into a single attitude or standpoint which may be called that of the 'generalized other.'"[24]

While Mead does not invoke the notion of an ideal communication community of the Habermasian sort, one that depends on a quasi-transcendental foundation, he does suggest that we can develop a critical distance from localized claims by invoking more abstract and relatively universal communities. For Mead, universals are first and foremost shared symbols, and a symbol, as a functional universal, can be called a universal even if it is shared by just two individuals. In this respect some symbols are more universal than others in being more widely shared, and there is a correlation between the potential for a symbol to be shared and its degree of abstractness. In an analogous manner, some communities or groups—for example, a scientific community—are more universal than others. Mead claims that "group solidarity, especially in its uniform restrictions, gives him [the child and the individual] the unity of universality. This I take to be the sole source of the universal. It quickly passes the bounds of the specific group.... Education and varied experience refine out of it what is provincial, and leave 'what is true for all men at all times.'"[25] Mead places scare quotes around the phrase "what is true for all men at all times," for he isn't naïvely ahistorical. While Mead shares in the Enlightenment's attraction to universalism, his thought is also attuned to romanticism's inclination to particularity.[26]

Mead, then, is advocating what might be called a contingent universalism, that is, the claim that individuals can move beyond the immediacy of local concerns by engaging others at different levels of abstraction. It is our capacity to distance ourselves from the local, to transcend the local, that provides a counterweight to the danger of moral myopia due to a preoccupation with localized sympathetic attachments. One of Mead's rather down-to-earth ways of expressing this is to say, "The only way in which we can react against the disapproval of the entire community is by setting up a higher sort of community which in a certain sense out-votes the one we find."[27] *We might even speculate that our sense of obligation, insofar as it requires a mediated response to suffering as opposed to the immediately visceral, is nurtured by the detachment afforded by the abstractions of generalized others.* And this tendency toward universality can be linked to Mead's account of the way in which a heightened degree of reflexivity and role-taking has developed in the modern world. We are simply more likely to inhabit various communities in the modern world, and our participation in them, as well as our movement between them, generates a tendency toward abstraction from the local.[28] This abstraction from the local helps to generate the "impartial spectator" that assists us in making moral decisions by transcending the provincial.[29] It should be noted that Mead doesn't equate tendencies toward universality (and "impartiality") solely with modernity.[30]

But if sympathy helps motivate us to act, what happens if we see ourselves first and foremost as members of relatively abstract communities? Isn't there a danger that these abstractions might displace or take priority over feelings, leading to diminished motivation to assist others? Isn't there a risk that sympathy will be displaced by an eviscerated universalism, one that cannot supply a sense of involvement and interest that leads to action? In other words, if we depend on abstractions to give strangers their due, don't we run the risk of turning agents into unemotional and unmotivated cosmopolitans? Are we not now facing a version of the struggle between the universal and particular, between a "bloodless" benevolent cosmopolitan and an "energized" sympathetic local agent?

For a pragmatist such as Mead, these oppositions may prove to be more conceptual or artificial than actual. The important questions for a pragmatist are the following: In practice, in actual situations, can and do individuals bring together elements of the universal and the particular? Can we join the particularity of sympathy with a more universally minded sense of obligation (via empathy)? Have people been able to reconcile these *seeming* opposites in their practices? Perhaps an example would best show how these "opposites" might be joined together in practice. The example I have in mind is the catastrophic loss of life, homelessness, and serious injury that resulted from the earthquakes and tsunamis in the Indian Ocean late in 2004 and early 2005.

Estimates have suggested that more than 150,000 people died, 500,000 were seriously injured, and 5 million were left homeless.[31] Nations responded to this catastrophe by offering various forms of assistance, including large sums of money, even appearing to compete with one another regarding the scope of their assistance. There were geopolitical reasons for this assistance, for example, concern about fragile and war-torn regimes in the region and a desire to appear altruistic toward Islamic cultures for propaganda purposes. But there also appeared to be a genuine aspiration to alleviate suffering, reflected not only in the actions of governments, which seemed to be supported by many of their citizens, but in the contributions made by individuals throughout the world. Of course, people felt different degrees of sympathy for the victims for various reasons, and there were those whose racism may have prevented them from seeing the humanity of those who suffered. Nevertheless, sympathy for the victims of the tsunamis appeared to be widespread.[32]

If we look at the world's response to this disaster, we can discern components of a moral psychology that is sensitive to the suffering of strangers, which I have been developing in light of Mead's work. First, many of those exposed to the images of death and destruction had an immediate, prereflective, sympathetic response to the distress of others, in spite of their physical and cultural distance. Second, for some, perhaps many, this immediate response set the stage for a more self-conscious taking of the perspective of those who suffered serious injury and/or the loss of loved ones. People began to see themselves as if they were the other (or perhaps it would be better to say, they began to step inside the shoes of the other). Third, the normative standards of generalized others came into play, bringing to bear "local" norms about dealing with those in distress, as well as more abstract perspectives that allowed the victims to be viewed as members of more "universal" communities, for example, those that encompassed both victims and the empathic individuals. Fourth, the sympathetic impulse, the taking of the perspective of others, and the normative dimension of generalized others helped to generate a sense of obligation, which entailed an appraisal of the effort that was needed to alleviate the suffering. Finally, this sense of obligation was acted on in various ways, for example, through monetary contributions or directly by those expending time and effort to help alleviate the suffering.

This said, it's important to note that not all, or even most, moral responses to suffering must begin with a visceral "feeling" for the other. We behave morally for various reasons. Abstract norms often guide our behavior. Our motives are often mixed. The pragmatist seeks to circumvent thinking that requires placing sympathy (feelings) and genuine morality at odds, such as one finds in Kant's or Levinas's ethics. The reality is that sympathy can play an important and salutary role in our ethical life, as can empathy, if at times only as necessary conditions for the obligatory. People are motivated to act in virtuous ways for various good reasons. The conceptual morass of the universal and particular need not block the path to goods that can be realized in practice.

~

Mead worried a great deal about war's role in undermining ethical behavior in the modern world. The psychology that helps lead to war can be viewed as the inverse of the psychology that nurtures acts of cosmopolitan benevolence. We have seen that Mead assumes that biological impulses play an important role in our sympathetic responses to others. For Mead, there are also impulses that play a role in the origin of war.[33] By exploring his views on war, and its relationship to nationalism, we can further clarify Mead's ideas on cosmopolitanism.

Mead thought that war was becoming an impossible course of action in the modern world. Following in Kant's footsteps, he argues that war is becoming increasingly and unacceptably dangerous.[34] Writing between the two world wars, he states, "Every war if allowed to go the accustomed way of wars will become a world war, and every war pursued uncompromisingly and intelligently must take as its objective the destruction not of hostile forces but of enemy nations in their entirety."[35] What has this to do with claims that Mead makes about sympathy? Mead is not only willing to posit a modifiable biological urge toward sympathizing with the plight of others but is also willing to claim that there are other impulses, including a hostile impulse. Human selves arise through the molding of these impulses by language, social interaction, and societal organization. "We are born with our fundamental impulses. . . . This primal stuff of which we are made up is not under our direct control. The primitive sexual, parental, hostile, and cooperative impulses out of which our social selves are built up are few—but they get an almost infinite field of varied application in society, and with every development of means of intercourse, with every invention they find new opportunities of expression."[36]

While we certainly would not want to confuse Mead with the Freud of *Civilization and Its Discontents*—he never posits overarching metapsychological and cosmological principles such as Eros and Thanatos, for example—for those used to a sanitized version of the American pragmatist tradition, one that avoids the "darker sides" of human nature, it is perhaps somewhat surprising to hear that Mead is quite prepared to say that there is an impulse to hostility. However, an impulse to hostility is only one factor in explaining war. For Mead, war is not simply a result of hostile impulses or power politics but depends on a desire for unity. "Society is unity in diversity. However there is always present the danger of its miscarriage. There are the two sources of its unity—the unity arising from the interconnection of all of the different selves in their self-conscious diversity and that arising from the identity of common impulses."[37]

Paradoxically, the source of hope in the modern world—the ability of human beings to abstract from the local and see themselves from ever-widening vantage points, thereby becoming participants in communities of increasing scope—can backfire if the promise of unity, community, remains unfulfilled. In this circumstance the impulse to unity, to affiliation, is not modified in the direction of intelligently guided social interaction and organization; rather, it is hijacked by social forces that prey upon primal needs for inclusion, which can lead to war. We then have identification and bonding with those we view as members of our community at the price of opposing those who are viewed as outsiders, as *not* members of our "club." There is no older story, but in the modern world we face an especially pernicious version of it.

> There is something profoundly pathetic in the situation of great peoples, that have been struggling up through long centuries of fighting and its attendant miseries, coming closer and closer to each other in their daily lives, fashioning unwittingly larger racial, lingual, liturgical, confessional, political, and economic communities, and realizing only intermittently the spiritual life which this larger community confers upon them, and realizing it only when they could fight for it. The pathos comes out most vividly in the nationalisms of the nineteenth and twentieth centuries. These nationalisms have meant the sudden realization that men belonged to communities that transcended their groups, families, and clans. . . . The pathos lies in the inability to feel the new unity with the nation except in the union of arms. It is not that men love fighting for its own sake, but they undergo its rigors for the sake of conjunction with all those who are fighting in the same cause.[38]

On the one hand, Mead advocates enlarging the social circles in which we engage in taking the perspectives of others, but on the other, he alerts us to forces that can turn this perspective-taking against others, that is, by limiting its scope to a given unit, say, a tribe or a nation, so that others are deemed as outside "our" community. If our sense of stability and community feel threatened, we may take such a turn. Given the destructive power available to us in the modern world, we must find a way to feel united with others in a peaceful, or at least a nonwarlike, fashion.

> There is only one solution for the problem [of war] and that is in finding the intelligible common objects, the objects of industry and commerce, the common values in literature, art, and science, the common human interests which political mechanisms define and protect and foster. . . . Within our communities the process of civilization is the discovery of these common ends which are the bases of social organizations. In social organization they come to mean not opposition but diverse occupations and activities. Difference of function takes the place of hostility of interest.[39]

These common interests are to be pursued within states and between states. Mead's thesis, in part, is that until there is a sense of unity in particular societies, developed through common ends and organizations that permit functional differentiation, there will be a temptation to war. This vision is certainly consistent with his view that unalienated integration into groups, the existence of different sorts of groups, and movement between them have the potential to nurture a kind of cosmopolitanism that will lessen hostility to "outsiders." One can immediately argue that Mead was simply naïve about political forces in the modern world and that functional differentiation can breed alienation as well as integration. I would, however, like to pass over a critique at this point in order to bring the discussion back to Mead's views on the psychology of sympathy. Certainly the mere reorientation of the psychology of individual actors will not prevent war, but I want to make a more modest claim that Mead's social-psychological approach has something interesting to say regarding what disposes individual actors to become responsive to the plight of others, which in turn can have consequences regarding how readily they take up arms. First, a caveat: Mead was well aware of the importance of institutional and legal safeguards, especially on the international plane. He was, after all, a booster of the League of Nations. This is not to say that he had a sufficiently robust theory of the procedural for dealing with domestic or international affairs. It is to say that he was not naïve enough to believe that efforts based on social-psychological insight alone are sufficient to address the problem of war.

As noted, Mead's position entails biological proclivities to sympathy and unity, whose origins are perhaps best understood in terms of natural selection; for example, human beings are relatively fragile biological organisms uniquely dependent on others of their kind for survival. We might also speculate that this fragility can in part account for the fear that people feel when they experience instability, social unrest, and alienation. Impulses or proclivities are molded, shaped, and informed by the way in which the self develops through linguistic interaction, role-taking, and the internalization of generalized others. However, while the reciprocity of social interaction is basic for Mead, it is not enough to guarantee unity. There must also be goals in common, which can be found in organizations whose functional distinctions permit the social integration of the actors. Without common goals and intelligent integration of social functions, Mead fears that war will result. Why? As we have seen, Mead argues that there is an organic drive for unity or social cohesion, which can be primed and activated by specific social conditions and sated by uniting with others in acts of war. Yet war, modern war in particular, is unacceptable to Mead. I want to offer a hypothesis, which Mead does not directly develop, but which should shed some light on how his cosmopolitanism and opposition to war are related.

If we take Mead's account of perspective-taking and sympathy seriously, one of the conditions that contributes to initiating and sustaining war is an inability to view others as those who can suffer undeservedly. This is surely a time-honored observation: war is made possible and sustained through the dehumanization of the enemy. Mead, however, is offering an account of the kinds of human capacities that have to be short-circuited if this is to occur. For example, if the so-called enemy were viewed as victims of a natural disaster, the sympathetic impulse, as well as our capacity to take their perspective, would diminish the urge to war. This is all the more true when pictures and videos of the human suffering involved in war are readily available. For individuals to stay motivated to carry out a war under these circumstances, they must be convinced that there is a genuine threat from an adversary or that the adversary deserves to suffer. Why did so many Americans mistakenly believe that Saddam Hussein and Iraq were responsible for 9/11? One might say that this misperception was due to effective propaganda. And one might also say that without this belief it would have been hard to justify the suffering that ensued. Undeserved suffering must become deserved suffering, which is viewed as deserved or acceptable because of what "they" did to us. Because of what they did to us, they cannot be like us, for if they were like us, they would not have acted as they did. They would have had sympathy for our suffering. Therefore, they must be inhuman.

Of course, "they" don't typically decide to do anything to us. "They" were not involved in the decisions of those who committed them to war, yet they undeservedly suffer from its consequences. For many, if not most, war should be viewed as a form of natural disaster. It arrives as a tidal force: dark, uncontrollable, and lethal. Yes, a populace can be stirred into a war frenzy, but this sort of mass hysteria only supports the view that people often have little control over the forces that give rise to war.

For Mead, prereflective sympathy and a capacity for taking the perspective of others are insufficient hedges against war, especially in the modern world. We need to become ever more cosmopolitan. We need to feel and know that others are capable of suffering as we do and that suffering is typically undeserved. And we need to develop a sense of obligation toward those who suffer. We need to transcend the local; but this will not be possible if nations and peoples are themselves divided, if alienation and (economic) instability are the rule, if political and economic situations undermine self-respect.

> What I am seeking to bring out is that the chief difficulty in attaining international-mindedness does not lie in the clash of international interests but in the deep-seated need which nations feel of being ready to fight, not for ostensible ends but for the sake of the sense of national unity, of self-determination, of national self-respect that they can achieve in no other way so easily as in the readiness to fight. National-mindedness and international-mindedness are inextricably involved in each other. Stable nations do not feel the need in any such degree as those that are seeking stability.[40]

If Mead's analysis is even partially on target, then he can be said to have understood factors working against the realization of his own cosmopolitan "vision," that is, *thwarted* expressivist sensibilities lodged in movements of national self-determination. Mead was never simply an adherent of the Radical Enlightenment's notion of universality. There was too much understanding of the romantic temper in his thought. Hence, national identity and self-determination need to be achieved before cosmopolitanism can come into its own. So once again we see an interweaving of the universal and particular for Mead. Perhaps the best that he could hope for in his lifetime was that tendencies to universality in the modern world would be nurtured and institutionalized—for example, through international organizations and agencies—while expectations for national and collective self-identity would be met in nonmilitaristic and nondestructive ways.

Mead's views on nationalism and war may seem old hat, a set of concerns from a time and place rapidly drifting into the past, especially as globalization in its myriad forms presses in around us. Or perhaps not. Du Bois, as we shall see in the next chapter, would have appreciated Mead's insights into the importance of self-determination and self-respect for different peoples.

§ 5   W. E. B. Du Bois
Double-Consciousness, Jamesian Sympathy,
and the Cosmopolitan

The Souls of Black Folk is W. E. B. Du Bois's most famous work. It is a short book, representing a small portion of his oeuvre.[1] It is a relatively early work, composed in large measure of previously published pieces. The famous first chapter, "Of Our Spiritual Strivings," was published originally as "The Strivings of the Negro People" in 1897, some six years before *Souls*.[2] This was during the period that Du Bois was researching one of his first major sociological studies, *The Philadelphia Negro*, seven years after he had graduated from Harvard, and a mere three years after graduate study in Germany.[3] He was a young man, at the beginning of a turbulent career that would extend into the 1960s.

The Souls of Black Folk has remained his most influential and widely read book, although Du Bois appears to have had some ambivalence about it. In his own review of the book, published a year after *Souls*, he states,

> One who is born with a cause is predestined to a certain narrowness of view, and at the same time to some clearness of vision within his limits with which the world often finds it well to reckon. My book has many of the defects and some of the advantages of this situation. Because I am a Negro I lose something of that breadth of view which the more cosmopolitan races have, and with this goes an intensity of feeling and conviction which both wins and repels sympathy, and now enlightens, now puzzles. . . . This is not saying that the style and workmanship of the book make its meaning altogether clear. . . . Nevertheless, as the feeling is deep the greater the impelling force to seek to express it. And here the feeling was deep.
>
> In its larger aspects the style is topical—African. This needs no apology. The blood of my fathers spoke through me and cast off the English restraint

of my training and surroundings. The resulting accomplishment is a matter of taste. Sometimes I think very well of it and sometimes I do not.[4]

I have quoted this self-review at some length because it not only addresses Du Bois's feelings about the book, at least in 1904, but also reflects several of the themes that will be addressed in this chapter—sympathy, race, and a Du Boisian notion of cosmopolitanism. As is well known, Du Bois took a turn toward Marxism later in his career. At the time he wrote *Souls*, his politics might be described as a progressive conservatism or a conservative progressivism. Commentators have different views on the extent to which Du Bois's early work is consistent with his later neo-Marxism. For example, Adolph L. Reed Jr. argues, "[T]hroughout his career Du Bois's writings rested on a conceptual foundation that is compatible with the collectivist outlook and . . . this orientation is evident in his attitudes about the importance of science in social affairs and the proper organization of the Afro-American population as well as in his specific concerns with political positions, such as Pan-Africanism and socialism."[5]

Defending or criticizing a claim of this nature is beyond the scope of this chapter. The goal here is more modest. I will argue that the philosophical and conceptual underpinnings of *Souls* can be located in four sources: (1) Williams James's interpretation of the Scottish theories of sympathy and impartiality; (2) notions of cultural or racial differences that can be traced back to Herder; (3) Hegel's concepts of recognition and self-consciousness; and (4) Du Bois's situated experience as an African American. In this chapter I will not be able to supply all of the biographical and historiographical material that would demonstrate that Du Bois was self-consciously drawing on these traditions. But I will supply sufficient textual and circumstantial evidence to defend the plausibility of this claim. Further, my goal is not simply archeological. I will argue that in *Souls*—specifically, in the passages in which he addresses the notion of double-consciousness—Du Bois moves beyond his own very nineteenth-century assumptions about race and provides a critical edge for rethinking theories of sentiment and sympathy that have informed Anglo-American ethical traditions. In doing so, he speaks to current debates regarding whether the sources of ethical life are best understood in terms of reciprocity. *Souls* also remains compelling because Du Bois is seeking to find a path that will allow him to respect and pay homage to cultural differences, to the particular, while defending the notion of a common humanity that informs this respect. The resolution of this seeming tension relates to the question of the reconciliation of the universal and the particular. How Du Bois tackles this issue not only looks back to the previous chapter but looks ahead to later chapters in which challenges to notions of self-determination and transcendence are addressed.

～

One of the central goals of *Souls* is to have its readership—in Du Bois's day primarily an educated Anglo audience—appreciate what it means to live behind what Du Bois refers to as "the Veil," where he locates the world of black experience. Du Bois stresses that he has been on both sides of the Veil, as well as above it. "Leaving, then, the world of the white man, I have stepped within the Veil, raising it that you may view faintly its deeper recesses,—the meaning of its religion, the passion of its human sorrow, and the struggle of its greater souls. . . . And, finally, need I add that I who speak here am bone of the bone and flesh of the flesh of them that live within the Veil?"[6] Du Bois hopes that if his audience can feel something of what he has felt, of what blacks in America have experienced, he will invoke a natural sympathy. Along with this sympathy, reason will play a vital role in helping us to overcome prejudice. Here are two passages from *Souls*, one that emphasizes reason; the other, sympathy and feeling.

> The nineteenth century was the first century of human sympathy,—the age when half wonderingly we began to descry in others that transfigured spark of divinity which we call Myself; when clodhopper and peasants, and tramps and thieves, and millionaires and—sometimes—Negroes, became throbbing souls whose warm pulsing life touched us so nearly that we half gasped with surprise, crying, "Thou too! Hast Thou seen Sorrow and the dull waters of Hopelessness? Hast Thou known Life?" And then all helplessly peered into those Other-worlds, and wailed, "O World of Worlds, how shall man make you one?"[7]

> Again, we may decry the color-prejudice of the South, yet it remains a heavy fact. Such curious kinks of the human mind exist and must be reckoned with soberly. . . . They can be met in but one way,—by the breadth and broadening of human reason, by catholicity of taste and culture.[8]

Some readers have been perplexed by the appeal to reason and to feeling in *Souls*, as if one had to choose one course over the other. However, if reason is understood as the rationality of the broad-minded and catholic impartial spectator—an understanding that Du Bois would have inherited from William James and the Scottish tradition and that is implicit in the passage just cited—then a good deal of the seeming tension evaporates.

Du Bois studied with William James at Harvard for two years, from 1888 to 1890. James's seminal *Principles of Psychology* was published in 1890. In *Dark Voices: W. E. B. Du Bois and American Thought*, Shamoon Zamir argues that in spite of Du Bois's own proclamations regarding his indebtedness to James, the relationship was a complex one from the start. No doubt Du Bois shared many of James's vitalist and volunteerist sensibilities during the period in which he wrote *Souls*, but even when he was James's student, he may have begun to raise questions about James's ahistoricism.[9] Zamir also argues that while James certainly appealed to the notion of an impartial spectator and sympathy in his ethics, Du Bois's "own recourse to sympathetic understanding . . . is closer to Boasian attempts at crosscultural understanding than it is to James's attitudes."[10] Zamir's position is well founded because James's ethical and political attitudes do not develop in the direction of sympathetic attachments to other cultures and their historical trajectories, as they do for Du Bois. Yet James's influence, and through him the Scottish theorists of sentiment, in particular Adam Smith, do play an important role in the psychological assumptions that inform *Souls*. It is because individuals have "Jamesian" souls, selves, that it is possible to motivate them to recognize cultural differences and move beyond parochialism. James's ideal self, a broad-minded impartial spectator, can help overcome prejudice and inspire African Americans to self-actualize, and it can help Anglos better understand the potentialities of another race. James's orientation also helps account for the manner in which reason or impartiality and feeling are interwoven in Du Bois's text. So before turning to the cultural and racial dimension of Du Bois's thought, and to the notion of double-consciousness, which has Hegelian roots, I explore in some depth James's account of the self in *The Principles*.

For those attuned to think of the self as a unitary phenomenon, James has a surprise in store in *The Principles*. In "The Consciousness of Self," he begins by speaking of multiple selves, which should be viewed as empirical: the material self, the social self, and the spiritual self; and a metaphysical pure ego. James remains agnostic about the pure ego. He will tell us at the end of the chapter that there may be metaphysical reasons for accepting a pure ego, whether in its spiritualist or transcendental incarnations, but this would carry "us beyond the psychological or naturalistic point of view."[11] The material self is easy enough to understand. In this category we find the body, clothes, family, and home. "All these different things are the objects of instinctive preferences coupled with the most important practical interests of life" (*PP*, 292). Here we should think of the body and its parts as a possession. For James there is "an . . . instinctive impulse" that "drives us to collect property" (293), which becomes part of our empirical self.[12] Further, following in John Locke's footsteps, James declares, "The parts of our wealth most intimately ours are those which are saturated with our labor" (293).

One might think that some of the things that James includes under the material self—clothing and property, for instance—should fall under the social dimension of the self, especially since James defines "a man's social self" in terms of "the recognition which he gets from his mates" (293). But let us leave aside the question of what should be denominated as material, and turn directly to the social. Generally speaking, the social is the domain of the acknowledgment or recognition of our actions and activities by others. There are in fact multiple social selves. "Properly speaking, *a man has as many social selves as there are individuals who recognize him* and carry an image of him in their mind. To wound any one of these his images is to wound him" (294). This observation is clearly one that Du Bois employs in discussing the damage done to the psyche of African Americans through the lack of appropriate recognition by Anglos. James also claims that the images that others have of an individual fall into classes, so "we may practically say that he has as many different social selves as there are distinct *groups* of persons about whose opinion he cares. He generally shows a different side of himself to each of these different groups" (294).[13] Du Bois utilizes this insight in *Souls* when he reflects on the ways in which African Americans have related to different social groups. And as we shall see, it is also an insight that sets the stage for Du Bois's notion of double-consciousness. Finally, the spiritual self should be viewed in terms of psychic dispositions or faculties,[14] for example, "our ability to argue and discriminate . . . our moral sensibility and conscience, . . . our indomitable will" (296).[15]

There is a hierarchy of selves: the merely bodily at the lowest level, the spiritual at the highest, with the extracorporeal material and social selves ranged similarly in the middle (313, 291–329). According to James, we learn to subordinate our lower selves to our higher selves. How does this happen? James tells us that there is a kind of moral education of the race, as well as direct ethical judgments (whose genealogy is not specified). And there are also judgments "called forth by the acts of others" (314). Here James borrows directly from the Scottish tradition. Our encounters with others lead us to judge ourselves and to develop a higher moral self. "But having constantly to pass judgment on my associates, I come . . . to see . . . my own lusts in the mirror of the lusts of others, and to *think* about them in a very different way from that in which I simply *feel*" (314).

James tells us that for each sort of self (material, social, and spiritual) there is a degree of potentiality for growth, for a widening of the self, that requires us to forgo immediate rewards. "Of all these wider, more potential selves, *the potential social self* is the most interesting . . . by reason of its connection with our moral and religious life" (315). James goes on to declare,

> I am always inwardly strengthened in my course and steeled against the loss of my actual social self by the thought of other and better *possible* social judges than those whose verdict goes against me now. The ideal social self which I thus seek in appealing to their decision may be very remote. . . . Yet still the emotion that beckons me on is indubitably the pursuit of an ideal social self, of a self that is at least *worthy* of approving recognition by the highest *possible* judging companion, if such companion there be. This self is the true, the intimate, the ultimate, the permanent Me which I seek. This judge is God, the Absolute Mind, the "Great Companion." . . . The impulse to pray is a necessary consequence of the fact that whilst the innermost of the empirical selves of a man is a Self of the *social* sort, it yet can find its only adequate *Socius* in an ideal world. (315–316)

Now this is an intriguing turn. Not only do we appear to have left the merely empirical for the ideal, but there is a tension present. On the one hand, the spiritual self we are told is the highest self, the most personal aspect of one's self, the sphere of conscience and will. On the other hand, the realm of morality, the realm in which we judge our actions to have moral worth, can be viewed as an extrapolation or development of our social self. And further, there is an inevitable press to the religious from within the social. "All progress in the social Self is the substitution of higher tribunals for lower; this ideal tribunal is the highest; and most men, either continually or occasionally carry a reference to it in their breast. The humblest outcast on this earth can feel himself to be real and valid by pursuit of this higher recognition" (316).

Once one starts down the path of seeking recognition, there seems to be a natural progression to an ideal sphere, one in which God recognizes one's actions. This is not to suggest that James dismisses the empirically spiritual. It is to ask how we are to understand the genesis of the moral self. If one remains nonmetaphysical, then it appears that James's examination of the self leads him in the direction of the social genesis of Adam Smith's man within the breast, the impartial spectator.

For James, the development of this wider, ideal, impartial self is linked to broadening our horizons through sympathy, and it would be impossible to develop this "wider" self if we were incapable of basic sympathetic attachments to others, that is, if we lacked an ability to place ourselves in the positions of others, what I have referred to as "empathy." Without sympathy or empathy, the impartial spectator could not evolve. Impartiality is equated here with a form of cosmopolitanism, a broadening of one's horizons, a capacity for seeing things from the vantage point of others. In addition, sympathy, in the sense of compassion for others, assists in the growth of the self through felt relations. Du Bois utilizes both notions of sympathy in *Souls*, that is, empathy (the taking of the perspectives of others) and compassion. These notions are seemingly blended in the following passage from James's *Principles*, which helps shed light on some of Du Bois's assumptions in *Souls*. In reading James's words, consider how Du Bois may have viewed their applicability to the children and grandchildren of freed slaves and the white southerners of his generation.

> All narrow people *intrench* their Me, they *retract* it. . . . People who don't resemble them, or who treat them with indifference, people over whom they gain no influence, are people on whose existence, however meritorious it may intrinsically be, they look with chill negation, if not with positive hate. Who will not be mine I will exclude from existence altogether; that is, as far I can make it so, such people shall be as if they were not. Thus may a certain absoluteness and definiteness in the outline of my Me console me for the smallness of its content. Sympathetic people, on the contrary, proceed by the entirely opposite way of expansion and inclusion. The outline of their self often gets uncertain enough, but for this the spread of its content more than atones. *Nil humani a me alienum*. Let them despise this little person of mine, and treat me like a dog, *I* shall not negate *them* so long as I have a soul in my body. They are realities as much as I am. What positive good is in them shall be mine too, etc., etc. (312–313)

Du Bois was in basic agreement with the sentiments that James espoused in the passage, which is evident in the passage quoted earlier, which began, "The nineteenth century was the first century of human sympathy,—the age when half wonderingly we began to descry in others that transfigured spark of divinity which we call Myself." However, Du Bois understood that this broadening of the self is seriously undermined, if not made impossible, by the Color Line. As long as the Veil is present, one cannot sympathize with the other. Thus, the Color Line limits the "expansion" of the self, which as we saw in Chapter 4, Mead also promoted. But the issue for Du Bois is not only a matter of getting individuals to expand their horizons by sympathizing with individuals who are members of other races. It is a matter of understanding that individuals have identities that are tied to their membership in a race, and these races have a life of their own. We must learn to recognize and treat other races, as well as individuals, "sympathetically."

~

Du Bois accepts the notion that there are great races, and he supports the actualization of the potentialities of these different races. As Siegland Lemke points out, there is good reason to believe that Du Bois was directly familiar with and influenced by Herder (whose ideas certainly found their way into nineteenth-century German letters).[16] It's worth comparing Herder's words with those of Du Bois. First, Herder from *Reflections on the Philosophy of the History of Mankind*, and then Du Bois from a talk that he gave in 1897 to the American Negro Academy.

> In every one of their inventions, whether of peace or war, and even in all the faults and barbarities that nations have committed, we discern the grand law of nature: let man be man; let him mould his condition according as to himself shall seem best. For this nations took possession of their land, and established themselves in it as they could. . . . Thus we every where find mankind possessing and exercising the right of forming themselves to a kind of humanity, as soon as they have discerned it.[17]

The following are the first two of seven points that Du Bois recommends as a creed for the Academy.

1. We believe that the Negro people, as a race, have a contribution to make to civilization and humanity, which no other race can make.

2. We believe it the duty of the Americans of Negro descent, as a body, to maintain their race identity until this mission of the Negro people is accomplished, and the ideal of human brotherhood has become a practical possibility.[18]

It appears that Du Bois relies not only on a Herderian notion of *Volk* and its right to self-determination but also on a Herderian notion of Humanity (*Menschheit* or *Humanität*) in order to give African Americans their due as a people and to argue for their contribution to a common humanity. According to Frank E. Manuel, "For Herder Humanity is one, and a *Volk*—unless corrupted (this is the implicit caveat)—can express only fully human values and ideas. Progress is the gradual expression of all possible *Volk* configurations."[19] While it is true that Herder views this process as unfolding over time, the central moral imperative of his vision is close to that of Du Bois in the period in which he wrote *Souls*.[20] The dignity of each race is linked to a common humanity that finds expression through each race. For Du Bois, it appears that Jamesian sympathy combined with the rationality of the broad-minded impartial spectator, and a Herderian notion of Humanity, are sufficient to generate the interracial communication and respect that he supports. And if Anglos in the United States developed these sensibilities, it would allow African Americans the space to nurture their own culture.

Yet Du Bois himself questions this conclusion through his analysis of double-consciousness in the first chapter of *Souls*. The sort of sympathy or impartiality that we have been discussing thus far suggests that reciprocity can be achieved through a degree of goodwill and education. However, the experience of double-consciousness undermines this goal. With the introduction of the notion of double-consciousness, Du Bois takes his place in a tradition that extends back at least to Rousseau, one that addresses the damage to the psyches, the "souls," of those who have been debased by slavery and servitude. For Du Bois, the threats to the self-actualization of black peoples and individuals are due not only to the explicit barriers of Jim Crow and apartheid but also to the psychological repercussions of racism.

Zamir argues that Du Bois's notion of double-consciousness can be directly linked to Hegel's analysis of self-consciousness in the *Phenomenology of Spirit*.[21] Specifically, he argues that we should understand double-consciousness as a form of "unhappy consciousness," the mode of consciousness with which Hegel closes the section on self-consciousness. There is a good deal of evidence that Du Bois had studied the *Phenomenology*. In all likelihood this study took place with George Santayana during Du Bois's second year at Harvard.[22] No doubt Zamir is correct regarding Hegel's influence. However, it is misleading to tie Du Bois's double-consciousness to Hegel's "unhappy consciousness."[23] The latter entails a split between the changeable and the unchangeable; it is a religious consciousness that is lost to itself. Du Bois is drawing in a more general way on the alienation and doubleness found throughout the section, especially in the master-slave dialectic, as well as on Hegel's notion of recognition.[24]

In brief, the Hegelian background to Du Bois's discussion can be located in the development of self-consciousness for Hegel. To be self-conscious requires a split within oneself; there is a distance between the consciousness that is aware and that of which it is aware. This consciousness experiences itself as alienated from itself and the world. In the master-slave dialectic, we discover that the "splitting" of self-consciousness results in the master's "essence" being found outside the master in the slave, and vice versa. The goal is to overcome this alienation of self in the other. This will occur only in a society in which mutual recognition is present, and Hegel provides a foretaste of this mutuality in the *Phenomenology* when he declares, "What still lies ahead for consciousness is the experience of what Spirit is—this absolute substance which is the unity of the different independent self-consciousnesses which, in their opposition, enjoy perfect freedom and independence: 'I' that is 'We' and 'We' that is 'I.'"[25]

Du Bois drew on Hegel's dialectical account of the alienation of the individual's consciousness from itself. This does not mean that he forsook the Jamesian view of the self as potentially an ideal, impartial self. Rather, he used Hegel and James to augment each other. Hegel demonstrated how a consciousness could be divided and experienced as a "twoness," and Du Bois drew on his insights in one of the most famous passages of *Souls*.

> After the Egyptian and Indian, the Greek and Roman, the Teuton and Mongolian, the Negro is a sort of seventh son, born within a veil, and gifted with second-sight in this American world,—a world which yields him no true self-consciousness, but only lets him see himself through the revelation of the other world. It is a peculiar sensation, this double-consciousness, this sense of always looking at one's self through the eyes of others, of measuring one's soul by the tape of a world that looks on in amused contempt and pity. One

ever feels his twoness,—an American, a Negro; two souls, two thoughts, two unreconciled strivings; two warring ideals in one dark body, whose dogged strength alone keeps it from being torn asunder.[26]

The problem is clear. If one has to expend too much of one's resources trying to see oneself through the eyes of the other, one loses oneself or one becomes split, a divided self. So the Jamesian model, and Mead's for that matter, which claims that impartiality is nurtured through individuals taking multiple perspectives, must come to terms with the reality that seeing oneself through the eyes of others can in fact be a damaging experience. Under certain conditions the self can as easily become alienated from itself as it can be led to expand its horizons through taking the perspectives of others.

Those who have a double-consciousness are in a unique position to achieve the impartiality of the spectator because of a heightened awareness of otherness and multiplicity. This in fact can be a resource for marginalized peoples. Multiple standpoints can lead to a breadth of vision and insight not possessed by dominant groups. Yet this advantage can be undermined through the alienation inherent in dominant/subordinate relationships. The participants in these relationships are not disembodied spirits. Those who are subordinate become frustrated and angry at those who compel them to see the world as they do. Du Bois confronts us with how asymmetry in power relations, which in his analysis is tied to racism, can undermine the best intentions of actors regarding sympathetic or impartial responses to others. To state the obvious, one cannot expect individuals to respond sympathetically under the yoke of oppression. In fact, the oppressed are confronted with a hostile, invasive "critic," who often appears under the guise of an impartial spectator. This is crucial. Those in the dominant position often have the luxury of *appearing* to be impartial or benevolent. But if there is no mutuality, no basic respect for the humanity of the other, the result is not impartiality but paternalism. The undermining of the "impartiality" of those who are subordinate through the interior "critic" cannot be separated from the way that the Veil prevents those who dominate, those who see themselves as more human than the other, from truly sympathizing with others. Asymmetrical relations undermine "natural" sympathetic responses for all those involved. For those who dominate, pity can become conflated and confused with sympathy. And pity infantilizes. It is no accident, then, that Du Bois lashes out against pity and the denial of "manhood" to the black race.

Du Bois has drawn on his experiences, his own standpoint as an African American, to challenge the possibility of mutuality and reciprocity, even as he promotes the latter. To place this in the context of contemporary debates about the relevance of recognition to our moral and political lives, on the one hand, Du Bois comes through as an advocate of mutual recognition, of symmetrical relationships of respect. On the other hand, he is a keen observer of the concrete conditions that make the realization of mutuality impractical or at minimum exceedingly difficult. The general framework of the problem, of course, would not be news to Hegel, given his analysis of the master-slave relationship. However, what Du Bois has accomplished is to generate an account of the repercussions of having a "consciousness" that is split between cultural or group identities in a society that is inherently racist, one in which the Veil remains opaque. Under these circumstances the Color Line promotes the presence of an invasive "critic," not a benign, impartial one. Du Bois has made explicit the psychological impact of this "critic," challenging Hegel's optimism that history is moving in the direction of a society of mutual recognition and Herder's great hope that all *Volk* will have their day. In fact, Du Bois's challenge plays on one of Herder's fears, the corruption of a *Volk* by foreign influences. Du Bois is telling us that there has been a corruption of the African American *Volk* through the continuous internal gaze of the other. Unless this gaze is overcome, self-actualization for African Americans as a people will remain unrealized. And, mutatis mutandis, the same is true for Anglos.

Yet *The Souls of Black Folk* is a testament to the hope that a way can be found around this impasse. Du Bois speaks of double-consciousness in the first chapter. He doesn't end the book on this note. Perhaps given the right conditions whites and blacks can view each other with sympathy, as complements in a larger American nation, so that double-consciousness will be overcome. The worlds of blacks and whites can be enlarged to include the experiences of each other. Herder's notion of Humanity will prevail. This is very much in keeping with James's program, and to a large extent that of other American pragmatists such as Dewey and Mead, regarding the enlargement of the self. As a matter of fact, in the first chapter of *Souls*, Du Bois presents a notion of complementarity that draws on the latter tradition, as well as a notion of development through the inclusion of differences that bears the mark of Hegel and of the humanism of Herder. It also relates to Mead's emphasis on the importance of working with others in a common enterprise to overcome alienation and social unrest.

> Work, culture, liberty,—all these we need . . . all striving toward that vaster ideal that swims before the Negro people, the ideal of human brotherhood, gained through the unifying ideal of Race; the ideal of fostering and developing the traits and talents of the Negro, not in opposition to or contempt for other races, but rather in large conformity to the greater ideals of the American Republic, in order that some day on American soil two-world-races may give each to each those characteristics both so sadly lack. We the darker ones come even now not altogether empty-handed: there are to-day no truer exponents of the pure human spirit of the Declaration of Independence than the American Negroes . . . all in all, we black men seem the sole oasis of simple faith and reverence in a dusty desert of dollars and smartness.[27]

The last line is perhaps a harbinger of Du Bois's future orientation, in which he came to question his early views, and in so doing he moved from psychology or cultural sociology to political economy. This is too large a topic for this chapter, but I would be remiss in not mentioning, however briefly, Du Bois's later work, for he came to understand racism primarily in terms of economic exploitation. In his autobiography, *Dusk of Dawn*, written many years after *The Souls of Black Folk*, Du Bois states, "[E]ven in the minds of the most dogmatic supporters of race theories and believers in the inferiority of colored folk to white, there was a conscious or unconscious determination to increase their incomes by taking full advantage of this belief. And then gradually this thought was metamorphosed into a realization that the income-bearing value of race prejudice was the cause not the result of theories of racial inferiority."[28]

I introduce these comments not to take a stand on Du Bois's later Marxist turn, nor to defend the position that racism can be explained solely in economic terms, but to provide an idea of how Du Bois came to question his earlier position. His comments speak to the limitations of notions of culture and race that Du Bois utilized in his earlier work. In order to understand oppression, we must focus more directly on an economic analysis of capital.

Part III
Sociological and Psychological Challenges to Transcendence

§ 6 Self-Concept in the New Sociology of Ideas
Reflections on Neil Gross's Richard Rorty: The Making of an American Philosopher

> Little by little, as sociologists of ideas worked side by side with intellectual historians to produce case studies that would result in better, more explanatory theories—at the same time that systematic empirical research was under way to test them—the development by thinkers of new ideas would stop seeming to be a miraculous, inexplicable act of genius or an expression of the zeitgeist or a simplistic manifestation of class interests and would start appearing for what it is: a more or less predictable outcome of the work lives and other quotidian social experiences of those fortunate enough to occupy the relatively limited number of occupational slots society sets aside for those deemed intellectuals.
> Neil Gross, *Richard Rorty: The Making of an American Philosopher*

> To see keeping a conversation going as a sufficient aim of philosophy . . . is to see human beings as generators of new descriptions rather than beings one hopes to be able to describe accurately.
> Richard Rorty, *Philosophy and the Mirror of Nature*

It seems indisputable that the intellectually gifted in any given generation of philosophers outnumber those who become well-known figures in their profession. What accounts for the "success" of some and the relative obscurity of others? Chance? Luck? Divine dispensation? Philosophers, like other academics, typically want to believe that their accomplishments and reputations stem from the uniqueness of their intellects, their drive, their creativity, their talents, and so on. What they don't want to hear is that their reputations are the product of affiliations with the "right" institutions and some fortunate strategic decisions. It seems implausible after all, given what we *seem* to know about differences in intellectual abilities and talents, that sociological factors may be responsible for success. Aren't there in fact those who are truly talented, and above and beyond those, geniuses? And don't those who are truly talented manage to create their own opportunities? But perhaps how we define talent and genius is influenced by those history has designated as the "winners," and the latter are not always so designated for their intrinsic merits. Others who may have had the potential to become significant thinkers, comparable in accomplishment and reputation to those whom guardians of the canon refer to as the "giants," were relegated to the dustbin of history because they were in the wrong place at the wrong time. They never entered the "conversation."

Neil Gross is not seeking to make claims quite as wide ranging as those that I have just set forth. He confines himself to the American academy. His goal is to provide a rich sociological account of the career of a single American philosopher—and by extrapolation, the careers of philosophers and professionals—in order to support his approach to the sociology of ideas. He argues that Rorty's renown is best understood not in terms of genius or exceptional gifts but as the result of a set of institutional affiliations and strategic decisions, as well as what Gross refers to as "self-concept." This is not to say that Rorty did not possess a very good mind. It is to say that the same mind would not have had the success that Rorty did without a unique confluence of sociological factors, that is, if one could imagine abstracting a mind in this fashion (which is precisely what Gross is arguing against). Gross is by no means claiming that his biography of Rorty proves his theory. As a matter of fact, he is careful to remind his readers that his book is only a case study. Nevertheless, he hopes that his study is sufficiently convincing that it will make further investigation of his theoretical orientation warranted.

My intention is not to write a book review of Gross's *Richard Rorty*. This chapter will differ from a review in that I will not do justice to the detailed account that he provides of Rorty's life. Among the many merits of Gross's biography is that it makes a very convincing case for *not* reading Rorty as a convert from analytic philosophy to pragmatism.[1] He shows how Rorty's attachment to metaphilosophy—from his days as an undergraduate at the University of Chicago studying Richard McKeon's taxonomy of philosophy, to his early work in metaphysics with Charles Hartshorne—marked Rorty as a historian of philosophy outside the analytic mainstream. But I am not concerned here with the details of Rorty's life. I am interested in exploring Gross's approach to the sociology of ideas, which draws on figures such as Pierre Bourdieu and Randall Collins, and in addressing some of the strengths and weaknesses of his theory of self-concept, especially as they relate to notions of transcendence and self-determination.

Gross is well versed in the history of ideas, and he is duly skeptical about the sociology of ideas as a discipline, given the way that it has typically been practiced, that is, with too much emphasis on reductive determinisms and too little attention to individual actors. Gross's ideas on sociology and the self are worth examining because they seem to promise a middle path between hard determinism and a Sartrean version of existential freedom while sustaining a commitment to the social nature of the self. Unfortunately, while avoiding cruder forms of determinism, he supports an account of human development that places too much emphasis on prediction and too little on self-determination and transcendence.

Gross seeks to displace models that overemphasize the role of the strategic in the development of the self. Nevertheless, the strategic plays an important role in his approach, and his account is indebted to Bourdieu. I begin with an exposition of the central theoretical chapter in Gross's book, "The Theory of Intellectual Self-Concept." Drawing on Rorty and Mead, I then critique Gross's model, contrasting it with an alternative account of the relationship between self-concept and self-formation, which borrows from approaches to choice and deliberation discussed earlier in this book.

～

Gross spends the first eight chapters of his book discussing Rorty's biography and presenting a preliminary articulation of the theory of intellectual self-concept, which he makes explicit in chapter 9. After addressing the notion of self-concept, he proceeds in chapter 10 to examine "critical junctures in Rorty's life . . . and how in each his thought was shaped by a combination of strategic and identity concerns" (300). How, then, does Gross develop his theory in chapter 9? He begins with discussions of Bourdieu and Collins, emphasizing the importance of the strategic in their sociologies, specifically in their treatment of philosophers.[2]

> Philosophers, Bourdieu and Collins suggest, are oriented first and foremost toward this field and have as their primary aim to obtain as much status and prestige as possible within it. Whether or not philosophers are conscious of

this goal—and both Bourdieu and Collins insist that often they are not—they enact career strategies in order to achieve it, and the philosophical positions they take should be seen as components of such strategies. (238)

A strategic move would be to seek a thesis adviser with the right sort of connections or to enter a well-funded graduate program that is highly regarded in the most influential philosophical circles (even if one's own interests don't align with the culture of the department). And publishing on topics currently in vogue at prestigious institutions certainly has its virtues as a strategy for professional advancement. Gross accepts that strategic considerations have played a fundamental role in the career paths of philosophers since the rise of the modern American university. And he addresses them in detail in his biography of Rorty.

What Bourdieu doesn't sufficiently appreciate, according to Gross, is the extent to which one's self-concept can undermine and displace strategic considerations. "But intellectuals—like all social actors—must also be seen as bearers of identities, and the identities that are important to them and form the core of their self-reflection cannot always be reduced to concerns over where they are located in status structures" (238–239). This seems reasonable enough. As important as one's position in the hierarchy of academic philosophy may be to professional philosophers, there are simply other considerations in life. Bourdieu, it seems, has paid insufficient attention to individual psychology.

> But while Bourdieu invests the individual with knowledgeability and the capacity to improvise, the human being as a whole becomes a vanishing point in his analysis. . . . [Bourdieu does address the body,] but the body, like the human being more generally, nevertheless ends up figuring as a tabula rasa in his account. . . . It does not represent an independent level of reality, governed by its own laws. The laws that would be important to consider in this regard are those of psychology. . . . Bourdieu hasn't much of a theory of individual or social psychology.[3] (247)

Gross will not make the same error. He will focus on the importance of individual psychology, specifically the role of self-concept. What then are the central features of Gross's theory that set his work apart from the work of Collins and Bourdieu?

Simply stated, the theory of intellectual self-concept holds that intellectuals tell themselves and others stories about who they are qua intellectuals: about their distinctive interests, dispositions, values, capacities, and tastes. These stories are typological—they involve a thinker describing herself or himself as an intellectual of a particular type—and once they become established they may exert a powerful effect on her or his future thought, inclining the thinker to embrace certain ideas over against others. (263–264)

In addressing the social-psychological foundations of intellectual self-concepts, Gross states that his first assumption is that his theory applies to intellectuals, and in his book, to philosophers (264).[4] For Gross, intellectuals should *not* be characterized as humanists who have special insight into the nature of morality or of the cosmos. "Definitions of this sort continue to animate work done today on such topics as the decline of the 'public intellectual' who 'speaks truth to power,' but most such work is at odds with the assumptions of the new sociology ideas" (264–265). He cites Edward Said's *Representation of the Intellectual* as an example of such work. And he goes on to explain why such work is at odds with the new sociology of ideas.

> This is so because new sociologists of ideas regard the efforts of knowledge producers to draw distinctions among themselves—between "heroic" public intellectuals and "mere" academics, for instance—as reflecting (among other things) strategies and tactics for amassing prestige and power in the intellectual field. . . . New sociologists of ideas prefer to define the term "intellectuals" expansively, to include all those whose occupational roles are centrally wrapped up with the formulation of knowledge claims. (265)

And how does Gross define a philosopher? "I define a philosopher in the modern era simply as someone who, having undergone the requisite training and credentialization and having submitted herself to the academic labor market, winds up in an occupational slot where she is paid to engage in an activity denoted as 'doing philosophy,' which typically involves some combination of teaching and research" (265).

Once the presentation of Gross's basic ideas is complete, I will raise criticisms about his approach to intellectuals, but I cannot let these passages, and the framework that stands behind them, pass without comment. Two points: First, Gross claims that older assumptions about intellectuals are no longer viable because, after all, public intellectuals can't really separate themselves from "mere" academics, since trying to distinguish oneself in this fashion ("among other things") is itself a strategy for gaining prestige and power. This strikes me as an exceedingly cavalier way to dismiss the tradition of the public intellectual in American culture. (Certainly Rorty would not want to see Dewey's public persona undermined in quite this fashion.) One might ask, on whose prestige meter does one judge the mix or balance of motives that may move an individual to become a "public intellectual" as opposed to a "mere" academic? Perhaps on Bourdieu's. "First, in its most highly developed form—which Bourdieu sees as expressed among philosophers—the academic habitus insists on and orients itself around the 'disinterested' character of academic pursuits. . . . But this is a ruse, for the second characteristic of the academic habitus is the tendency for academics to gravitate toward work that will in fact bring them the most intellectual prestige" (243–244).

Isn't prestige trumped by other motives in the careers of intellectuals? Of course it is, and this is Gross's own position in much of the book. So it is curious that when he sets out to describe (public) intellectuals, he falls into this sort of rhetoric. This reinforces a concern that I will address later, that Bourdieuean (or mutatis mutandis, Nietzschean) commitments, which are not empirical, may play a larger role in Gross's (new) sociology of ideas than is apparent at first.

Second, it seems that a theory that is going to claim great powers for institutions in molding and shaping intellectuals, philosophers, has stacked the deck if those whom it studies have already bought into the institutional system in a particular fashion. Gross focuses on Rorty, and those like Rorty, philosophers who have "chosen" to submit themselves to a labor market with the goal of occupying academic positions (that will lead to tenure), and whose livelihood and success depend on doing philosophy in a specific (institutionally sanctioned) fashion (265, 345).[5]

To return to the exposition of Gross's theory: after Gross discusses to whom the theory is intended to apply, American academic philosophers, his next step is to develop "an approach to understanding identity" (266).[6] In order to do so, Gross draws on three intellectual traditions. The first is Anglo-American social psychology, "which is much indebted to William James and George Herbert Mead" (266). From it he borrows "the assumption that among the components of selfhood is self-concept, which Morris Rosenberg defines as 'the totality of the individual's thoughts and feelings having reference to himself as an object'" (266–267). I assume that this notion of the self is related to Mead's concept of the "me."[7] Gross discusses this dimension in terms of social roles and notes that in different social domains people have different self-concepts.[8] Regarding the latter, he appears to have in mind the way in which different Generalized Others define different social selves. For Gross, self-concepts are connected to the sorting of persons and things into categories that organize experience, and our plans of action depend on the categories that we use to organize the social world(s).

> I argue that intellectual self-concepts serve to position thinkers in cultural taxonomies. I have already suggested that intellectual self-concepts are typological—they involve a thinker characterizing herself as an intellectual of a certain type—and insofar as this is so, they indicate where thinkers see themselves as located in terms of ideas, values, character, capacities, and so forth, in relation to other intellectuals in some more or less shared classificatory matrix. (267)

But roles and typologies will only get us so far. They are too static. They don't tell us enough about the nature of an intellectual self-concept. Roles and typologies are insufficiently individualized to provide rich identities. What we need are narratives, stories uniquely our own and that have a temporal spread. This introduces the second intellectual tradition, one that "sees much of identity to be a matter of narrative" (268). However, some psychologists have argued that self-concepts should be kept separate from life narratives. Gross argues that the sociology of ideas does not require such a move. Roles and narratives should be viewed as intertwined in a manner that produces stories that can be spoken of as self-concepts. "[Intellectual self-concept] refers to the stories that intellectuals tell themselves and others about who they are as intellectuals, stories that weave together the totality of their reflexive thoughts and feelings" (269).

And why are such self-concepts important? For one thing they serve as motives for certain kinds of actions.

> Beyond suggesting that actors are motivated to protect the integrity of their self-concepts against efforts to "spoil" their identities and lower their self-esteem, social psychologists argue that there is a "motive to act in accordance with the self-concept and to maintain it intact in the face of potentially challenging evidence. People behave in a fashion consistent with the pictures they hold of themselves and interpret any experience contradictory to this self-picture as a threat."[9] (269)

Gross claims that there is general agreement among social psychologists that people are motivated to sustain their self-concepts. They dismiss feedback that is inconsistent with them and seek interaction with those who reinforce them. What is contested is "the mechanisms through which [this motive] exerts its effects. Those working in the tradition of 'processual symbolic interactionism' have generally followed its founder, Herbert Blumer, in suggesting that there is considerable variation in self-concept from situation to situation and Mead in proposing that social action unfolds as a negotiation between the history of the 'me' and the novelty of the 'I,' a negotiation whose outcome can never be known in advance" (270).[10] This position is countered by structural interactionists. Adhering to more mechanistic models, they might appeal to the metaphor of human beings as thermostats. "With their identities 'set' in certain ways, actors will evaluate reflected appraisals they receive, experience distress if those reflections do not match their pregiven identity settings, and adjust their behavior so as to bring about self-concept congruence" (270). After making the latter statement, Gross launches into a general critique of these two camps.

From the perspective of the sociology of ideas, both forms of interactionism fail to clarify "the relationship between self-concept and intellectual production. Processual symbolic interactionists . . . would resist the urge to explain why, in causal terms, intellectual products end up taking one form rather than another. For them indeterminacy is part of reality" (270). The structuralist approach, on the other hand, simply cannot account for "the complexity of action involving the manipulation of thousands of symbols" (270). What then is the alternative? Rather surprisingly, Gross turns to the ego psychology of Erik Erikson, which constitutes the third intellectual tradition, arguing that his work deserves reevaluation.

According to Gross, Erikson's approach provides constructive ways for thinking about how identities are formed and held together. Individuals "seek to develop identity schemes that tie together the disparate identity elements they have been endowed with by virtue of their psychosocial experience" (271). Exactly what, one may wonder, does a claim of this sort add to the model that Gross has been developing? We have already seen that human beings appear to shun inconsistencies in their self-concepts. For Erikson, most people are willing to accept prefabricated "ideological systems" as ways to manage potential threats, but there are those who address identity crises by inventing new ways of resolving them. Erikson considers these the creative individuals. Perhaps they are best positioned "to develop identity schemes that tie together the disparate identity elements." Yet Gross challenges Erikson's dichotomy between those who are creative and those who accept the prefabricated, claiming that this distinction has not survived sociological scrutiny. So, again, we must ask, what then is Erikson's contribution to Gross's theory?

> I suggest that intellectuals are motivated to develop or attach themselves to ideas that, while counting as important contributions to their fields, also function to give expression to and tie together in a satisfying manner what they understand to be the core features of their intellectual self-concepts. It is not the desire for simple self-concept consistency that forms the basis for this motivation, but the overall drive for ego coherence in an institutional and cultural environment where one's intellectual output is seen as an essential feature of oneself. (272)

So it is not consistency alone that ties intellectual commitments and self-concept together but a drive for *ego coherence* in which "one's intellectual output is seen as an essential feature of oneself." Of course, one could raise questions at this juncture about the concept of "coherence" and how it differs from "consistency," but perhaps the more striking question is how Gross's model would work in a culture that is not driven by "output" or the performance principle,[11] to borrow a phrase from Marcuse.[12] Setting aside these questions, what we do know is that the drive for ego coherence is not to be understood mechanistically, for it entails "complex moments of intellectual synthesis in which identity elements, knowledge of one's field, and intellectual vision and intention fuse" (272). After highlighting these points, Gross then summarizes his theory of intellectual self-concept. *"Thinkers tell stories to themselves and others about who they are as intellectuals. They are then strongly motivated to do intellectual work that will, inter alia, help to express and bring together the disparate elements of these stories. Everything else being equal, they will gravitate toward ideas that make this kind of synthesis possible"* (272).

A thinker's self-narrative will significantly influence the work that he or she produces, although "the precise form taken by the resulting work can never be fully predicted in advance" (272). Gross assures us that self-concepts can and do change. In fact, as thinkers work on their projects, their activity may help transform their self-concepts. In this sense, "the relationships between self-concept and intellectual choice can thus be bi-directional" (273).

In the last chapter of the book, Gross seeks to use Rorty's life to show how strategic considerations interact with "the quest for self-concept coherence." To properly demonstrate the relationship, one must have a sense of "the origin of intellectual self-concepts in thinkers' social experiences over the life course" (276). In my view, the most successful sections of Gross's book, which make up by far the largest portion of it, are those in which he shows how Rorty's professional ambitions had to adjust to, and reconcile themselves with, his conception of himself as an intellectual and philosopher. The latter, of course, was not stagnant. It changed, sometimes in response to strategic considerations.

I have been focusing on the pages in which Gross sets forth his theoretical model. While his work is an improvement over simplistic approaches that have viewed intellectual activity as merely epiphenomenal to assorted ideologies, Gross's approach is inadequate in a number of ways, to which I have already alluded. I now turn to a more detailed treatment of the limitations of his model, which will address the nature of reflection, novelty, anticipatory experience, and creativity.

～

Gross is correct in criticizing the overemphasis on the strategic in Bourdieu. But, as we have seen, Gross is not seeking to dismiss the strategic. He is seeking to supplement it with a more nuanced account of motivation and behavior, and for Gross the counter to the strategic for philosophers (intellectuals) is to be found in their self-concepts. I have briefly addressed how Gross understands the strategic. Before I focus directly on the limitations of his theory of intellectual self-concept, a few additional comments are in order.

While there are many ways to approach strategic behavior, for example, various rational actor theories, Gross has chosen to draw on Bourdieu. Given this decision, note that Bourdieu's emphasis on the strategic has affinities with Nietzsche's understanding of the human condition, especially with regard to the pervasiveness of the agonistic. Neither Nietzsche's nor Bourdieu's approach has gone uncontested.[13] And Gross seems to be aware of the fact that Bourdieu's notion of the strategic is open to challenge; however, at times it seems that he doesn't fully appreciate the extent to which Bourdieu's position is suspect, not only empirically and historically but philosophically. I will not prove this here. Instead, I will provide an example that reveals something of the uncritical manner in which Gross adopts features of his position. While discussing factors that "help predict whether the transfer of an identity from an institution to a person . . . will occur" (280), Gross makes the following claim.

> I want to suggest that the identities treated as sacred by institutions are especially likely to be absorbed if those identities provide a way for people to feel morally superior to others. *The anthropological drive to distinguish oneself from others in moral terms* may feed into larger processes of social stratification and may be cited as ideological justification for inequality, but it is not merely a function of such processes and lends a natural advantage to institutions . . . that can provide meaningful moral distinctions to those who affiliate themselves with them.[14] (281–282, emphasis added)

This passage appears to contain an undefended claim about human nature, namely, there is a "drive" in human beings to achieve moral superiority. I assume that Gross would argue that the presence of this drive leads to struggles between individuals to achieve superiority, which in practice requires strategic behaviors. The fact that this drive is described as "anthropological" suggests that it is transhistorical and, therefore, unavoidable (at least in some form). An assumption of this sort about (moral) superiority lends weight to the notion that Gross at times, contra his own intentions regarding self-concepts, is too ready to accept Bourdieu's commitment to the pervasiveness of *illusio* or interest in (winning) whatever "game" we are playing,[15] and the consequent use of strategic behaviors in order to "win."[16] In terms of philosophers this cashes out in assertions about the importance of a quest for status and the strategic behaviors it initiates. Gross is aware that his theory is historically circumscribed, much of the time, yet he appears comfortable making generalizable claims about human nature that have consequences for behavior. This suggests that there may be more determinism in Gross's account than he is willing to admit, but the degree of determinism that he is willing to admit is itself problematic.

Gross's model seeks to account for current "choices" that intellectual actors may make and ideas that they may devise, based on past and present positions in fields (in Bourdieu's understanding of the term) and self-concepts. Fostering the capacity of sociologists to predict these "decisions" is one of his aims, and this goal entails drawing on laws.

> The theory of intellectual self-concept is intended to be complementary to the theories of Bourdieu, and Collins, and others. At the same time, the theory suggests that many of the self-concepts that come to be important to thinkers

cannot be reduced down to concerns over field position and involve a broader set of self-understandings. These self-understandings, according to the theory, are key variables that *help predict* which choices thinkers will make in a variety of intellectual matters. (264, emphasis added)

In the last passage of the book he tells us that as a consequence of better theories,

> the development by thinkers of new ideas would stop seeming to be a miraculous, inexplicable act of genius or an expression of the zeitgeist or a simplistic manifestation of class interests and would start appearing for what it is: *a more or less predictable outcome* of the work lives and other quotidian social experiences of those fortunate enough to occupy the relatively limited number of occupational slots society sets aside for those deemed intellectuals. (350, emphasis added)

And recall Gross's criticism of Bourdieu's account of the body: "It does not represent an independent level of reality, governed by its own laws. The laws that would be important to consider in this regard are those of psychology. . . . Bourdieu hasn't much of a theory of individual or social psychology" (247).

I am not suggesting that Gross is seeking to predict the behavior of intellectuals with the accuracy with which physicists can predict the decay of uranium atoms. What he is seeking is "a more or less predictable outcome" (350), one in which "the precise form taken by the resulting work [of an intellectual] can never be fully predicted in advance" (272). Nevertheless, when you combine his soft quest for prediction with his willingness to accept much of what Bourdieu offers regarding the strategic, the package fails to do justice to the reflexive and creative capacities of agents. Insofar as philosophers have alternative self-concepts, or can appreciate tensions in their self-concepts, they are in a position to bypass the determinism implied by a model that invokes the notion of more or less predictable outcomes. A philosopher's self-concept is a feature of a reflexive relationship to self, and this brings with it a capacity for selecting different courses of action, which are in principle not predictable in advance. For example, philosophers may consider the reasons for following one course of action rather than another or even (in unusually transformative moments) the reasons for having one self-concept rather than another. Reasons, when understood in terms of deliberation, can lead or "cause" one to act in different ways. One does not have to accept the entire Habermasian framework to agree with him that giving reasons is an important component of freedom (although I would prefer to say, of a family of activities that fall under the rubric of freedom).[17]

> Once reasons for or against an action come into play, we must assume that the conclusion that we first wish to arrive at as a result of weighing reasons is not fixed from the outset. Were the question as to how to decide not open to begin with, we would not need to engage in deliberation at all. A will is formed, however imperceptibly, *in the course of* deliberations. And because a decision *comes about* as the result of deliberations, however fleeting and unclear they may be, we experience ourselves as free only in the actions that we perform to some degree consciously.... Only a reflective will is free.... The motivating role of reasons cannot be understood on the model of an observable event being caused by a prior state of affairs. The judging process *empowers* the agent as the author of a decision. The agent would feel disempowered, i.e. robbed of initiative, by a causally explicable natural process.[18]

Although one can view reasons as types of "self-conscious" causes, this is not the way Gross is using the term "cause" when he speaks of influences that move us to choose x over y. His view of causality is too closely aligned with (more or less) predictable outcomes. It is a form of efficient causality, even if the actor is aware of a motivating self-concept, as he or she can be for Gross. In my view, the process of developing a self-concept entails a degree of reflexivity, and this allows us to view ourselves in the context of alternative courses of action, for which different reasons can be offered. In becoming so conscious, we can to some extent escape being "caused" to follow certain (career) trajectories. Gross would not deny that this is possible, since he doesn't view us mechanistically. But there is no theory or developed argument about the place of this kind of reflection in his book. Further, a developed version of such a theory would pose a challenge to Gross's hopes for "laws" and predictions about career paths. The more that we discuss this capacity, the more that we examine the nature of reflexivity—and the "freedom" and "self-determination" it helps make possible—the more we learn about how a subject can achieve a better purchase on courses of action. This is, of course, not to say that a subject becomes a fully "rational" actor always in control of the "decisions" that he or she makes. Nor is it to claim that there aren't patterns of human behavior. It is to say that reflection, insofar as it entails anticipatory experience, can provide an opportunity for deliberating about alternative courses of action that allows for a transcendence of the given or the expected.

This cashes out in an obvious sort of way. I cannot "choose" to opt out of the institutional game of status seeking unless I can see alternatives. Gross will say that the opting out is based on a self-concept, but part of the issue here is how one develops a self-concept that leads one to opt out. And here is where creativity, at least in terms of seeing alternatives, comes into play.[19] Creativity of this type emerges as we interact and develop socially. And when it emerges (in relationship to self-concepts), it allows for choices that may not appear psychologically "lawful" according to the schema that Gross has developed.[20] Why? Because "creativity" here entails having a self-concept that is open to novel alternatives, which can become part of a feedback loop that helps to transform our self-concept(s). Gross suggested a similar idea when he spoke of the bidirectionality of the intellectual's work, that is, how one's work can transform one's self-concept, and vice versa. However, Gross's model is not fully bidirectional. Why? Because the model is geared toward accounting for present "choices" based on past and present institutional affiliations and self-concepts. To borrow Sartre's jargon, it appears as if we have projects that thrust us toward the future in various ways, but these projects are fundamentally conditioned by institutional considerations and certain drives, whether they be for coherence or prestige. This represents a reversal of the early Sartre's view, for whom it is ultimately our "decisions" and projects that "define" our current self-concepts. We do not have to go as far as the early Sartre does in advocating freedom as pure spontaneity. We can, however, agree that the way we orient ourselves toward possibilities helps to influence our choices in the present. And these possibilities, and our orientation toward them, can be more open ended than Gross's theory would lead us to believe. Further, it is one of the ironies of Gross's book that his subject, Richard Rorty, would have found aspects of his theory problematic in just these areas. The goal here is not to offer Rorty as an alternative to Gross but as a foil who can help highlight limitations in the latter's position.

As we saw in Chapter 1, toward the close of *Philosophy and the Mirror of Nature*, Rorty invokes Sartre to help clarify his own position.

> There are great philosophers who dread the thought that their vocabulary should ever be institutionalized, or that their writing might be seen as commensurable with the tradition. . . . The later Wittgenstein and the later

Heidegger (like Kierkegaard and Nietzsche) are of the latter sort. . . . Great edifying philosophers are reactive and offer satires, parodies, aphorisms. They know their work loses its point when the period they were reacting against is over. They are *intentionally* peripheral. Great systematic philosophers, like great scientists, build for eternity. Great edifying philosophers destroy for the sake of their own generation. . . . Edifying philosophers want to keep space open for the sense of wonder . . . wonder that there is something new under the sun. (*PMN*, 369)

As readers of Rorty know, and as Gross makes abundantly clear, Kuhn's notion of normal and abnormal science was important in the maturation of his thinking. Combined with the work of the later Wittgenstein, it helped Rorty develop a way of thinking about how the language games of philosophers could be seen as historically circumscribed, while allowing for the possibility of the appearance of new language games, new philosophical "worlds." While Rorty may not have been comfortable with the language of existentialism, there is certainly something of the existentialist in Rorty, as I argued earlier. Rorty wants to help us avoid surrendering to the language of normal science or accepted language games. Another way of describing this is to say that he wants us to remain open to transcendence. I repeat the quotation that was cited as at the close of Chapter 1:

[Kant] created new forms of philosophical bad faith—substituting "transcendental" attempts to find one's true self for "metaphysical" attempts to find a world elsewhere. By tacitly identifying the moral agent with the constituting transcendental self, he left the road open to ever more complicated post-Kantian attempts to reduce freedom to nature, choice to knowledge, the *pour-soi* to the *en-soi*. This is the road I have been trying to block by recasting ahistorical and permanent distinctions . . . in terms of historical and temporary distinctions between the familiar and the unfamiliar, the normal and the abnormal. (*PMN*, 383–384)

Paradoxically Gross's theory, and his account of Rorty's development, downplay the capacity for creative transformation of the self, or perhaps I should say, transcendence of the given and familiar, that was central to Rorty's work. This feature of Gross's theory can be seen in the way in which he dismisses aspects of Mead's thought.

When Gross discusses Mead, one of the points he makes is that for Mead, "social action unfolds as a negotiation between the history of the 'me' and the novelty of the 'I,' a negotiation whose outcome can be never known in advance" (270). And he goes on to say about the tradition that Mead gave rise to, "Processual symbolic interactionists . . . would resist the urge to explain why, in causal terms, intellectual products end up taking one form rather than another. For them indeterminacy is part of reality, and their interest would be in the fluid, idiosyncratic, and always unpredictable processes through which self-conceptions and the content of thought come to be mutually adjusted" (270).

For these reasons processual symbolic interactionism will not "shed much light on the relationship between self-concept and intellectual production" (270). I will not attempt to speak here for the entire school of symbolic interactionism. I will say that with regard to Mead these claims are misleading. Gross has set up a straw man. He is making it appear as if the unpredictable is so pervasive in Mead's cosmos that "causal" explanations are hardly worth his attention. In fact, Mead's philosophy depends on a fine balancing act between the systemic, which can be analyzed causally, and the novel. Yes, it is true, for Mead there is a moment of spontaneity in all of our interactions. But in practice this spontaneity does not typically undermine the systematicity of our interactions. Mead's model of the development of the self is predicated on symbols, language, maintaining a degree of consistency over time. In other words, our actions and the actions of others must be relatively predictable, that is, capable of being anticipated. It is true that our reactions are never absolutely identical to prior responses, an idea that reaches back to James's understanding of the stream of consciousness. When I tell you to close the window, my words are always somewhat different than they have been in the past, but they remain functionally equivalent. So Mead's approach does not leave us mired in the world of indeterminacy; for example, self-concepts can remain quite constant over time.

However, contra Gross, Mead insists that people do behave in novel ways, that is, ways that are *in principle* unpredictable. (In this sense there will be too much "indeterminacy" in his model for Gross.) Mead argues that this is an empirically verifiable claim, even if we cannot explain the physics or biology (yet). One must understand novelty in two ways here. There is the novelty of the play made by a second baseman that he has never made before and that he did not plan. For example, he spontaneously twists his glove in an unusual way to make a catch, and in so doing, he acts in a way that is different from how he has acted in the past. After the fact, this new play can become part of his or baseball's repertoire.

But this is not the only form of novelty. There is also the novelty that results from reflections on problems encountered. Human beings develop, through interaction with others and the world, and through sociality, the capacity to see alternative paths. When they encounter problems, they utilize this capacity. They devise new solutions to problems at hand. Scientific experimentation is a systematized form of this activity.

For Mead, "sociality" is the capacity to exist in a state of limbo between two systems and is an integral feature of the most developed forms of human reflexivity. As we have seen, when a new or novel organism is introduced into an ecosystem, a state of sociality can occur, that is, a state of being betwixt and between, when the old system is no longer what it was and the new system has yet to emerge. Selves can be thought of as systems, as "me" systems. What is peculiar about these systems is that they are tied to an organism that learns that it often exists betwixt and between, whether between social roles, institutional arrangements, or old and new conceptions of the self. We utilize these potentially reflective states to help determine new "me" systems, that is, to engage in self-determination. Further, many of the situations in which we are called on to live betwixt and between are not predictable. We don't know what interactions we might have, or even what changes there might be in our bodies, say, a sudden loss of seeing or hearing, that would involve us in a state of sociality. We learn to live with this reality, or as the cliché teaches, we come to expect the unexpected. Self-concepts require reflection, but as reflective creatures we become aware of novelty, which in turn transforms the manner in which we are self-conscious. At minimum, it intensifies it. Novelty is not simply an add-on, an accident that selves possessing self-concepts can dismiss.

For Mead, when we encounter "problems" in our self-concepts, when we are pushed and pulled by different dimensions of our experience—for example, by alternative values—we can react by transforming (and enlarging) the self (and our self-concept). There doesn't appear to be a theory in Gross's book that explains how individuals can play a significant role in the reconstruction of their self-concepts, that is, how they can help determine their self-concepts. There are descriptions of Rorty thinking about where he wants to go with his life, but there is no theory, for example, about how the capacity to reflect is related to these decisions. There is a gesturing in the direction that human beings are not simply identity "sponges" and that we must be clear that an actor's self-understanding plays a vital part in his or her career decisions. For Gross, however, "These self-understandings . . . are key variables that *help predict which choices thinkers* will make in a variety of intellectual matters" (264, emphasis added).

For Gross, what is problematic about Mead, and Rorty's philosophy for that matter, is that they simply are not with the program, that is, a social science program that would like to predict the paths that intellectuals take based on strategic considerations and concepts of self. For Rorty, we (some people more than others) have a capacity to create new metaphors and language games that will reshape our self-concepts in ways that we can't predict. As we have seen, the prediction game is the language game of normal science. Rorty wants to use "abnormal" science as a metaphor for possibilities that have yet to be imagined. Mead, in a somewhat neo-Hegelian fashion, wants to claim that reflection, involving as it often does anticipatory experiences, opens the door to processes of self-reconstruction. This capacity, when combined with the reality of novelty and spontaneity, doesn't make predictions impossible; it just limits their scope. Or better still, the fact is that while we can make reasonable predictions about how people will behave, they have a capacity to surprise us and themselves. This may seem obvious and trivial in light of Gross's project, which entails learning how to gauge and predict the influence of institutional factors. Yet it ends up creating an interesting methodological problem for Gross. You can't really know how any given intellectual is going to respond to circumstances because of his or her capacity for reflection and novel responses. Therefore, any certainty about your predictions will only be retrospective. One needs to wait until a life is over to place the pieces in the puzzle. Of course, Gross can respond that his model is not meant to supply certainty. Fair enough. But just how much predictive capacity can his (or any) model actually offer regarding individual human actions? If Mead is correct, it will be less than Gross hopes, but more than the early Sartre would expect.

My intention in invoking Rorty, the subject of Gross's study, is not to suggest that we replace Gross's project with his. It is to suggest that something of the balance between what philosophers or academics (or people) are and are not capable of, with regard to recasting their own narratives and self-concepts, has been lost in Gross's theory. Rorty addresses how we go about redefining ourselves through the activities of strong poets and those who won't be cowed by "normal" science. Mead walks a middle ground between Rorty and Gross that seems more on the mark, one that makes novelty more mundane than does Rorty and relates it to the development of reflection and our self-concepts. In Chapter 8 we will examine additional features of Mead's approach to transcendence, contrasting his views with Hegel's. We turn first to a discussion of ways that the instinctual may relate to our capacity for self-determination.

§ 7   Eros and Self-Determination

> The reign of such a one-dimensional reality does not mean that materialism rules, and that the spiritual, metaphysical, and bohemian occupations are petering out. On the contrary, there is a great deal of "Worship together this week," "Why not try God," Zen, existentialism, and beat ways of life, etc. But such modes of protest and transcendence are no longer contradictory to the status quo and no longer negative. They are rather the ceremonial part of practical behaviorism, its harmless negation, and are quickly digested by the status quo as part of its healthy diet.
>
> —Herbert Marcuse, *One-Dimensional Man*

Thus far we have focused primarily on figures indebted to the pragmatic and existential traditions, so the reader may wonder why Marcuse, a critical theorist deeply indebted to Freud, is being introduced at this juncture. There are several compelling reasons. First, Marcuse's work is sufficiently informed by Hegel and existentialism to make transcendence a central motif. For Marcuse, the ability to contradict the status quo, to negate the given, is a mode of transcendence, one that makes self-determination possible. Second, for most of Marcuse's career he struggled with the implications of Freud's determinism, seeking to show how reading Freud in a dialectical fashion could make self-determination a possibility. In the previous chapter we addressed an approach to the sociology of ideas whose deterministic implications might undermine the model of self-determination developed earlier in this book. In this chapter we find Marcuse grappling with a singular challenge to self-determination, namely, how Eros, a potential source of transcendence, may pose an insuperable threat to a free civilization that nurtures self-determining subjects. Third, Marcuse's solution to this threat, as I will argue, requires that he take a turn toward Hegel and the existential, which he does. As a matter of fact, his invocation of the "project" and "determinate choice" can be read as an attempt to reconcile existentialism and Marxism. It can also be read as an attempt to reconcile existential and pragmatic sensibilities, without requiring an acceptance of a Freudian interpretation of Eros. Unfortunately, Marcuse never turned directly to pragmatism. Had he done so, I believe that his work would have been less susceptible to the charge of aestheticism, although I make no attempt to prove this claim here.

In the penultimate chapter of *Eros and Civilization*, Marcuse is quite succinct regarding the threat posed by Eros to "the idea of a free civilization," one that allows for transcendence of the given and self-determination. He declares, "The mere fact that, in the choice of its objects, the sex instinct is not guided by reciprocity constitutes a source of unavoidable conflict among individuals—and a strong argument against the possibility of its self-sublimation" (226). At least two points appear to follow: reciprocity would reduce conflict, and it is not only the death instinct and surplus repression that make a free civilization problematic but the nature of Eros itself. Paradoxically, one of the major arguments of the book—that the death instinct can and should be neutralized in order to strengthen Eros—becomes questionable if Eros is itself a source of unavoidable conflict. In order to grapple with the latter challenge, Marcuse takes an interesting tack. He suggests that Eros may be most fully realized when it encounters internal limitations and boundaries, which are utilized to intensify and broaden the range of the erotic. These claims are linked to notions of self-determination and sensuous rationality. But his approach to the challenge at hand appears to leave Marcuse in a bind. What would be the ground for limiting Eros if not a form of determinate negation (which could be tied to Thanatos), or learned behaviors, that is, modifications of behavior that prevent immediate responses to certain stimuli? The latter strategy, however, invokes a behavioral sensibility that is typically viewed as unacceptably positivistic by Marcuse, whereas the former raises basic questions about how determinate negation would actually function in this context.

In this chapter I explore two avenues for interpreting Marcuse's attempt to avoid the sabotage of a "free civilization" and self-determination by Eros: Hegel's dialectic of limit, which Marcuse addresses in *Reason and Revolution*, and determinate choice and the project, which Marcuse fastens on in *One-Dimensional Man*. These discussions will highlight the relationships and tensions between Marcuse's dialectical method, which depends on determinate negation and contradiction, his claims regarding Eros's capacity for self-limitation, and his emphasis on determinate choice and the project in *One-Dimensional Man*. I offer a possible solution to Marcuse's dilemma regarding Eros by focusing on his notion of determinate choice. In doing so, I read Marcuse (to some degree) against Marcuse by appealing to his affinity for the existential (and existentialism) in order to undermine his commitment to Freud and the deterministic implications of the latter's thought.

∼

Near the close of *Eros and Civilization*, Marcuse introduces the notion that Eros may be a source of lasting conflict. Although this notion certainly doesn't take readers totally by surprise, given that the instinctual does not readily heed reason and lacks self-restraint, the nature of the threat posed by Eros presents a unique challenge to Marcuse's project.

> It is not the conflict between instinct and reason that provides the strongest argument against the idea of a free civilization, but rather the conflict which instinct creates in itself. Even if the destructive forms of its polymorphous perversity and license are due to surplus-repression and become susceptible to libidinal order once surplus-repression is removed, instinct itself is beyond good and evil, and no free civilization can dispense with this distinction. The mere fact that, in the choice of its objects, the sex instinct is not guided by reciprocity constitutes a source of unavoidable conflict among individuals—and a strong argument against the possibility of its self-sublimation. (226)

Marcuse then goes on to pose a question and offer a possible solution to the dilemma of an Eros that is inherently uncontrollable and therefore a threat to civilization.

> But is there perhaps in the instinct itself an inner barrier which "contains" its driving power? Is there perhaps a "natural" self-restraint in Eros so that its genuine gratification would call for delay, detour, and arrest? Then there would be obstructions and limitations imposed not from the outside, by a repressive reality principle, but set and accepted by the instinct itself because they have inherent libidinal value. (226)

Freud, we are told, understood the value of such restraint because "'unrestrained sexual liberty from the beginning' results in lack of full satisfaction" (226). Marcuse cautions that we must be careful not to let the forces of repression misuse the latter insight to justify the denial of instinctual gratification. Nevertheless, he does not want to let the notion that Eros may be able to limit itself slip away, because "'natural obstacles' in the instinct, far from denying pleasure, may function as a premium on pleasure if they are divorced from archaic taboos and exogenous constraints. Pleasure *contains an element of self-determination* which is the token of human triumph over blind necessity" (227, emphasis added). And he goes on to say,

> What distinguishes pleasure from the blind satisfaction of want is *the instinct's refusal to exhaust itself in immediate satisfaction, its ability to build up and use barriers for intensifying fulfillment.* Though this instinctual refusal has done the work of domination, it can also serve the opposite function: eroticize non-libidinal relations, transform biological tension and relief into free happiness. No longer employed as instruments for retaining men in alienated performances, *the barriers against absolute gratification would become elements of human freedom;* they would protect that other alienation in which pleasure originates—man's alienation not from himself but from mere nature: his free self-realization. Men would really exist as individuals, *each shaping his own life;* they would face each other with truly different needs and truly different modes of satisfaction—*with their own refusals and their own selections.* The ascendancy of the pleasure principle would thus engender antagonisms, pains, and frustrations—individual conflicts in the striving for gratification. But these conflicts would themselves have libidinal value: they would be permeated with the rationality of gratification. This *sensuous* rationality contains its own moral laws. (227–228, all but final emphasis added)

The passages I have been citing are found on little more than two pages of Marcuse's text. I find them extraordinary, and I am tempted to respond by exclaiming, "Hallelujah!" but I am afraid that this would not be especially helpful. My problem here is that I simply cannot understand from the arguments thus far offered in *Eros and Civilization* how Eros's capacity for self-limitation arises. While I can certainly imagine a behavioral explanation, that is, people learn over time what sorts of restrictions and activities conduce toward an increase of pleasure, I cannot understand how from Marcuse's Freudian assumptions he can be make this claim. Notice that he is not claiming that the ego or the superego is responsible for this (self-)limiting of Eros but that the instinct refuses to exhaust itself by setting up barriers, which reflects a "sensuous rationality."

To be fair to Marcuse, I must qualify my last statement about the superego, for after the passages just cited, he provides an account of the superego in which it is *not* the unambiguous representative of the reality principle. We learn that the superego may be able to form an alliance with the id, "defending the claims of the id against the ego and the external world" (228). Marcuse then speculates about a libidinal morality that can be understood in terms of a *superid*. The latter is wrapped up with a pregenital morality shaped by identification with the mother. But this discussion does not appear to provide a "mechanism" by which Eros can limit itself. Rather, it leads to the possibility that there may be a narcissistic-maternal unity that we wish to reestablish, one in which "the 'maternal' images of the super ego convey promises rather than memory traces—images of a free future rather than of a dark past" (230–231).[1]

Marcuse then moves on to make some interesting and compelling observations about time, forgetfulness, memory, and the manner in which the conflict between life and death diminishes as the Nirvana principle takes center stage. This discussion, however, only highlights the problem with which we began, because with the convergence of the pleasure principle and the Nirvana principle, "Eros, freed from surplus repression, would be strengthened, and the strengthened Eros would, as it were, absorb the objective of the death instinct" (235). This certainly would be a positive outcome in terms of neutralizing aggression, but in terms of our original problem—that Eros is not guided by reciprocity and leads to conflict between individuals—it appears the situation may have become even more dangerous, or at least potentially more dangerous. If Eros becomes too dominant, if its expression is not sufficiently checked, then it threatens to undermine civilization for the reasons Marcuse spelled out earlier in the chapter.

It does not appear that Marcuse worked out a "mechanism" for Eros's self-limitation, or if he has, I have not been able to locate it in his reflections in *Eros and Civilization*. His explanation for the self-limitation of Eros in terms of a superid is simply undeveloped and unconvincing. If we assume that Marcuse did *not* work out a Freudian or Freudian-inspired account of the self-limitation of Eros, and we want to be generous readers of his text, then we should assume that he must have been drawing on some other source in order to defend the possibility. In fact, Marcuse's speculations gain a degree of coherence when they are framed in terms of his understanding and familiarity with Hegel's dialectic of limit. Marcuse often utilizes a dialectically inspired heuristic to address a problem at hand, without making explicit the fact that he is doing so or the details of the process. In the case under consideration, this proclivity may be leading him to make claims about the "self-determination" of Eros, which he cannot adequately defend on the basis of a libidinal morality and a superid. Standing behind these claims are basic insights into how the dialectic operates, which Marcuse applies to Eros, as if Eros were a subject that could indeed limit itself. An alternative way of stating this is that Marcuse joins at the hip the subject's capacity for self-determination and Eros's alleged capacity for self-limitation. This move is in many ways a classic Hegelian one, in that "things," concepts, or forces and their relations can be viewed as self-positing because of their relationship to the development of the subject or spirit.

∽

Although the details of Hegel's dialectic of limit are beyond the scope of this chapter, Marcuse's account of the beginning of Hegel's *Science of Logic* in *Reason and Revolution* (hereafter cited as *RR*) provides insights salient to the topic at hand, the self-limitation of Eros. We learn that things may be said to have certain qualities because they have limits, and the latter are to be understood in terms of negation. "Every qualitative determination is in itself a limitation and therefore a negation" (*RR*,132). But things do not remain static. They undergo transformation. Marcuse emphasizes the manner in which the inherent potentialities of a thing, the proper nature of a thing, come into conflict with "the actual state or condition of the thing" (134), which Marcuse refers to as its talification. He tells us that "since the thing is conceived as a kind of subject that determines itself through its relations to other things, its existent qualities or talifications are barriers or limits (*Grenzen*) through which its potentialities must break. The process of existence is simply the contradiction between talifications and potentialities; hence, to exist and to be limited are identical" (135–136).[2] And he goes on to cite a famous passage from Hegel, which I quote in part. "When we say of things that they are finite, we mean thereby . . . that Not-Being constitutes their nature and their Being. Finite things are; but their relation to themselves is that they are related to themselves as something negative, and in this self-relation send themselves on beyond themselves and their Being. . . . The finite does not only change. . . . [T]he hour of their birth is the hour of their death" (136). So we can say that "things" are defined by their limits, and they have a negative relation to themselves because as limited (finite), they are negated and superseded. The latter can be viewed as either the destruction (death) of the thing or the realization of its inherent potentialities.

It may seem at first that when Marcuse speaks about the boundaries that Eros may be able to erect for itself, they cannot be the kind discussed by Hegel. After all, it would appear to be a peculiar sort of Eros—an instinct that "seeks" union or even fusion—that would depend on negation as a principle for self-limitation.[3] However, if we assume that Eros shares with other finite things, concepts, or "forces" a need for a limit, then there would appear to be no great mystery in thinking of Eros in terms of negation. Marcuse would have taken the notion of determination through negation for granted, and we will return shortly to why this notion may be of assistance in understanding the relationship between boundaries and the self-limitation of Eros. Before doing so, we might once again note just how peculiar Marcuse's claims are about the self-limitation of Eros. On the one hand, Eros requires a limit insofar as it resembles other finite forces or powers; on the other, Eros does not appear to honor limits. It knows no bounds. The nature of this instinct is to overcome otherness and not heed limits, to gratify itself even if the price is conflict. For these reasons Marcuse worries about Eros and why the idea of its self-limitation would be so appealing. Yet he doesn't want to fall into the trap of simply praising Eros for its self-limitations, for glorifying the latter could end up serving the forces of repression. So we are offered two reasons in *Eros and Civilization* for why self-limitation is a good idea: it will lead to more intense and heightened gratifications, and it will create an opening for free self-realization. However, as noted, no satisfying mechanism for how Eros can self-limit is offered even though this activity appears to be crucial for human flourishing. Perhaps employing dialectical language may prove to be of some assistance after all.

In order to fully express itself, to intensify itself, Eros must not only be able to overcome what is different from itself and press toward unity. It must also be able to become alienated from its own immediate self-expression so that it does not become a victim of its own auto-affective nature. The immediate needs to be mediated. Eros must be limited; negation must be present. If an appeal to dialectical language appears to be unduly speculative at this juncture, I offer the following. After Marcuse tells us in *Eros and Civilization* that "Pleasure contains an element of self-determination which is the token of human triumph over blind necessity" (227), he quotes Horkheimer and Adorno from the *Dialectic of the Enlightenment*. Here is Marcuse's translation of their words from the German. "Nature does not know real pleasure but only satisfaction of want. All pleasure is societal—in the unsublimated no less than in the sublimated impulses. *Pleasure originates in alienation*" (227, emphasis added). Marcuse then asserts, "What distinguishes pleasure from the blind satisfaction of want is the instinct's refusal to exhaust itself in immediate satisfaction, its ability to build up and use barriers for intensifying fulfillment" (227). In these remarks Marcuse has distinguished pleasure from the mere satisfaction of want, invoked the societal nature of pleasure, and affirmed that pleasure originates in alienation.[4]

In terms of how helpful the dialectic may be in understanding Eros, Marcuse's own language is telling. He is prepared to invoke the notion of alienation in the context of discussing "the instinct's . . . ability to build up and use barriers for intensifying fulfillment." The alienation that he refers to here is certainly not the capitalist-specific alienation of Marx's *Manuscripts of 1844*. One would be on good ground in arguing that what we have here is a notion of alienation tied to the concept of negation in the dialectic. If alienation is basic to pleasure or Eros, then it is not a large step for someone schooled in dialectical modes of thought to assert that Eros is not unitary but "contains" negation. In this regard Eros can be spoken of as alienated from itself insofar as it is not a sheer immediacy. Once Eros is viewed as "containing" negation, then Marcuse's claim that a sensuous rationality exists becomes more plausible. Eros's "rationality" is manifest in its capacity to be intensified through the presence of limits.

However, this can't be the whole story, for there is a big difference between the presence of negation or a limit, and the active and reflective movement of self-limitation. Asserting that finite things or forces require and relate to barriers, negations of themselves, is quite different from claiming that they engage in the activity of creating limits for themselves, which appears to entail a kind of reflexivity. And here is where a notion of the subject becomes crucial. Thus far we have only provided a necessary condition for self-limitation, the presence of negation "within" Eros, and not a sufficient condition. Once again, I suggest that we look at Marcuse's language. What appears to be taking place is that resources that should be credited to a subject, a conscious or potentially conscious agent of self-transformation and self-determination, are being ascribed to the instinct of Eros itself. Notice in this regard how Marcuse explicitly ties alienation to self-realization by declaring, "No longer employed as instruments for retaining men in alienated performances, the barriers against absolute gratification would become elements of human freedom; they would protect that other alienation in which pleasure originates—man's alienation not from himself but from mere nature: his free self-realization" (227). Containment of Eros makes self-realization possible, but not simply containment from the "outside," so to speak, in the form of an oppressive superego, but a "self-determining" containment from "within."

~

So here is the place to lay my cards on the table. Marcuse is going to have to appeal to the subject's capacity for self-determination in order to rein in Eros in a manner that leads to free self-realization, and this is going to entail a move from "determinate negation" to "determinate choice." However, before I introduce the latter notion, a summary of some of the basic points discussed thus far is in order. In the context of addressing the barriers that Eros might "contain," we learned that such barriers are a step toward free self-realization, for they remove us from being subservient to the caprice of nature in the form of the merely instinctual. This claim brought with it a puzzle. If Eros is to limit itself to serve self-realization, it must be able to alienate itself from itself as the merely natural. But if Eros is the merely natural, how then can it create a barrier or limit to its own expression? Marcuse's tentative solution to this conundrum involved the notion of a superid and a libidinal morality. A more plausible course, given Marcuse's engagement with the dialectic, is to invoke the power of the negative. If we dismiss behaviorism and its commitment to learned behaviors and their somatic instantiation, which Marcuse appears to do, then what alternative is there to the power of the negative to limit Eros? Perhaps fantasy and art. Yet they too appear to depend on internal, as well as external, barriers insofar as they are modes of sublimation. They too would require the presence of negation. So it appears that Eros must be able to "accommodate" negation, as we have seen.

But even if Hegel's dialectic of limit can provide resources for understanding how Eros might "contain" negation, or be susceptible to barriers, what still appears to be absent is a way to understand how Eros can be self-limiting, especially if one ties this notion to the self-realization of the subject. It's one thing to learn that finite things are related to what they are not in terms of a boundary or limit, and quite another to suggest that they can posit this limit for themselves. The latter brings with it a component of reflexivity and self-determination that we typically associate with subjects. Let's turn to Marcuse's use of the notion of the "project" to see if we can clarify how Eros might be capable of self-limitation.

I have been arguing that there is a latent or even parasitical use of the dialectic of limit in *Eros and Civilization*. Determinate negation plays a role in the constitution and life of Eros. The notion of negation and determinate negation is also important in *One-Dimensional Man*, especially when Marcuse is dealing with the conceptual. Consider the following passage, for example.

> The world of immediate experience—the world in which we find ourselves living—must be comprehended, transformed, even subverted in order to become that which it really is. In the equation Reason = Truth = Reality, which joins the subjective and objective world into one antagonistic unity, Reason is the subversive power, the "power of the negative" that establishes, as theoretical and practical Reason, the truth for men and things—that is, the conditions in which men and things become what they really are. (123)

Although Marcuse trades on notions of determinate negation and the dialectical nature of reason and history in *One-Dimensional Man*, he also takes a turn toward the existential. In chapter 8, Marcuse addresses the notion of historical transcendence, and in doing so, he finds that he must shift his language from that of determinate negation to "determinate choice," which is tied to his notion of the "project." It is this latter turn that opens a path for a possible way of thinking about how the subject can come to limit Eros, which appears as Eros's own self-limit.

> The object-world is thus the world of a specific historical project, and is never accessible outside the historical project which organizes matter, and the organization of matter is at one and the same time a theoretical and a practical enterprise. I have used the term "project" so repeatedly because it seems to me to accentuate most clearly the specific character of historical practice. It results from a determinate choice, seizure of one among other ways of comprehending, organizing, and transforming reality. The initial choice defines the range of possibilities open on this way, and precludes alternative possibilities incompatible with it. (219)

In the middle of this discussion Marcuse must grapple with a challenge: history may not involve determinate choices but only determinate negations. And he asks, "If the historical continuum itself provides the objective ground for determining the truth of different historical projects, does it also determine their sequence and their limits?" (220–221). In other words, when all is said and done, are we left with determinism? After raising the possibility of the negation of a given historical reality through its own potentialities, he goes on to ask, "Is this negation a 'determinate' one—that is, is the internal succession of a historical project, once it has become a totality, necessarily pre-determined by the structure of this totality?" (221). And he answers,

> If so, then the term "project" would be deceptive. That which is historical possibility would sooner or later be real; and the definition of liberty as comprehended necessity would have a repressive connotation which it does not have. All this may not matter much. What does matter is that such historical determination would (in spite of all subtle ethics and psychology) absolve the crimes against humanity which civilization continues to commit and thus facilitate this continuation. (221)

To counter this deterministic picture, Marcuse then immediately offers an alternative to determinate negation. "I suggest the phrase 'determinate choice' in order to emphasize the ingression of liberty into historical necessity; the phrase does no more than condense the proposition that men make their own history but make it under given conditions" (221).

So what then does this have to do with the problem of the self-limitation of Eros? Recall that one of the reasons that Marcuse gave for the importance of Eros limiting itself was to create an opening for free self-realization. He hoped that a way could be found for Eros to limit itself so that nature, in its unhumanized form, would not crowd out human flourishing. In *One-Dimensional Man* Marcuse worries that changes in history may be viewed as determinate negations within a totality, which do not yield an open-ended dialectic but confront us with the System, which in turn absolves crimes against humanity. Much preferable is the Marxian formulation that "men make their own history but make it under given conditions." However, it would seem that men can make their own history only if Eros provides enough room for free self-realization, and they can only truly flourish if Eros is allowed to intensify itself through not being immediately expressed. Yet if Eros's self-limitation depends on a form of auto-affective determinate negation, then we as historical actors are at the mercy of determinate negations that may not be as insidious as those located in Hegel's System but that surely undermine the human capacity for self-determination. Transcendence and free self-realization cannot be left to the urges of an instinct that mysteriously manages to constrain itself through determinate negations.

Here is my suggestion for acknowledging Marcuse's efforts in *Eros and Civilization*, while seeking to move beyond them. I propose that we take the problem of the self-limitation of Eros (or the instinctual) as a stand-in for a host of problems about how to self-limit, and borrow from Marcuse's insights into the dialectic, determinate negation, determinate choice, and the project. But we then make a move that the Marcuse of *Eros and Civilization* and *One-Dimensional Man* would view as problematic. We bring in learned behaviors and habits and combine what we know about how habits arise with Marcuse's commitment to determinate choice. This does not mean that we opt for a crass decisionism. It means that we take an existential pragmatism seriously. Projects are historical and require the molding and shaping of given conditions, as does Eros itself. Eros, if there is in fact an instinct by that name, is never experienced as first nature, at least not by social and historical beings, as Marcuse was well aware. I suggest that the existential dimension of Marcuse's thought be combined with a sensitivity to material conditions, but not only material conditions in a Marxian sense, which Marcuse would have readily recognized, but material conditions in terms of habits and learned behaviors. Or if we prefer Bourdieu's terminology, mutatis mutandis, with the habitus. We can learn, and we do learn, as subjects, when it is profitable to restrict Eros (or the instinctual). The latter is not a separate cosmic principle. It is part of our biological endowment. This endowment is subject to modification in various ways, as Marcuse well knew. Eros (or the instinctual) is constrained not by itself but by a productive conspiracy with (self-conscious) agents who have learned how to produce circumstances that enhance and hinder the expressions of Eros, and they have done so in part by promoting certain habits. Less talk of sublimation and art, and more about the conditions under which determinate choices can help initiate beneficial patterns of behavior, would be of assistance here.

The concluding chapter seeks to give the habitual, the biological, and the existential their due through reinterpreting Hegel's master-slave dialectic in light of Mead's work and Jean Baker Miller's neo-Freudianism.

§8 What If Hegel's Master and Slave Were Women?

In the Introduction I referred to Hegel's master-slave dialectic, which is embedded within his dialectic of recognition, as an urtext for divining the social nature of the self. Hegel's dialectic can be viewed as setting the stage for Mead's understanding of how the self develops through actions and symbolic gestures that are affirmed by others. His text is also valuable because it provides a way of thinking about transcendence that influenced twentieth-century theoreticians such as Sartre and Marcuse. Yet Hegel fails to offer a sufficiently ontogenetic account of the self's development, and he remains an obstinately pre-Darwinian thinker. In this chapter I turn to Hegel to demonstrate (once again) his lasting value in addressing contemporary social issues, such as how we are to think about gendered relationships, but also to suggest some of his limitations, principally, his lack of appreciation for how the instinctual or impulsive may serve as modes of transcendence in particular contexts. The goals for this chapter, then, are fourfold: first, to provide a reading of Hegel's dialectic that shows how the notion of transcendence as negation is operative in perhaps the most famous of his texts; second, to show how Mead would reinterpret and criticize Hegel's dialectic, especially his concepts of self-consciousness and recognition; third, to present an approach to gendered relationships that parallels Hegel's master-slave dialectic; and finally, to suggest an alternative to notions of "cultural transcendence" that we find in Hegel by highlighting the biological or physiological dimension of emotions.[1] But before we turn to an exposition of Hegel's text, a more detailed introduction to this chapter is in order.

There are at least two questions lodged in the one question of the title of this chapter: could both master and slave in *The Phenomenology of Spirit* be women, and, hypothetically speaking, if one or both were women, how would the dialectic be different? From within the narrow confines of the introduction to the section that includes the master-slave dialectic in Hegel's *Phenomenology of Spirit*, it should make no difference whatsoever if the master and slave were both women. At the start of the dialectic, we are operating at a level of universality that should transcend differences of gender. When two individuals, two self-consciousnesses, initially encounter each other, each experiences this encounter as a loss, because each self sees its essence, pure self-consciousness, as "out there," in the other.[2] Each then proceeds to supersede this apparent loss by "defining" this essence as its own. The self and other *appear* at this juncture to be neutral with regard to gender, that is, if we assume that both genders are capable of at least a modest degree of self-consciousness. However, given Hegel's views regarding the development of the subject, the roles of women and the family in history, and the fact that there is a battle to the death in the dialectic (one that Hegel would not have associated with women), it is implausible that the lords and servants in this section of the *Phenomenology* are female (in Hegel's mind). And to reinforce this point, we know that the chapter that follows the master-slave dialectic deals with Stoicism, a philosophical position that Hegel links to male figures such as Epictetus and Marcus Aurelius.

It certainly appears that Hegel has men in mind when he speaks of master and slave. As we shall see, it can even be argued that the dialectic would end (for Hegel) if the participants were women. However, by abstracting the dialectic from the development of spirit in the *Phenomenology*, the dynamics of the relationship are such that a plausible case can be made for viewing dominants as male and subordinates as female. Simone de Beauvoir makes such a case in *The Second Sex*, as does the psychiatrist Jean Baker Miller in *Toward a New Psychology of Women*, which was first published in 1976. Although Hegel is an important presence in Beauvoir's work, Hegel does not make an appearance in Miller's book, nor does Beauvoir for that matter, with whom Miller shares a good deal. Miller does not seem to be aware of Hegel's dialectic. Nevertheless, she presents a picture of relationships between men and women that is similar in important ways to Hegel's account of master and slave. Many have commented on how Hegel's dialectic can be used to illuminate gendered interactions, while acknowledging that a reading of this sort is outside the scope of Hegel's intentions in this section of the *Phenomenology*. Yet this type of reading is legitimate, so long as it doesn't conflate Hegel's views with those that can be developed from his insights. Many have also stated that using Hegel in this manner is a bit old hat and have turned to what have been denominated postmodern readings. I am going to be old-fashioned here.[3] I am going to present Miller's views and interweave them with insights from Hegel's text. I take it to be of interest that a psychiatrist, working within the psychoanalytic tradition and writing in the 1970s, has developed insights similar to Hegel's. It is also of interest that Miller would challenge both Hegel and the Beauvoir of *The Second Sex* on the priority of culture over nature as a path to transcendence. For Miller, transcendence of fixed roles and patterns of behavior involves accommodating impulses or instincts that help to generate emotions. For women to transcend the limitations placed on them in particular societies, their members (male and female) are going to have to learn to accept a different sort of balance between the cultural and the biological. Miller does not advocate some sort of primitivism but an appreciation for the extent to which biologically grounded needs can inform the emotions and the behavior of social actors. Transcendence is suspect if it merely reinforces accepted prejudices about the relationship between first and second nature.

The model of self-determination that I have been developing can sustain a turn to the biological; think here of the influence of Darwin on Mead and Dewey, and Mead's claims about biological impulses. However, it might still be argued that biology, properly contextualized, has yet to be given its due as a potential counter to, and source of, transcendence. Miller appears to offer a counterweight and an alternative to viewing transcendence from the vantage point of a Sartre or a Hegel, although I certainly don't believe that her position undermines the basic claims of this book, for example, because, as I will argue, she is in fact closer to Mead than one might expect. And this proximity will allow a recapitulation of some of Mead's basic claims about human nature.

Before I proceed, two caveats are in order. First, I am not suggesting that one can find in Hegel the psychological insights or the commitment to egalitarianism that are at the heart of Miller's analysis. Nor am I claiming that Miller should be read as a dialectical philosopher. I am claiming that Miller's book has the potential to illuminate Hegel's text, and vice versa. Second, Miller's work is of limited value philosophically because of the extent to which she uncritically relies on the psychoanalytic tradition;

for example, she does not work through the tensions between Freud's determinism and the claims for human freedom and creativity that she espouses. But hers is not a philosophical work, and I am not turning to it for resolution of these issues. I am choosing to close *Transcendence* with an examination of her ideas in order to emphasize the fact that transcendence is possible in a multitude of ways, including heeding the biological, a point that Marcuse would certainly find congenial. I now turn to the promised exposition of Hegel's master-slave dialectic, which sets the stage for Mead's and Miller's insights.

~

In the section in the *Phenomenology* on self-consciousness, in which we find the dialectic of master and slave, we enter the narrative as consciousness comes to view itself as the object of knowledge. Prior to this there were modes of consciousness that attempted to engage the sensuous world by perceiving and interpreting "external" objects. Now consciousness has itself for its object. It is the I = I, or the consciousness that is immediately aware of itself through an act of reflection. It is the cogito. How can there be an *immediate* reflection of this sort? For Hegel, there cannot be.[4] Reflective knowledge entails mediation (an insight that Mead endorses but develops in a different manner). It turns out that self-consciousness is not only aware of itself; it is still aware of the sensuous world, the so-called world of externality. Self-consciousness is not merely an I = I, a pure self-consciousness, because it also "contains" the "awareness of" the sensuous world that it seemingly left behind. Although self-consciousness would like to dismiss this world of appearance, it "haunts" self-consciousness, as Sartre might say. Self-consciousness, the "I" that takes itself to be unitary, cannot rid itself of otherness that undermines its unity.[5] It is, we are told, "*Desire* in general" (105).

What self-consciousness desires is to be in unity with itself, that is, without otherness.[6] It seeks to assert that it has no ties to the independent objects of the sensuous world. After all, it is supposed to be a pure self-consciousness. In order to maintain its purity, its identity, in the face of that which is different from itself, it negates the objects that it encounters in the external world. "Self-consciousness is thus certain of itself only by superseding this other that presents itself to self-consciousness as an independent life" (109). But the drive to overcome the otherness of these independent objects is complicated by the fact that the so-called independent objects are not simply "out there," simply external. Self-consciousness is aware of them in the activity of superseding (some of) them; hence, they are an element of its consciousness.[7] Notice that thus far I have not referred to self-consciousness as male or female. There is nothing about the argument up to this point that requires that self-consciousness be male. As a matter of fact, self-consciousness should be thought of as a genus (110). However, as we will see shortly, there is good reason for believing that Hegel has men in mind even at this juncture.

Self-consciousness is in a state of continuous unrest. It desires to be an immediate unity—that is, it does not "wish" to be "outside" itself caught up in externality—so it must confront the otherness of the independent objects of the world. The fact of the matter is that this otherness is actually "within," because the individual is conscious of the sensuous world; however, self-consciousness acts as if the otherness is only "out there," in the world. Its response, as we have seen, is to seek to rid its world of this otherness. "It destroys the independent object and thereby gives itself the certainty of itself as a *true* certainty, a certainty which has become explicit for self-consciousness itself *in an objective manner*" (109). How does it accomplish this? It might be as simple as eating and digesting that which is other. Of course, this relationship to the external world will not achieve what self-consciousness wishes. "In this satisfaction, however, experience makes it aware that the object has its own independence" (109).[8] At this stage of the dialectic, then, self-consciousness depends on the independent other that it wishes to supersede, to transcend if you will, for it only realizes itself in the process of negating this other. Not only is it aware of the external world but its "essence" now lies in the activity of negating the independent objects of this world. In other words, the "I" requires the activity of transcending independent objects in order to be a self-conscious "I." But the "I" does not want to accept the fact that it requires the mediation of objects in an external world. It cannot admit that it depends on the other (nor that the other is part and parcel of its own consciousness).

What to do? Well, a good trick would be to have that which is other negate itself—that is, do away with itself—so that self-consciousness would not have to deal with it. This cannot ultimately work, as we shall see, but for now self-consciousness favors this move. "On account of the independence of the object, therefore, it can achieve satisfaction only when the object itself effects the negation within itself" (109). This seemingly would free self-consciousness from the need to grapple with independent objects. However, this kind of self-negation is not to be had in nature. Things and animals do not negate themselves, or at least do not do so in a way that could be satisfying to self-consciousness.

We learn that "*[s]elf-consciousness achieves its satisfaction only in another self-consciousness*" (110). Why should this be so? We will not fully understand why until we are much further along in the *Phenomenology*.[9] Nevertheless, it is clear at this juncture that a self-consciousness cannot hope to overcome otherness through the negation of merely natural objects. It can never "conquer" all of the objects of the external world, and it actually needs these objects for its activity of negation. In order to overcome "otherness," self-consciousness must find another route. Its task is not an easy one. It must locate a form of otherness that is sufficiently different from itself that its activity of negation can continue, but which is also sufficiently similar to itself so that overcoming this otherness is not insuperable. Only another human being can potentially fulfill these conditions. Hegel famously remarks, "A self-consciousness exists *for a self-consciousness*. Only so is it in fact self-consciousness; for only in this way does the unity of itself in its otherness become explicit for it" (110).[10] If a self could recognize itself in another, and see the other as itself, the individual would no longer need to negate independent external objects in order to realize and assert its self-consciousness. Its activity of negation would be confined to overcoming the otherness of another self-consciousness. In other words, by mutually recognizing each other as selves, each self-consciousness would have its relationship to itself mediated by the other. They would "*recognize themselves as mutually recognizing one another*" (112).[11]

We are, however, far from achieving this explicit unity of self and other. Recall that the activity of negating defines self-consciousness at this point. The initial reaction to the discovery of another self-consciousness is to seek to negate this other. This is similar to the reaction to "external objects" that we saw earlier. But the intensity of the reaction is compounded by the unique threat that another self-consciousness poses. The individual finds its essence out there in the other, because the other is another self. Its own essence is now tainted with otherness (because it sees itself in the other). The individual wishes to negate this otherness in order to be at home with itself. This preoccupation, instead of leading to mutuality, at this stage of the dialectic leads to another reality, inequality, that is, master and slave. Why does the dialectic take this turn?

In addition to the desire of self-consciousness to destroy that which threatens its identity, and to rid its world of otherness in general, self-consciousness also seeks to define itself as above the merely natural, as not merely a part of the external world. It wants to be recognized as a pure self-consciousness. To do so, it must rise above its own biological life, which from the perspective of pure self-consciousness is part of the external world. It must transcend the limits of the merely biological. "The presentation of itself, however, as the pure abstraction of self-consciousness consists in showing itself as the pure negation of its objective mode, or in showing that it is not attached to any specific *existence*, not to the individuality common to existence as such, that it is not attached to life" (113). As a pure self-consciousness it is more than willing to risk its own biological life in seeking to kill the other, who threatens its identity.[12] By risking its life in this manner, self-consciousness hopes to demonstrate that it is above the merely biological and to rid its world of the pretender to its throne. And of course, the other self-consciousness has identical hopes. Hence, a battle to the death ensues.

However, Hegel declares that without biological life there can be no self-consciousness. If both self-consciousnesses die in the struggle, the dialectic would end, and the merely natural would win out, namely, death. So at least one consciousness must choose life, and another must choose self-consciousness over life. This will assure that that spirit's development can continue. "[T]here is posited a pure self-consciousness [the master], and a consciousness which is not purely for itself but for another, i.e. is a merely *immediate* consciousness, or consciousness in the form of *thinghood* [the slave]. Both moments are essential" (115).

Before we turn to the master-slave dialectic, it is worth highlighting that in "the battle to the death" Hegel is without a doubt speaking about male agents. In support of this claim I offer the following passage from Hegel's *Philosophy of Right*, in which he is discussing the family, a much more developed social relationship than the one we are currently addressing but that still reflects his basic assumptions about males and females.

> Thus one sex [male] is mind in its self-diremption into explicit personal self-subsistence and the knowledge and volition of free universality. . . . It follows that man has his actual substantive life in the state, in learning, and so forth, *as well as in labour and struggle with the external world and with himself so that it is only out of his diremption that he fights his way to self-subsistent unity with*

himself. . . . Woman, on the other hand, has her substantive destiny in the family, and to be imbued with family piety is her ethical frame of mind.[13]

This is perhaps the place to answer one question raised by the title of this chapter: What if Hegel's master and slave were women? The answer is rather straightforward for Hegel. We would never have arrived at the distinction between masters and slaves had the burgeoning self-consciousnesses been women, because women would have clung to life and avoided the "the trial by death" (114). On the other hand, men might have killed each other off in their quest to rise above the merely biological. Fortunately, some men were willing to become slaves in order not to die. But such men are not really men. They are womanly in that they prefer the biological to transcendence. As a matter of fact, if this presentation of Hegel's position is reasonably on target, one can see why Beauvoir's analysis of woman as Other is such a plausible extension of Hegel's text. Women, like slaves, have been mired in the biological, the natural, and the nontranscendent. In Beauvoir's words, "Spirit has prevailed over Life, transcendence over immanence. . . . In woman are incarnated the disturbing mysteries of nature, and man escapes her hold when he frees himself from nature."[14]

The master has power over the thinglike consciousness because by risking his life, he has proven that he is above the merely biological. The slave was not willing to risk life, so it is fitting that the master or lord should hold him in bondage (115). For the master, the objects of the world are seemingly no longer a threat to his independence, for he has the servant to act as a buffer between himself and the world of things. The slave works on the world for the master. "The lord relates himself mediately to the thing through the bondsman" (115–116). To put it quite simply, the master enjoys the fruits of the bondsman's labor, while the bondsman appears to be mired in animality and thinghood. The master is seemingly desire satisfied. And he appears to have achieved recognition of his status, because he has the slave to acknowledge his (pure) self-consciousness and mastery.

Of course, there is something not quite right in all of this. For the master to achieve independence, the other who recognizes him should be independent, a peer of the master. A dependent creature cannot recognize an independent one. The master cannot gain the satisfaction that he needs, the certainty of himself, for the inessential cannot acknowledge the essential. Further, we have here a contradiction—the master's alleged independence is in fact a dependence on the slave. A role reversal has seemingly taken place. How does the slave come to recognize this reversal? The bondsman has two experiences to draw on to help raise his consciousness, work and fear. Work is desire held in check. And fear allows the worker to experience the power of the negative.

At this juncture we can break off the overview of Hegel's master-slave dialectic. We can reasonably conclude that Hegel assumes that he is discussing men in the life-and-death struggle and in the master-slave dialectic. Yet the manner in which Hegel describes the relationship between the master and the slave has allowed commentators to view slaves or servants as women. This is the move that Simone de Beauvoir makes and the one that Jean Baker Miller would make, had she engaged Hegel. We will turn to Miller shortly. First, I want to address how Mead might respond to Hegel's notions of self-consciousness and recognition.

~

Mead would certainly agree that self-consciousness is a fundamental feature of human experience, but it is not essential, at least not in the neo-Aristotelian way that Hegel thinks of it as essential. Mead is, after all, a post-Darwinian, and "essentiality" is either transitory (e.g., a species or a role) or defined in terms of interest; for example, a chair can be defined as having an "essence" relative to the interest of human beings who sit in such objects. Mead would want to ask Hegel an obvious question: How do we arrive at the point of having a consciousness that is capable of reflection, an I = I, either in terms of the individual or the species? We need a (nonspiritual) mechanism that can account for reflection, the turning back of experience on itself that is entailed in self-consciousness. Hegel doesn't explain this phenomenon. He assumes that there is an "I" that is aware of itself at the very beginning of the section on self-consciousness, which is tantamount to assuming that self-consciousness has always been present in human beings, however "primitive" it might be. In other words, spirit's essence has always entailed some form of the genus self-consciousness. Hegel, after all, was an antievolutionist.

The *Phenomenology* begins with a section on consciousness, which is followed by the one on self-consciousness that we have been discussing. This might lead readers to conclude that Hegel has a developmental model that can explain how individuals or the species moves from consciousness to self-consciousness. This would be the wrong inference. The chapters in the *Phenomenology* on consciousness present modes of consciousness that do not fully appreciate the limitations of their own claims, for example, the claim that the senses can provide certain knowledge. They are ultimately of no assistance in understanding how self-consciousness emerges, unless one is talking about the self-conscious subject as it is found in German idealism. The early chapters intertwine philosophical positions with developmental claims in an idiosyncratic fashion that simply doesn't address this issue. They do, however, assume that self-consciousness is implicit in the various modes of consciousness, without acknowledging the degree to which consciousness is already a form of self-consciousness.

Hegel would claim that self-consciousness is implicit in the chapters on consciousness and will become explicit in the chapters to follow. From Mead's vantage point, self-consciousness is more evident (explicit) than Hegel acknowledges in these early chapters. The proof of this claim is to be found in Hegel's appeal to language in the very first chapter of the *Phenomenology* on sense-certainty,[15] for the presence of language suggests that there is a more sophisticated form of self-consciousness present than Hegel allows.[16] As we have seen, language for Mead implies that self-consciousness, or at least a proto-self-consciousness, is present. Yes, it is true that for Mead there can be a limited use of language without the presence of a self or self-consciousness, for example, in very young children.[17] But in practice, if we are talking about *Homo sapiens* who possess language and live in social groups, and therefore have generalized other(s), then we can be fairly certain that the adults in such communities would be self-conscious. Hegel is so fixated on undermining sense-certainty and perception as forms of "knowing" in the early chapters of the *Phenomenology* that he doesn't examine the degree to which self-consciousness is explicit in these forms, except insofar he uses the presence of the "I" to undermine the pretenses of these particular forms of consciousness.[18] From Mead's perspective the book really should have begun with an exploration of social interaction, because consciousness, as Hegel presents it, is already a form of (social) self-consciousness, and an explanation is called for regarding its appearance and genesis.

We have seen that for Mead the genesis of self-consciousness, both in terms of phylogenesis and ontogenesis, is intimately connected to the development of language. Self-consciousness requires not only the reflexive vocal gesture but the capacity for role-taking, which itself requires a degree of mastery of anticipatory experience. Without being able to take the role of the other, one would not be able to anticipate and retrospect in a fashion that makes taking the perspective of the generalized other possible. And without the generalized other, the genus "self-consciousness" that Hegel examines—that is, a self that is aware of itself as a unity—is absent for Mead.

Hegel claims that self-consciousness experiences its essence outside itself and must negate this externality. Mead would say that this overcoming of externality through negation is unnecessary. Why? Because self-awareness is built on forms of reciprocal or mutual recognition from the outset, not in the sophisticated sense of recognizing the dignity of the other but in a basic sense that selves would not develop without individuals mutually recognizing their attitudes and behaviors in each other.[19] For Mead, recognition involves a re-cognition of one's own attitudes (or preparations for action) and behaviors. I may be (prereflectively) aware of my behaviors, but I don't re-cognize them as my own, as "part" of my (burgeoning) self, until I can see and affirm them as if I were the other. This requires an affirmation by the other, a "signal" from the other, a recognition by the other, that I am actually "getting it right," that I understand the meaning of certain (shared) attitudes and behaviors. In other words, through mutual or reciprocal recognition I learn to trust that I am accurately taking the perspective of the other and the generalized other, which in turn helps generate a self as a cognitive object. Whether we are focusing on the phylogenetic or the ontogenetic, mutual recognition precedes the quest for affirmation through a struggle with the other. From Mead's vantage point, there is confusion in Hegel's account between the role of recognition in the process of the development of self-consciousness and the desire on the part of a specific consciousness to have his or her uniqueness affirmed in a particular way, that is, as a pure self-consciousness (and then as a master). Mead's account provides the conditions for the possibility of the specific dynamic that Hegel addresses in the struggle between two self-consciousnesses.[20]

Mead doesn't dismiss the importance of what he calls self-assertion. However, self-assertion is the result of having a personality with a specific set of interests and goals, which may include seeking status in a community. A willingness to transcend the biological in order to achieve self-consciousness, which for Hegel entails being recognized as willing to transcend the biological, is simply not as pivotal in Mead. In this regard, Mead would be more amenable than Hegel to Miller's position, as we shall see.

In *Toward a New Psychology of Women* Miller tells us, "Dominant groups usually define one or more acceptable roles for the subordinate. Acceptable roles typically involve providing services that no dominant group wants to perform for itself" (6).[21] We also learn from Miller that "subordinates themselves can come to find it difficult to believe in their own ability" (7). If subordinates take on the characteristics that they are expected to, often childlike qualities, then "they are considered well-adjusted" (7). In Hegel's terms, the subordinate is expected to set aside her own needs in order to serve the master. She is the inessential. He is the essential.

Throughout most of Western history women's efforts have kept the household functioning. For most of American history, women have made sure that the "trivial things" of the household—for example, children's needs, cooking, cleaning—are not allowed to intrude on their husbands' activities or even their states of mind. The husband, as the dominant, has a sense of himself as above such things, much as Hegel's master is above the merely natural and biological. To engage in these domains, a man would have to relinquish his special humanity, his claim to manhood. Much like Hegel's master, men have lived a lie by not acknowledging the dependent side of themselves, while women, like Hegel's slave, cannot (at first) see their potential for independence. Ideally, men and women would acknowledge both sides of themselves. However, it is typically the case that women have functioned as servants, and as servants they feel that they must please their masters. In order to do so, women must learn about men. In this regard women possess what Du Bois refers to as a double-consciousness, which entails an internalization of the dominant as an internal critic. In Miller's words, "Subordinates often know more about the dominants than they know about themselves. If a large part of your fate depends on accommodating to and pleasing the dominants, you concentrate on them. Indeed, there is little purpose in knowing yourself" (10–11).

Men fear dependence, which is just what relationships of domination and subordination can breed. In terms of Hegel's dialectic of master and slave, we can say that the master depends on the slave but cannot acknowledge this dependence, while the slave is actually competent in managing the affairs of the household. Yet competence is of no assistance in enhancing one's self-esteem if the slave's contributions are seen as fundamentally less valuable than the master's. And this has surely been true of so-called women's work. As noted, so-called women's work has had to do with many of the most basic concerns of life, concerns that men in Western cultures have typically sought to escape, such as child rearing. And here is an interesting connection to psychoanalysis, for the latter has dealt with just those areas that have been relegated to the domain of women: the bodily, the childish, and the sexual. Men have denied parts of themselves that psychoanalysis helps us explore.

> Freud focused on bodily, sexual, and childish experience and said that these are of determining but hidden importance. More recent psychoanalytic theory tends to emphasize the deeper issues of feelings of vulnerability, weakness, helplessness, dependency, and the basic emotional connections between an individual and other people. . . . One might even say that we came to "need" psychoanalysis precisely because certain essential parts of men's experience have been very problematic and therefore were unacknowledged, unexplored, and denied. Women, then, become the "carriers" for society of certain aspects of total human experience—those aspects that remain unsolved. (This is one reason why women must be so mistreated and degraded.) The result of such a process is to keep men from fully integrating these areas into their own lives. (22–23)

Hegel's master can be viewed as rejecting behaviors and attitudes that are associated with mere animal life, because to be self-conscious is to rise above the merely biological. For Miller, this "rising above the merely biological" would be interpreted in terms of men's rejection of states of vulnerability and emotional attachment. Men define them as feminine and in so doing reject aspects of themselves that are required for human flourishing. Women are left to do the work of keeping men connected to these parts of their lives. They mediate the natural for men. Miller asks, can we not view the current women's movement in light of how women have been "the bearers of these human necessities for the social group as a whole?" (24).[22]

From the perspective of the dominant male culture, weakness, vulnerability, and helplessness are negatives to be avoided or denied. But they are fundamental parts of life, and women have dealt with them in ways that men have not. This should be viewed as a strength. The master, after all, denies large portions of experience by having the slave take care of them for him. In Miller's terms, he denies his feelings of vulnerability and weakness. On the other hand, "by having to defend less and deny less, women are in a position to understand weakness more readily and to work productively *with* it" (32).

By acknowledging vulnerabilities, Miller is not suggesting that women should remain attached to them. Women, as a matter of fact, must learn how "to let go of their belief in the *rightness* of weakness" (32), in order overcome their "fear of *not* being weak" (32).[23] In a parallel fashion, Hegel's slave must let go of viewing himself as the inessential, as weaker than the master who was willing to sacrifice life. However, there is an important difference between Miller and Hegel here. Hegel argues that through living in fear and through work in service to the master, the slave overcomes the mentality of a slave. Through transforming the world and seeing himself in his transformations, he is liberated from the master's definition of him. "Through his service he rids himself of his attachment to natural existence in every single detail; and gets rid of it by working on it."[24] The slave transcends the given by transforming it. Notice that Hegel is arguing, as Beauvoir does, that attachment to the merely natural hinders the development of the individual. Miller challenges this notion. The natural must be given its due, as we shall see. (Of course, with regard to women's role in history, Beauvoir's argument is more nuanced than this, but in the final analysis Miller would view *The Second Sex* as ceding too much ground to culture, to a form of "transcendence," while underestimating the virtues of the "biological.")

For Miller, women play a role in maintaining the present state of affairs by propping men up, for example, by rescuing men when they feel emotionally threatened. Subordinates often perform this role. It is reasonable to assume that Hegel's slave (qua slave) sought to recognize his master in a way that satisfied the master's self-image (or perhaps in light of Gross's work we should say, the master's "self-concept").[25] Women, for Miller, allow men to be dependent without having to acknowledge their dependence, that is, they support their sham independence. To use current psychological jargon, both women and slaves enable the dominants. Yet it is important to note how difficult it is for women to do the right thing. For example, faced with a spouse suffering from certain kinds of anxieties, the woman is often left in a no-win situation, as in the case of two of Miller's clients, Charles and Ruth.

> He harbored the seemingly contradictory wish that his wife would somehow solve everything for him with such magic and dispatch that he would never

be aware of his weakness at all. She should do this without being asked....
The fact that Ruth did not instantly accomplish this feat for him was a deep-seated cause of his anger at her. Instead, she confronted him with an attempt to deal with the problem, and by doing so, reminded him of his feelings of weakness and vulnerability. But even if she had done nothing, her very presence would have caused him to face the frustration of his wish for total caretaking and problem solving. (33)

These are precisely the kinds of binds, according to Miller, that we fall into by failing to acknowledge the damage to ourselves and to our relationships that is produced by a lack of reciprocity. The master's insistence on dominance and his unwillingness to acknowledge his dependence are at the heart of Hegel's dialectic of master and slave. And the inequities of the lordship-and-bondage relationship will only fully resolve themselves for Hegel when there is a society of mutual recognition, a reciprocity between self and other.

Leaving aside Hegel's rather parochial views on women, his vision of the good society is one in which differences flourish. For Miller, women's liberation is not a matter of simply taking over current men's roles and values but occurs in part through the creation of new roles and relationships, that is, by allowing differences to flourish. This is quite in line with Mead's argument that in the modern world a healthy social system is one in which there is a growing diversity of roles and functions. And he argued that women should not be confined to traditional roles.[26]

This transformation is, of course, easier said than done. If women move beyond currently prescribed boundaries, they are viewed "as either attacking men or trying to be like them" (17). If women try to assert their own needs, they will have to be prepared to be "seen as creating conflict and must bear the psychological burden of rejecting men's images of 'true womanhood'" (17). (How often have we heard women mouth the line that they are not feminists, even as they are engaged in just the sorts of activities that feminists would approve of, for example, asserting their rights to a career?) Women "are encouraged to concentrate on forming and maintaining a relationship to one person. In fact, women are encouraged to believe that if they do go through the mental and emotional struggle of self-development, the end result will be disastrous—they will forfeit the possibility of having any close relationships" (18–19).

So through the fear of isolation and conflict women "are diverted from exploring and expressing their needs" (19). To do so would not only be to risk conflict with powerful institutions and men but to turn away from the ideas of womanhood that they have internalized. Women instead "are encouraged to 'transform' their own needs" (19); that is, to come to see someone else's needs as their own, in a manner similar to that of Hegel's slave. Miller tells us, "Conflict is denied and the means to engage openly in conflict are excluded" (13). She goes on to note, "In sum, both sides are diverted from open conflict around real differences, by which they could grow, and are channeled into hidden conflict around falsifications. For this hidden conflict, there are no acceptable social forms or guides because this conflict supposedly doesn't exist" (13).

To overcome merely living for the other will entail what Miller calls good conflict.[27] "Conflict, seen in its fullest sense, is not necessarily threatening or destructive. . . . Growth requires engagement with difference and with people embodying that difference" (13). Miller's remark on growth is apt not only in terms of describing ways of improving male and female relationships but is also well suited to describing a central feature of the form of cosmopolitanism that was addressed in earlier chapters of this book. Her reference to good conflict, translated into Hegel's terms, entails making implicit contradictions or conflicts explicit. Both Hegel and Miller would agree that conflict and contradictions must be engaged, although the ways in which psychoanalysis and Hegel overlap and divide on the nature of conflict is a question that is beyond the scope of this chapter.

∼

Miller and Hegel clearly disagree on the instinctual or impulsive. For Hegel, the instinctual trials of the body are ultimately superseded by culture and history, at least for men. Not so for Miller, since the needs produced (in part) by biological impulses, such as a need for emotional attachment, remain omnipresent, even if they are often denied by men as they seek to assert their masculinity. For Miller, there is certainly a sense in which "transcendence" would involve overcoming aspects of traditional roles through a willingness to give emotions, many of which have their origin (at least in part) in instinctual or bodily needs, their due.[28] In this regard she bears some kinship to Marcuse in the manner in which he turns to transhistorical (but historically informed) instincts, for example, Eros, as a ground for rejecting common cultural assumptions about well-being. The instinctual provides a route for transcending one-dimensional society. Where I believe Miller and Marcuse would differ is on the degree to which Marcuse emphasizes sublimation of the instinctual in order to create an aesthetic that could challenge one-dimensional society.[29] (This is not to say that Miller is somehow opposed to sublimation. But I suspect that she would be skeptical about the value of a "mediated" aesthetic that requires a loss of connection to more immediate feelings.)

Miller's understanding of the dangers presented by approaches such as Hegel's and Beauvoir's, which too often dichotomize nature and culture, is in line with Mead's understanding of the biological and physiological. He is, after all, a post-Darwinian, neo-Hegelian, for whom we are first and foremost biological and social organisms with an unusual set of capacities that permit the development of extensive social networks and self-reflection. He views biological impulses as ongoing, "sublimated" and "non-sublimated," facts of human life.[30] No doubt society molds and shapes the impulses for Mead. But recall that in Chapter 4 we saw that there is an impulse to affiliate, which continues even in so-called civilized times, and can lead to war. Also recall Mead's language in the following passage.

> We are born with our fundamental impulses.... This primal stuff of which we are made up is not under our direct control. The primitive sexual, parental, hostile, and cooperative impulses out of which our social selves are built up are few—but they get an almost infinite field of varied application in society, and with every development of means of intercourse, with every invention they find new opportunities of expression.[31]

Notice that Mead is arguing that these impulses (primal stuff) do not atrophy, although they find new and different routes of expression. Fundamental impulses are rarely ever "extinguished." As we saw in Chapter 4, Mead speaks of the visceral, prereflective response that we have to the suffering of others. For example, it seems that only the pathological are completely without sympathy for others.[32] "The kindliness that expresses itself in charity is as fundamental an element in human nature as are any in our original endowment. The man without a generous impulse is abnormal and abhorrent."[33] While it is true that our obligations to others involve more than feelings, we shouldn't dismiss their importance, for example, in helping to move us to assist others.

Mead would find Miller's insistence on the biological foundations of certain needs compelling and applicable to *both* men and women. For Hegel, women retain a closer connection to the "biological world" than men do (or at least than "spiritually" evolved men do). This is not to suggest that

Hegel dismisses the "natural." But Mead and Hegel clearly have a different understanding of how men and women relate to the "natural world" and associated forms of life. It's worth repeating in this context Hegel's words from the *Philosophy of Right* that I cited earlier in this chapter.

> Thus one sex [male] is mind in its self-diremption into explicit personal self-subsistence and the knowledge and volition of free universality. . . . It follows that man has his actual substantive life in the state, in learning, and so forth, *as well as in labour and struggle with the external world and with himself so that it is only out of his diremption that he fights his way to self-subsistent unity with himself.* . . . Woman, on the other hand, has her substantive destiny in the family, and to be imbued with family piety is her ethical frame of mind.[34]

After the phrase "he fights his way to self-subsistent unity with himself," Hegel goes on to say, "In the family he has a tranquil intuition of this unity, and there he lives a subjective ethical life on the plane of feeling." In other words, although the family is not crudely natural for Hegel, it is a form of ethical life dominated by feeling. It is where men experience an *intuition* of a *deeper unity* that will be realized in the State and in Absolute Spirit. Hegel's hierarchy is clear and clearly demarcated.

Mead, on the other hand, like Miller, is a political egalitarian, and an egalitarian in regard to feelings and their place in human life. Miller derives her insights from clinical work and psychoanalytic literature. Mead's work is informed by Scottish theorists of sentiment, as well as early twentieth-century research into physiology. These are different worlds. Yet Mead and Miller would agree that we would be ill-advised to become insensitive to the "feeling" dimension of our lives. There are times when this dimension can assist us in transcending rigid cultural or legal assumptions about what is morally praiseworthy or acceptable. (For instance, we feel for the suffering of the slave, even though slavery is legally permissible. Or as Marcuse might suggest, there are times when instinctual gratification reminds us of utopian possibilities, the promise of a world that transcends the parochialisms of one-dimensional society.) Both Miller and Mead would argue that all human beings are in principle equally tied to this sphere of feeling.[35] Mead, for example, is definitely not just speaking about women in the following passage.

> We choose our business associates . . . but we *fall in* love, and whatever action we take upon this primal premiss [*sic*], it is not a matter of our own choice.

> We say that we instinctively help a child who has fallen down. . . . [T]he impulse to helpfulness is just as much an endowment as the impulse of hostility. This primal stuff of which we are made up is not under our direct control.[36]

So to some degree we have come full circle. In the first chapters of this book we saw how an existential understanding of transcendence is present in Dewey, as well as in Sartre and Rorty. But we also observed how for Dewey and Mead, the existential moment is balanced by the social and the organic.[37] In Chapter 4 we learned that a theory of cosmopolitanism built on Mead's work depends on sentiments, which can be prereflective "initiators" of behavior even in highly socialized individuals. This theory requires acknowledging the impulsive, while appreciating the importance of obligation, which develops through the emergence of the social self and the "impartial spectator."

Although Hegel didn't dismiss the body, he thought that spirit transcended it, for spirit is free and self-determining, but the body is weighed down by matter. No doubt Mead's understanding of the interaction between self and other owed much to Hegel. There is a dialectic of self and other in Mead. However, Mead sought to transform Hegel's dialectic from a story about spirit's development to one about the genesis of the self through language and social interaction. Mead set out on this path early in his career when he became intrigued by physiology and the social sciences, during a time that he was still captivated by Hegel. His dual interests are reflected in a letter that he wrote to his friend Henry Castle as a young assistant professor at the University of Michigan. It's a good note on which to end this chapter, for it shows in a delightful fashion Mead bringing together Hegel, who helped teach Dewey and Mead how to think about the social and transcendence, and Mead's commitment to the body and the biological sciences, which helped shape his branch of pragmatism.

> I have at last reached a position I used to dream of in Harvard—where it is possible to apply good straight [physiological psychology] to Hegel, and I don't know what more a mortal can want on earth.[38]

Reference Matter

Notes

Introduction
1. "Each *Volk* contained the principle of its individuality within itself; it was a self-respecting monad. The Christian Pietist conception of souls equal in the eyes of God was extended to peoples throughout world history." Manuel, "Introduction," in Herder, *Reflections*, xvii.
2. Herder, *Reflections*, 84.
3. I hasten to add that this assertion is not to be construed as defending peoples or states that act perversely and immorally, for example, Nazi Germany. I do not believe that the "right" to self-determination is an absolute right. It is a right, or perhaps more accurately, a good, when certain minimal normative criteria are met. However, for the purposes of the present discussion, I want to bracket the normative issues involved in judging different social groups or cultures. I will note that one of the characteristics of Nazi Germany was its xenophobia, which is an anticosmopolitan stance, to say the least.
4. One example of a set of sensibilities that is often associated with cosmopolitanism, an openness to and regard for those from different cultures and religious backgrounds, can be found in "The Edicts of Asoka." A warlike Indian emperor (ca. 274–232 BC) who experienced a change of heart about morality and war, Asoka had his teachings and pronouncements about morality inscribed on rocks, pillars, and caves throughout his kingdom; for example, "Since I am convinced that the welfare and happiness of the people will be achieved only [through growth in dharma], I consider how I may bring happiness to the people, not only to relatives of mine or residents of my capital city, but also to those who are far removed from me. I act in the same manner with respect to all. I am concerned similarly with all classes. Moreover, I have honored all religious sects with various offerings." Asoka, *Edicts*, 36. Asoka's sensibilities bear comparison

with those of the Stoics. However, both Asoka and the Stoics lived in times that accepted slavery.

5. I am using *peoples* and *nations* largely synonymously. I assume that nations by definition have unique cultures, whereas (nation-)states may or may not be (highly) culturally pluralistic, for example, the United States and Iceland. Because of increased mobility, migration, and communication, perhaps the notion of a "people" will someday seem passé. But we have not yet arrived at this world.

6. See Aboulafia, *The Mediating Self* and *The Cosmopolitan Self*.

7. "Sociality" refers to the way in which biological and social systems change and transition from one state to another.

8. See Lear, *Radical Hope*.

9. Taylor, *Sources of the Self*, 374–375 (emphasis added).

10. This statement would require qualification for several important existentialists, for example, Søren Kierkegaard.

11. "There is an ideal, natural way to self-fulfillment for each *Volk* analogous to an individual's development from birth to the grave. Unfortunately, peoples have broken the bounds of their natural habitat, have destroyed and been destroyed, have contaminated other cultures and been contaminated. The tragic, unnatural episodes of world history are the subjection of cultures to the vicissitudes of such experience. Herder is a moral historical judge: the monad of *Volk* individuality can be lost and has been. That which is mixed is rarely good, that which imitates is a defilement, and that which is forced lacks authenticity." Manuel, "Introduction," in Herder, *Reflections*, xviii.

12. The mission of the cosmopolitan may be difficult, but it certainly isn't impossible. As a matter of fact, it appears to be less a mission and more a daily challenge as we move into an increasingly mobile and transactional twenty-first century. Following Mead, I speculate about why cosmopolitanism may be on the rise, especially in Chapter 4, but this is a topic for another book, one that would draw on empirical work in the social sciences.

13. Sartre, *Transcendence of the Ego*, 98–99. The translation cited here is a revision of Williams and Kirkpatrick's translation of Sartre by Robert Denoon Cummings, *Philosophy of Jean-Paul Sartre*, 54. In *Being and Nothingness* Sartre modifies his position. The for-itself is not an impersonal spontaneity but one that has a "sense of self."

14. Lear, *Radical Hope*, 42. The goal of Lear's book is not to argue for determinism but to show that hope and transcendence are still possible in the face of the destruction of one's culture. "The Crow hoped for the emergence of a Crow subjectivity that did not yet exist. There would be ways of continuing to form oneself as a Crow subject—ways to flourish as a Crow—even though the

traditional forms were doomed. This hope is radical in that it is aiming for a subjectivity that is at once Crow and does not yet exist" (104).

15. Given the variety of standards for how cultures do or do not make forms of excellence central, certainly Lear would not wish to generalize about specific features of Crow culture. It is also worth noting that Lear, following Kierkegaard, is concerned to show that what becomes impossible, when a culture's way of life is made impossible, is subjectivity understood as a "never-ending task." In this case the chief, Plenty Coups, could no longer pursue his project of becoming an outstanding chief because the latter role no longer made sense in the new cultural context of the reservation. Lear is clear that his work is interpretive, as it must be when it imports a notion of subjectivity from a nineteenth-century Danish existentialist to assist in explaining the experience of a Crow chief.

16. See Aboulafia, *The Mediating Self*, especially 73–101.

17. In ancient Greece, before the Stoics were the Sophists, who may have been the first true philosophical cosmopolitans of the Greek world, leaving aside the clannish, and idiosyncratically broad-minded, Pythagoreans. However, neither the Stoics nor the Sophists argued for the notion that all peoples (as different and unique peoples) were inherently worthy of respect and entitled to develop themselves as they saw fit. And both camps, if the Sophists can be called a camp, accepted slavery.

18. No doubt there were individuals who held some of these attitudes, mutandis mutatis, before modern times. It's the package and its pervasiveness that are unique.

Chapter 1

1. See Sartre, *Transcendence of the Ego; Being and Nothingness*, part 1, chap. 1; part 2, chap. 1; and part 4, chap. 1; and *Existentialism Is a Humanism*.

2. Sartwell, "Rorty: In Memoriam." Sartwell observes in the same piece that "Rorty had encyclopedic knowledge and an accessible public voice rare in academic philosophy. But above all else, he was a provocateur." He also notes that Rorty misinterpreted others, but even when challenged, he continued to insist on referring to their works in ways that he found congenial.

3. Given Rorty's concerns, his recent death brings to mind Sartre's claim about death and the *en-soi*, that is, death as the end of transcendence and our ability to influence how we are defined by others.

4. In *Richard Rorty*, Neil Gross provides a careful account of Rorty's intellectual development, which clearly shows that Rorty came to analytic philosophy after exposure to, and an interest in, nonanalytic readings of the history of philosophy.

5. Regarding the strong poet and creativity, a conversation that I had with Rorty during the same visit may be of interest. During this conversation he expressed his dismay over the state of philosophy in the United States. When I pitched the notion that the most confining versions of analytic philosophy, for example, those that excluded the history of philosophy, appeared to be contracting in influence, he would have none of it. He felt that "old-fashioned" analytic philosophy would continue to hold sway over the most established and influential philosophy departments in the United States for the foreseeable future. So what, I asked, is going to change things? Dick sank back into his seat and said (to paraphrase), "Probably nothing until the next pathbreaker [read, strong poet] turns up on the scene, and there is no predicting such an event."

6. "When such edifying philosophers as Marx, Freud, and Sartre offer new explanations of our usual patterns of justifying our actions and assertions, and when these explanations are taken up and integrated into our lives, we have striking examples of the phenomenon of reflection's changing vocabulary and behavior" (*PMN*, 386). Needless to say, it may seem peculiar to think of Freud, Marx, and Sartre as nonsystematic thinkers. One has to bear in mind Rorty's idiosyncratic understanding of the differences between systematic thinkers, who build for eternity, and those thinkers who may seem systematic but who ultimately turn out to be primarily edifying.

7. See, for example, James, *Principles of Psychology*, vol. 1. All subsequent references refer to volume 1.

8. For example, for Mead, there are metaphysical dimensions to novelty; in fact, temporality is dependent on novelty. Mead, *Philosophy of the Present*.

9. Sartre would certainly challenge an exclusive connection between the *pour-soi* and reflection, since the for-itself is primarily a prereflective spontaneity. However, I don't believe that Rorty intended to confine the *pour-soi* solely to reflection by this comment. In any case, continuing to follow my course of an "unfettered" reading of Rorty, I would prefer to focus here on his notion of "choosers of alternative vocabularies."

10. "Thus, there is no human nature since there is no God to conceive of it." Sartre, *Existentialism Is a Humanism*, 22.

11. Rorty appears to believe that Sartre was not radical enough in his approach to the notion of "essence." Hence we find him stating in a footnote in *Mirror of Nature*, "It would have been fortunate if Sartre had followed up his remark that man is the being whose essence is to have no essence by saying that this went for all other beings also. Unless this addition is made, Sartre will appear to be insisting on the good old metaphysical distinction between spirit and nature in other terms, rather than simply making the point that man is always free to choose new descriptions (for, among other things, himself)" (361–362).

12. See, for example, James, *Principles of Psychology*, especially 314–316; and

Mead, *Mind, Self, and Society*. (In a personal note that Rorty sent me years ago, he mentioned that he had felt a special attachment to Mead because his mother, Winfred Raushenbush, had lived with the Meads while she was in school at the University of Chicago.)

13. Rorty goes on to say, "The torturers and the brainwashers are, in any case, already in as good a position to interfere with human freedom as they could wish; further scientific progress cannot improve their position" (*PMN*, 354).

14. Sartre, *Being and Nothingness*, 23.

15. Dewey, *Experience and Nature*.

Chapter 2

1. Dewey to Daniels, November 17, 1947, *Correspondence of John Dewey*, vol. 3.

2. Dewey to James, May 6, 1891, *Correspondence of John Dewey*, vol. 1. Quoted in Good, *Search for Unity in Diversity*, 146. Dewey goes on to note, "But Hegel seems to me intensely modern in his spirit, whatever his garb, and I don't like to see him dressed up as Scholasticus Redivivus—although of course his friends, the professed Hegelians, are mainly responsible for that."

3. James, *Principles of Psychology*, 304.

4. See James, "Does 'Consciousness' Exist?" and "The Notion of Consciousness," in *Writings of William James*, 169–194.

5. Mead, "The Social Self," in *Selected Writings*, 142–149.

6. Dewey interprets James's account as in line with his reading of Hegel. It seems that for Dewey in 1891, Hegel offers an account of consciousness that does not posit a unifying ego, and Dewey believes that he is following Hegel when he claims that one does not need to posit a unifying thinker or consciousness to produce a unified self. The world will supply the unity.

7. Good, *Search for Unity in Diversity*, 187; Dewey, *Psychology*, 216. A major difference between the early Sartre and Dewey appears to center on the extent to which Sartre stresses the destabilizing, detotalizing "nature" of consciousness, whereas Dewey emphasizes unity as a necessary condition for the self and, as a corollary, for self-consciousness. But so stated, this difference, which seems undeniable, is misleading. When one actually delves more deeply into the positions of these thinkers, similarities become more apparent. Both, for example, would have agreed that James was on the right track when he sought to undermine the role of a transcendental ego, and this undermining is tied to ideas that are central to the positions of both thinkers. Dewey, as a committed post-Darwinian, targets many of the same types of thinkers whom Sartre appears to have in his sights when he criticizes those who treat the self as an essence or substance.

8. An exception to the dearth of work on Dewey and Sartre is William R. Caspary's article, "Dewey and Sartre on Ethical Decisions," 367–393. Caspary's piece focuses on the relationship between Dewey's notion of dramatic rehearsal and Sartre's commitment to radical choice. The article also provides a summary of several points of comparison between Sartre and Dewey; specifically, the author mentions ten points of comparison between Dewey and Sartre, for example, engagement, invention, freedom and responsibility, contingency, anxiety, self-formation, and the ethical dilemma. The heart of Caspary's piece is an analysis of Sartre's famous example of the student who must decide whether to go to war or stay home with his mother, in light of the role of dramatic rehearsals in Dewey's approach to ethical dilemmas. There is something to be said for this sort of comparison, although there is a danger of exaggerating the extent to which Sartre himself would be willing to employ the method of dramatic rehearsal, especially if the result is a notion of a harmonized or unified self or act, which is the goal for Dewey, according to Caspary.

9. Detmer, *Freedom as a Value*, 154.

10. Cohen-Solal, "Introduction," in Sartre, *Existentialism Is a Humanism*, 10.

11. Jean-Paul Sartre, "Post-Lecture Discussion," in *Existentialism Is a Humanism*, 55 (emphasis added).

12. Ibid., 57 (emphasis added).

13. See Detmer, *Freedom as a Value*, 177–215.

14. See ibid., 56–80.

15. If we take Sartre at his word in *Being and Nothingness*, he is attempting to present an ontology, and a dualistic one at that. Dewey would no doubt dismiss this approach as old school, in spite of the jargon of twentieth-century phenomenology. But without rehearsing the debates here about whether or not *Being and Nothingness* is a successful and consistent phenomenological ontology, we can certainly say that informed readers have argued that Sartre imports empirical observations in a manner that raises difficulties for his ontology. One of the most significant challenges that Sartre faces in this regard involves his claim that the Other does not alter the ontological structure of the for-itself, yet nevertheless permanently alters the relationship of the for-itself to itself. Sartre declares, "Being-for-others is not an ontological structure of the For-itself. We can not think of deriving being-for-others from a being-for-itself. . . . Of course our human-reality must of necessity be simultaneously for-itself and for-others, but our present investigation does not aim at constituting an anthropology. It would perhaps not be impossible to conceive of a For-itself which would be wholly free from all For-others and which would exist without even suspecting the possibility of being an object. But this For-itself simply would not be 'man.'" Sartre, *Being and Nothingness*, 282 (hereafter cited as *BN*). From the perspective of the pragmatist, this passage suggests that Sartre is seeking to create a difference that

doesn't make a difference. There is a hypothetical that is invoked here, the possibility of a for-itself without others that is simply not man. The invocation of this hypothetical is supposed to help us avoid philosophical anthropology. It is a reasonable question to ask whether in this and other cases Sartre manages to do so. In my view, much of *Being and Nothingness* can be read as philosophical anthropology, not ontology, and this is the language that Sartre appears to translate his philosophy into in "Existentialism Is a Humanism."

16. Sartre, *BN*, 565.
17. Detmer, *Freedom as a Value*, 40–50.
18. Sartre, BN, 483.
19. Detmer, *Freedom as a Value*, 63. Sartre asserts, "It is necessary, however, to note that the choice, being identical with acting, supposes a commencement of realization in order that the choice may be distinguished from the dream and the wish. Thus we shall not say that a prisoner is always free to go out of prison, which would be absurd, nor that he is always free to long for release, which would be an irrelevant truism, but that he is always free to try to escape (or to get himself liberated); that is, that whatever his condition may be, he can project his escape and learn the value of his project by undertaking some action" (*BN*, 483–484).
20. In one place in "Existentialism Is a Humanism," Sartre warns his readers not to confuse will and choice. "What we usually understand by 'will' is a conscious decision that most of us take after we have made ourselves what we are. I may want to join a party, write a book, or get married—but all of that is only a manifestation of an earlier and more spontaneous choice than what is known as 'will'" (23). This passage is in line with statements in *Being and Nothingness*. The problem is that in other passages in "Existentialism Is a Humanism" Sartre is not so careful about making this distinction, and a reader can easily come away with the impression that he is talking about something like free will and self-conscious choice. In fact, even this passage appears to suggest the possibility of self-conscious decisions, which involve reflection or deliberation, if one thinks about wanting to join a party, write a book, or get married as being in the same ballpark as deciding to go off to war and leave one's mother behind, that is, as having at some point involved a weighing of options. (It turns out that the "confusion" about "choice" is no accident. In spite of Sartre's commitment to the spontaneity of consciousness, a form of deliberation appears to be a feature of practical freedom. Sartre is being less than careful in his presentation, but he is not just being lax. The topic is complex for him.)
21. Sartre distinguishes impure and pure reflection. The former deals with the objectification of psychic states and is oriented to the past, whereas the latter entails an unmediated transparency of (self-)consciousness to itself. "Pure reflection [is] the simple presence of the reflective for-itself to the for-itself

reflected-on" (*BN*, 155). We will be concerned with impure reflection in this chapter. See ibid., 150–170.

22. Sartre, *Transcendence of the Ego*, 98–99. The translation cited here is a revision of Williams and Kirkpatrick's translation of Sartre by Robert Denoon Cummings, *Philosophy of Jean-Paul Sartre*, 54. Sartre continues in the same paragraph, "The will orients itself toward states of consciousness, emotions, or things, but it never turns back upon consciousness. We are well aware of this from the occasions on which we try to *will* a consciousness (I *will* fall asleep, I *will* no longer think about that, etc.). In these various cases, it is essentially necessary that the will be maintained and preserved *by the consciousness which is radically opposed* to the consciousness the will would bring about (if I *will* to fall asleep, I stay awake; if I *will* not to think about this or that, I *thereby* think about it)."

23. Dewey declares, "Unless there is a direct, mainly unreflective appreciation of persons and deeds, the data for subsequent thought will be lacking or distorted. A person must *feel* the qualities of acts as one feels with the hands the qualities of roughness and smoothness in objects, before he has an inducement to deliberate or material with which to deliberate. Effective reflection must also terminate in a situation which is directly appreciated, if thought is to be effective in action." Dewey and Tufts, *Ethics*, 268–269. The passages of *Ethics* quoted in this chapter were written by Dewey.

24. Dewey, *Ethics*, 286.
25. Sartre, *BN*, 462.
26. Ibid., 95.
27. Ibid., 102.
28. This may in part be due to the influence of a Hegelian notion of negativity. For Dewey, the synthetic aspect of Hegel's dialectic remains congenial. For the early Sartre, his model of consciousness can be approached as a truncated Hegelian dialectic, in which the negative is linked to the subject, as it is in Hegel, but is transformed into a negative that separates consciousness from itself, yielding a prereflective and then a reflective consciousness.
29. Dewey, "Need for a Recovery in Philosophy," in *Middle Works*, 9–10.
30. Dewey, *Logic*, 189.
31. Dewey, "Reflex Arc Concept in Psychology," in *Early Works*, 96–109.
32. Sartre, *BN*, 483.
33. Dewey, "Need for a Recovery of Philosophy," 44–45.
34. Sartre, *BN*, 23.
35. Ibid., 476.
36. Dewey, *Ethics*, 290–291.
37. Sartre, *BN*, 476–477.
38. Dewey, *Ethics*, 306.
39. Ibid., 296.

40. Ibid., 306–307.
41. Sartre, *BN*, 468.
42. A long discussion is possible here regarding the relationship of projects to what Sartre calls an original or initial project, but this would take us too far afield. For our purposes it is sufficient to acknowledge that Sartre argues that there are initial projects that frame our other projects, for example, "choosing myself as inferior in the midst of others" (*BN*, 471). These original projects may be pursued in different ways without changing the original project. What is crucial for the analysis offered in this chapter is that no project is fixed for Sartre. "I can refuse to stop [walking to the city] only by a radical conversion of my being-in-the-world; that is, by an abrupt metamorphosis of my *initial project*—i.e., by another choice of myself and of my ends. Moreover this modification is always possible" (464, emphasis added).
43. Ibid., 450.
44. For Dewey, groups engaged in intelligent or scientific inquiry have a decided advantage over individuals in determining successful courses of action.
45. See Sartre, *Search for a Method*.
46. Detmer, *Freedom as a Value*, 136–137.
47. Dewey, *Ethics*, 267. Dewey also notes, "The results of prior experience, including previous conscious thinking, get taken up into direct habits, and express themselves in direct appraisals of value. Most of our moral judgments are intuitive, but this fact is not a proof of the existence of a separate faculty of moral insight, but is the result of past experience funded into direct outlook upon the scene of life" (266).
48. Sartre, *BN*, 444.
49. Dewey, *Ethics*, 286.
50. Ibid.
51. Ibid.
52. Sartre, *BN*, 450–451.
53. Ibid., 451.
54. Ibid., 450.
55. Ibid.
56. A turn to Sartre's account of existential psychoanalysis might prove helpful in further clarifying Sartre's position, but this is beyond the scope of this chapter. See ibid., 557–575.
57. See note 15 in this chapter, and Aboulafia, *Mediating Self*, especially 45–69, for a discussion of ways in which Sartre's ontology is intertwined with the empirical.
58. Sartre, *Existentialism Is a Humanism*, 23–25.
59. Dewey, *Ethics*, 303–304.

Chapter 3

An earlier version of this chapter was published as "A (neo) American in Paris: Bourdieu, Mead, and Pragmatism," in *Bourdieu: A Critical Reader*, ed. Richard Shusterman (Oxford: Blackwell Publishers, 1999); reprinted by permission of Blackwell Publishers.

1. Bourdieu describes fields in the following fashion:

The school system, the state, the church, political parties, or unions are not apparatuses but fields. In a field, agents and institutions constantly struggle, according to the regularities and the rules constitutive of this space of play (and, in given conjunctures, over those rules themselves), with various degrees of strength and therefore diverse probabilities of success, to appropriate the specific products at stake in the game. Those who dominate in a given field are in a position to make it function to their advantage but they must always contend with the resistance, the claims, the contention, "political" or otherwise, of the dominated. (Bourdieu and Wacquant, *Invitation*, 102)

2. See Kestenbaum, *Phenomenological Sense of John Dewey*, and Ostrow, *Social Sensitivity*.

3. Bourdieu and Wacquant, *Invitation*, 122. Bourdieu goes on to say: "At bottom and in short—I cannot consider here all the relevant commonalities and differences—I would say that the theory of practical sense presents many similarities with theories, such as Dewey's, that grant a central role to the notion of habit, understood as an active and creative relation to the world, and reject all the conceptual dualisms upon which nearly all post-Cartesian philosophies are based: subject and object, internal and external, material and spiritual, individual and social, and so on." In contrast to the Platonic vision of like nurturing like, perhaps we should refer to Bourdieu's speculations here as his prototheory of the reactive habitus: opposition to the same breeds the similar.

4. Given Bourdieu's repeated disparagements of theory for theory's sake, or the mere comparison of theories for the sake of contrasting them, I find myself in a bit of a quandary. Bourdieu would no doubt prefer that my time be spent utilizing his approach to investigate the genesis of fields that could produce such similarities. Since this is neither the place nor the time to analyze or dispute Bourdieu's complex relationship to the theoretical, I suggest that those who share his aversion to the merely theoretical view this chapter as supplying information for a possible future study. See, for example, Bourdieu and Wacquant, *Invitation*, 159–160.

5. This chapter will also prove of assistance in discussing Neil Gross's new sociology of ideas in Chapter 6. Gross both accepts and criticizes important features of Bourdieu's social theory.

6. Bourdieu, *Logic of Practice*, 50 (hereafter cited as *LP*).

7. Bourdieu, "A Lecture on the Lecture," in *In Other Words*, 190. (Translators differ on whether to italicize the word *habitus*. In *Transcendence* I have followed the translators' wishes. In my own text, I have not italicized it.)
8. James, *Psychology: The Briefer Course*, 10.
9. Ibid., 11–12.
10. Mead, *Mind, Self, and Society*, 352–353 (hereafter cited as *MSS*).
11. Mead, "Scientific Method and the Moral Sciences," in *Selected Writings*, 258. See also "Philanthropy from the Point of View of Ethics," in *Selected Writings*, 397.
12. Bourdieu would in all likelihood respond to Mead on ethics and politics as he has to Dewey on art and education. "Dewey, however laudable his stances in matters of art and education, did not escape this kind of moralism [that is, by rejecting the dichotomy between popular and high culture, one could make it disappear] fostered by both his epoch and his national philosophical and political traditions" (*Invitation*, 84).
13. The parentheses around *self* in this chapter are meant to draw attention to the distinction between a fully developed consciousness of self, in which one is directly reflecting on who one is—that is, one's identity—and the awareness one has of one's actions or the meaning of one's words. In the latter case the parentheses will be used. This distinction is suggested by Mead's approach; whether and to what degree it can be maintained are beyond the scope of this chapter.
14. Bourdieu, *LP*, 80.
15. Mead, *MSS*, 43.
16. Bourdieu, *LP*, 80–81.
17. Ibid., 50–51.
18. Mead, *MSS*, 47.
19. Mead is well aware that hand sign languages allow one to respond to one's own gestures as the other does, because one can see and feel a hand sign as the other sees it. Mead, however, views the vocal gesture as ultimately more suited to this task.
20. Mead, *MSS*, 134.
21. Cook, *George Herbert Mead*, 79.
22. Bourdieu, *LP*, 19.
23. Habermas, "Individuation Through Socialization," in *Postmetaphysical Thinking*, 149–204.
24. There are times when Mead refers to the self as a combination of the "I" and the "me," a self, as opposed to solely the "me," while at other times the "me" does not appear to require quite the level of sophistication that is suggested here. Part of the problem lies in the fact that so much of what we have from Mead is drawn from students' or Mead's lecture notes. Mead never published a book on

his social psychology or philosophy. In addition, it appears that he wanted to retain some flexibility in his functional distinctions.

25. Mead, *MSS*, 154 (emphasis added).

26. There is an agonistic dimension to fields that is not typically a basic feature of Mead's "systems." See Bourdieu's comments in note 1 in this chapter.

27. Mead, *MSS*, 157.

28. Bourdieu, *LP*, 60. Bourdieu goes on to tell us that "'personal' style, the particular stamp marking all the products of the same *habitus*, whether practices or works, is never more than a deviation in relation to the style of a period or class" (ibid.).

29. Mead, *MSS*, 175.

30. Ibid., 174.

31. Bourdieu appears to associate project-oriented or "controlled" spontaneity with Sartre, but the absence of a posited self on the prereflective level for Sartre complicates this reading.

32. Bourdieu, *LP*, 56.

33. Whether Mead can succeed here is beyond the scope of this chapter. See Aboulafia, *The Mediating Self*, 45–69.

34. Mead, *Philosophy of the Present*, 1, 33. No doubt the metaphysical questions surrounding the status of novelty—just how novel is novelty?—are rather breathtaking and worthy of attention but are clearly beyond the scope of this chapter.

35. Bourdieu, *LP*, 60–61.

36. Bourdieu and Wacquant, *Invitation*, 132–133.

37. Ibid., 133. Bourdieu continues, "Having said this, I must immediately add that there is a probability, inscribed in the social destiny associated with definite social conditions, that experiences will confirm habitus, because most people are statistically bound to encounter circumstances that tend to agree with those that originally fashioned their habitus. . . . From [the categories already constructed by prior experiences] . . . follows an inevitable priority of originary experiences and a *relative* closure of the system of dispositions that constitute habitus (*Invitation*, 133; bracketed comment by Bourdieu). This is not Bourdieu's complete answer. He goes on to discuss the relation of habitus to certain social structures.

38. Bourdieu, "A Reply to Some Objections," in *In Other Words*, 116.

39. Bourdieu, *LP*, 55.

40. Mead, *Philosophy of the Present*, 47.

41. See Aboulafia, *The Mediating Self*, 73–101.

42. Bourdieu, *LP*, 91.

43. Socrates, as Nietzsche glibly and humorously teaches, was a dialectician and educator, and as such, a degenerate, one who fell from true excellence, and

this sort of excellence needs none of his rhetorical strategies. Nietzsche, *Twilight of the Idols*, in *The Portable Nietzsche*, 473–479.

44. Bourdieu, *LP*, 103.
45. Bourdieu, *In Other Words*, 5.
46. Rosenthal and Bourgeois read Mead as very close to Merleau-Ponty; hence they tend to see a prereflective sphere in Mead's thought that has many of the attributes of Merleau-Ponty's lived body. My own view is that Mead bifurcated the reflective and nonreflective at times to an unnecessary degree, although I find his approach generally more congenial than Bourdieu's with regard to the relationship between reflective and nonreflective experience. I agree with Rosenthal and Bourgeois that there is a sensitivity to experience in Mead that could easily be developed in the direction of Merleau-Ponty's work. Our disagreement is over the degree to which he actually accomplished this end. I discuss the relationship between the prereflective and the reflective in my book *The Mediating Self*. See Rosenthal and Bourgeois, *Mead and Merleau-Ponty*.
47. Mead, *MSS*, 196.
48. This, of course, would not surprise Bourdieu, who has few compunctions about categorizing Dewey's moralism in terms of American cultural traditions.
49. Bourdieu and Wacquant, *Invitation*, 116–117. This reference to the Stoics brings to mind Adam Smith, who was influenced by them. Bourdieu seems to take a special delight in criticizing what he takes to be the notion of the *impartial spectator*, which suggests to him objectivity from the mountaintop, the aloofness of the theoretician (*LP*, 31). Mead, on the other hand, would feel comfortable with this notion if it were understood in the spirit of certain aspects of Adam Smith's work, that is, not as objectivity from on High but as a constant claim on us to attempt to take the perspective of others and thereby gain some distance from our own interests. Smith may have increasingly moved toward a notion of the Judge on High as he revised successive editions of *The Theory of Moral Sentiments*, but from the first there was a strong social bent and practical impulse behind the phrase.
50. Mead, *MSS*, 386.
51. Membership in these groups allows for "definite social relations (however indirect) with an almost infinite number of other individuals . . . cutting across functional lines of demarcation which divide different human social communities from one another, and including individual members from several (in some cases from all) such communities" (*MSS*, 157). Mead took this process to be part and parcel of the growing interdependence of the modern world. He did not view such groups as necessarily destroying more localized ones but as existing at different levels of abstraction.

Chapter 4

Material in this chapter derives from my essay "Mead on Cosmopolitanism, Sympathy, and War," in *Pragmatism, Nation, and Race: Community in the Age of Empire*, ed. Chad Kautzer and Eduardo Mendieta (Bloomington: Indiana University Press, 2009); reprinted by permission of Indiana University Press.

1. There is much riding on the term "undeserved": what are the source and nature of the judgment that this suffering is in fact undeserved? For the purposes at hand, all I ask is that the reader accept the claim that people suffer through no fault of their own, whether because of the calculations of human beings or to natural disasters.

2. See Aboulafia, *Cosmopolitan Self*, 7–27.

3. Arendt, "The Crisis in Culture," in *Between Past and Future*, 220. Arendt continues, "The power of judgment rests on a potential agreement with others, and the thinking process which is active in judging something is not, like the thought process of pure reasoning, a dialogue between me and myself, but finds itself always and primarily, even if I am quite alone in making up my mind, in an anticipated communication with others with whom I know I must finally come to some agreement. From this potential agreement judgment derives its specific validity."

4. The way in which I am using the term "empathy" is in line with the non-evaluative dimension of Martha Nussbaum's definition of the term. "'Empathy' is often used, as I shall later use it, to designate an imaginative reconstruction of another person's experience, without any particular evaluation of that experience; so used, obviously, it is quite different and insufficient for compassion; it may not even be necessary for it." Nussbaum, *Upheavals of Thought*, 301–302. As we will see, if empathy simply refers to "taking the perspective of others," it can be viewed in nonevaluative terms. However, for Mead there are circumstances in which the evaluative dimension of taking the perspective of others comes directly into play, for example, with certain generalized others.

5. Mead, *Movements of Thought*, 60.

6. Ibid., 63.

7. Mead asserts, "It is only because this new self had gone back into the past that such an organized past arose at all. . . . [W]e have to recognize that history does not exist except in so far as the individuals of the present in some sense put themselves back into the past. It is only in a process of memory—memory of the people, if you like, that history can be created. And such a reconstruction of the past is possible only when we have, so to speak, reached some such point that we can become aware of ourselves" (ibid., 70).

8. I will sidestep here the immensely challenging question of the relationship between the sensibility that we call romantic and the material conditions that

helped to generate it. Mead was certainly aware of the importance of material conditions, but in my view he did not have sufficiently critical tools to assess them.

9. If one thinks of the significance of a figure such as Herder, and the resonance of his position regarding cultural diversity, Mead's hypothesis is at least plausible, even if what we call romanticism is due at least in part to a transformation in material conditions.

10. I am confident that Mead would have argued that this sensibility did not remain confined to the West.

11. Mead, "The Social Self," in *Selected Writings*, 148 (emphasis added).

12. Arendt, *Lectures*, 74–75.

13. I am simplifying the story of how selves became more expansive in the modern world for Mead. It is a story that involves the rise of modern science as well as new methods of communication, and it would require its own chapter. In passing I should note that romanticism's role in this development is complex, for it tends to focus us on the individual self, but it does so in a manner that opens up the possibility of relating to others in new ways. While the reflexivity it emphasizes can turn us inward, it also sets the stage for enlarging our social lives.

14. Mead, "Philanthropy," in *Selected Writings*, 392.

15. Ibid., 400 (emphasis added).

16. Mead, "National-Mindedness," in *Selected Writings*, 358.

17. No doubt membership in different groups influences how we behave within a specific group. But even allowing for this influence, I think it fair to say that there are differences in behavior that cannot be explained solely by this sort of sociology, that is, there still remain psychological differences.

18. Smith, *Theory of Moral Sentiments*, 9.

19. There has been considerable debate in social-psychological circles regarding the sources of empathy, or what I have been referring to as "sympathy." There are those who argue for an empathy-altruism model, in which altruism is viewed as fundamentally independent from egoism (see, for example, Batson et al., "Is Empathy-Induced Helping due to Self-Other Merging?" 495–509). And there are those who find the source of empathy (sympathy) in the perception of an overlap between self and other, which grounds empathy in self-interest (see, for example, Cialdini et al., "Reinterpreting the Empathy-Altruism Relationship," 481–494). Needless to say, this is a debate that we cannot enter directly into here. In a sense, features of both positions can be found in the model that is being developed, and they both support one of its important assumptions, that empathetic (sympathetic) attachment to others increases the likelihood that people will seek to help those in need.

20. It is important to emphasize that sympathetic attachments, insofar as we are defining *sympathy* as a synonym for *compassion*, are not the original source

of perspective-taking. Role-taking in developmental terms is related to language development and therefore is weighted to the cognitive, although it can and does have emotional resonances.

21. Dewey states in his *Ethics*,

> To put ourselves in the place of others, to see things from the standpoint of their purposes and values, to humble, contrariwise, our own pretensions and claims till they reach the level they would assume in the eye of an impartial sympathetic observer, is the surest way to attain objectivity of moral knowledge. Sympathy is the animating mold of moral judgment not because its dictates take precedence in action over those of other impulses (which they do not), but because it furnishes the most efficacious *intellectual* standpoint. It is the tool, *par excellence*, for resolving complex situations. Then when it passes into active or overt conduct, it does so *fused* with other impulses and not in isolation and is thus protected from sentimentality. In this fusion there is broad and objective survey of all desires and projects because there is an expanded personality. (270)

Dewey appears to be combining "empathy" and "sympathy" in the section of the *Ethics* from which this quotation is drawn, that is, if the terms are understood as they have been defined in this chapter.

22. Mead, *Mind, Self, and Society*, 157 (hereafter cited as *MSS*).

23. What Mead says about rights sheds light on how he views universality. "In the community there are certain ways of acting under situations which are essentially identical, and these ways of acting on the part of anyone are those which we excite in others when we take certain steps. If we assert our rights, we are calling for a definite response just because they are rights that are universal—a response which everyone should, and perhaps will, give" (ibid., 260–261).

24. Ibid., 90.

25. Mead, "Behavioristic Account of the Significant Symbol," in *Selected Writings*, 245.

26. I would add that this feature of Mead's thought is one that he shares with many other pragmatists, in particular Dewey.

27. Mead, *MSS*, 167–168.

28. No doubt material conditions play a significant, if not primary, role in this process, for example, new technologies for communication and transportation, and the corporate organization of labor.

29. Both Dewey's and Mead's appeal to impartiality is qualified by an appreciation for the role of interest in our lives.

30. For example, religions in earlier eras have certainly laid the groundwork for, or supported, forms of universalism. Mead tells us, "Even in the immediacy of the situation that seemingly involves only the giver and the recipient, there is the implication of a community in which the good has a universal value—'which of them was neighbor to him that fell among thieves?' It is, however, an implication that can become explicit only when the social structure and the

ideas behind it make it possible to regard others as neighbors. The generalization of the prophetic message, its conception of the community as the children of Jehovah, made this possible" ("Philanthropy," in *Selected Writings*, 401).

31. *New York Times*, January 2, 2005, 1, 9.

32. Note the appeal for assistance made by Susilo Bambang Yudhoyono, Indonesia's president: "I appeal to the world community to contribute to the reconstruction of Indonesia that has been hit by disaster and we welcome those contributions as a manifestation of global unity" (*New York Times*, January 2, 2005, 1). After the disaster(s), U.S. newscasts talked about the potential dangers of earthquakes and tsunamis in the United States. While these newscasts can be viewed as cynical attempts to increase ratings through appeals to fear and self-interest, they also had the practical effect of motivating viewers to take the perspective of those who were suffering, that is, those with whom they may have had more in common than they realized.

33. It's important to note that Mead preferred the term "impulse" to "instinct" because he saw the former as more malleable than the latter.

> Human behavior, or conduct, like the behavior of lower animal forms, springs from impulses. An impulse is a congenital tendency to react in a specific manner to a certain sort of stimulus, under certain organic conditions. Hunger and anger are illustrations of such impulses. They are best termed "impulses," and not "instincts," because they are subject to extensive modifications in the life-history of individuals, and these modifications are so much more extensive than those to which the instincts of lower animal forms are subject that the use of the term "instinct" in describing the behavior of normal adult human individuals is seriously inexact. ("Supplementary Essay I," in Mead, *Mind, Self, and Society*, 337)

34. Kant, "Idea for a Universal History," in *On History*, 11–26.
35. Mead, "National-Mindedness," in *Selected Writings*, 362–363.
36. Ibid., 358–359.
37. Ibid., 359.
38. Ibid., 364–365.
39. Ibid., 365.
40. Ibid., 367.

Chapter 5

Previously published as "W. E. B. Du Bois: Double-Consciousness, Jamesian Sympathy, and the Critical Turn," in *The Oxford Handbook of American Philosophy*, ed. Cheryl Misak (Oxford: Oxford University Press, 2008); reprinted by permission of Oxford University Press.

1. Du Bois, *Souls*.
2. Du Bois, "Strivings of the Negro People," 194–198. "The Strivings of the

Negro People" is not identical to the first chapter of *Souls*. For example, in the article we find the following line: "The freedman has not yet found in freedom his promised land" (195). In the first chapter of *Souls* the line reads, "The Nation has not yet found peace from its sins; the freedman has not yet found in freedom his promised land" (7).

3. Du Bois, *The Philadelphia Negro*.

4. Du Bois, "On *The Souls of Black Folk*," in *Oxford W. E. B. Du Bois Reader*, 304–305.

5. Reed, *Du Bois and American Political Thought*, 22.

6. *Souls*, 1–2. Du Bois also states, "Then it dawned upon me with a certain suddenness that I was different from others; or like, mayhap, in heart and life and longing, but shut out from their world by a vast veil. I had thereafter no desire to tear down that veil, to creep through; I held all beyond it in common contempt, and lived above it in a region of blue sky and great wandering shadows" (4).

7. Ibid., 178.

8. Ibid., 76.

9. Zamir, *Dark Voices*, 51.

10. Ibid., 44.

11. James, *Principles of Psychology*, 401 (hereafter cited as *PP*).

12. At the beginning of the chapter, James has little problem providing a rather striking definition of the nontranscendental self, which, as Shamoon Zamir points out in *Dark Voices*, is weighed down with a good deal of ideological baggage. "It is telling that James begins his chapter titled 'The Consciousness of Self' with a definition of self as a structure of commodity fetishism. '*In its widest possible sense*,' he writes, '*a man's Self is the sum total of all that he CAN call his*, not only his body and his psychic powers, but his clothes and his house, his wife and children [!], his ancestors and friends, his reputation and works, his lands and horses, and yacht and bank-account'" (157–158; bracketed exclamation added by Zamir).

13. These insights are developed by Mead when he discusses the generalized other in *Mind, Self, and Society*. For James, the individual who has the greatest power over us in terms of recognition is the person with whom we are in love.

14. We must bear in mind that James is speaking of the spiritual self here as an empirical self. As such it is "a man's inner or subjective being, his psychic faculties or dispositions, taken concretely; not the bare principle of personal Unity, or 'pure' Ego" (*PP*, 296).

15. James claims that the common experience of the "spiritual self" is of an "*active* element in all consciousness" (*PP*, 297). We can also address the spiritual self in terms of the stream of consciousness, either as a segment of the stream or in terms of its totality. In so doing "our considering the spiritual self at all is a reflective process . . . the result of our abandoning the outward-looking point

of view, and of our having become able to think of subjectivity as such, *to think of ourselves as thinkers*" (296). James is not suggesting that the spiritual self is always actively reflective, that is, actively thinking about itself as a thinker. The spiritual self may arise due to one's awareness of bodily adjustments, actions and reactions, which generate a form of awareness of self that does not entail active reflection.

16. Lemke, "Berlin and Boundaries," 63–64. "Obviously, it would be simplistic to ascertain a direct connection between Herder and Du Bois. But it is very likely that Du Bois came across Herder's writings in William James's philosophy course at Harvard and in Wilhelm Dilthey's lectures on the history of philosophy at the University of Berlin. Herder's insistence on the elevating effect of poetry, his definition of the *Volk*, and his sustained concept of *Seele* literally resonate throughout *The Souls of Black Folk*." (Although it should be noted that Herder actually opposed the notion of race. He argued that there is in fact only one human race with an almost endless number of *Volk*. See *Reflections*, 6–7.)

17. Herder, *Reflections*, 84.

18. Du Bois, "Conservation of the Races," in *Oxford W. E. B. Du Bois Reader*, 46. In the same speech Du Bois makes the following claims about race.

> If [the division of human beings into races] be true, then the history of the world is the history, not of individuals, but of groups, not of nations, but of races, and he who ignores or seeks to override the race idea in human history ignores and overrides the central thought of all history. What, then, is a race? It is a vast family of human beings, generally of common blood and language, always of common history, traditions and impulses, who are both voluntarily and involuntarily striving together for the accomplishment of certain more or less vividly conceived ideals of life. (40)

Although there is little doubt that Du Bois insisted on racial difference during the period that he wrote *Souls*, it is also the case that he was familiar with challenges to strict, essentializing definitions of race. This can be seen in his report "The First Universal Races Congress," in *Oxford W. E. B. Du Bois Reader*, 55–59.

19. Manuel, "Editor's Introduction," in *Reflections*, xx–xxi.

20. It's worth highlighting the reference to corruption in Manuel's account of Herder. Peoples can be tarnished and damaged by outside forces. This is a problem that Du Bois worries about in terms of the repercussions of slavery, which he believes may have left some African Americans with unacceptable sexual mores and a general lack of discipline.

21. Hegel, *Phenomenology of Spirit*, 104–138.

22. Zamir, *Dark Voices*, 113, 248–249n2.

23. Ibid., 144.

24. Hegel's master-slave dialectic is sufficiently familiar to require little by

way of introduction, and it will be discussed in detail in Chapter 8. However, given the previous discussion of James's and Du Bois's relationship to Scottish philosophy, we should note that Hegel was familiar with Adam Smith, as well as the Scottish theorists of sentiment. Smith's influence can readily be seen, for example, in the introduction to Hegel's *Lectures on the Philosophy of History* (see Hegel, *Reason in History*). The notion that the self can judge itself only through the looking glass provided by the other would have been well known to any reader of Smith. Of course, the influences on Hegel are legion. But let us speculate. Let us consider the possibility that when Hegel was thinking about the relationship of master and slave, and developing his model of mutual recognition, he drew on the social interactionism of Smith. No doubt Hegel radicalized the interaction, for instead of assuming that the self learns about what is right and wrong from its interactions with others, the self is viewed as coming into being through its interactions with others. And it does this in such a way that the spirit of different times informs its constitution. We are only selves insofar as we are recognized as selves, and this is precisely why neither master nor slave can be said to have a fully developed sense of self. Each self is contaminated by its relationship with an other who is either idealized or seen as less than human. The power of the negative leads to the eventual sublation of the asymmetry between master and slave.

25. Hegel, *Phenomenology of Spirit*, 110.

26. Du Bois, *Souls*, 5. In Du Bois's article "The Strivings of the Negro People," he refers to "self-consciousness" in this passage and not to "true self-consciousness" as he does in *Souls*. From a Hegelian vantage point this is a significant clarification. Forms of alienated self-consciousness are "self-consciousnesses" for Hegel, but they are not yet truly and fully self-conscious. This achievement requires historical development. Du Bois's addition of "true" can be interpreted as an attempt to avoid leaving his readers with a false impression about those who experience double-consciousness, namely, that they lack any form of self-consciousness. What they lack is *true* self-consciousness. Du Bois goes on to assert, "The history of the American Negro is the history of this strife—this longing to attain self-conscious manhood, to merge his double self into a better and truer self. In this merging he wishes neither of the older selves to be lost" (*Souls*, 5).

27. *Souls*, 11–12. Both Herder and Hegel would have a problem with how Du Bois conceptualizes historical "progress" in this passage, but for different reasons. For Herder, Du Bois would be insufficiently attuned to cultural differences, blending what should not be blended. For Hegel, Du Bois's treatment would be insufficiently dialectical. It would be mere edifying discourse.

28. Du Bois, *Dusk of Dawn*, 129.

Chapter 6

1. Another very good book on this issue is Hall, *Richard Rorty*. (All page citations in this chapter are to Gross's *Richard Rorty: The Making of an American Philosopher* unless otherwise indicated.)

2. I am focusing here on Bourdieu, rather than Collins, because of my familiarity with the former and because he was the subject of Chapter 3. But it makes little difference to a presentation of Gross's basic ideas since they serve similar functions in his model and are often treated as a package. Although ultimately critical of Bourdieu, Gross is sympathetic to his analysis of how actors employ cultural, social, economic, and symbolic capital in a strategic fashion (237–246).

3. Notice that the problem here for Gross is not about whether the individual has a greater capacity to make decisions that are not law governed than Bourdieu would allow. On the contrary, his problem with Bourdieu is that he doesn't have a theory that yields psychological laws. However, as we saw in Chapter 3, the problem with Bourdieu isn't a lack of psychological laws; it is that the capacity to improvise is circumscribed and not readily explicable. Or perhaps I should say, undertheorized. Yes, there is improvisation, but it appears to arise when one has a foot in more than one "field," so to speak, and can transfer elements of the habitus from one field to another. There is a good case to be made that this "mechanism" is simply insufficient to account for the diverse forms of improvisation of which people are capable. In other words, Bourdieu doesn't have a theory to address adequately the pluralism of the improvisational. And Gross does not appear to be concerned about this.

4. Although Gross is clear that his theory is meant to apply to American academic philosophers (265), he doesn't always confine himself to this group, especially in his more general theoretical claims. In fact, he utilizes a theoretical apparatus that by definition includes populations that are not American academics. (Who doesn't behave strategically? Who doesn't have a self-concept?) In other words, the pool that he is studying via Rorty, American academic philosophers, depends on utilizing conceptual tools that by definition apply to a larger pool. On one level, there is no problem with this. He is merely giving us an example of how ideas that may have wider applicability work in one case or for one set of individuals. But my point here is that Gross's theoretical claims often go far beyond American academics, or academics in general. So a rather peculiar situation arises. The concepts have so much breadth that the evidence used to support them, Rorty's trajectory, is underwhelming. And Gross's recognition of the fact that he needs to gather more evidence does not dig him out of the hole here. Why? Because the problem with the theory is not only due to a lack of evidence. The problem is a lack of evidence combined with a theory that itself

needs refinement, and until it is refined, the evidence provided, Rorty's life, can seem like special pleading.

5. Gross may have a somewhat jaundiced and narrow view of American philosophers, which is on display in his convictions about how they deal with status. In his conclusion, Gross discusses status in his summary of the main themes of his book. Point eleven begins, "Given the relatively small number of assistant professor slots that open up each year in elite departments and the relatively large number of Ph.D.'s such departments produce, it is inevitable that a significant number of young academicians will experience downward mobility with their first jobs, winding up with lower-status positions than they may have hoped to attain. The majority of such persons end up adjusting their expectations downward and come to live more or less productive and happy lives at second- or third-tier institutions. . . . Some, however, will formulate a plan to move up to a higher-status job after a few years" (345). Leaving the issue of tone aside, is Gross describing a large number of philosophers? Yes. Is he describing as many philosophers as he thinks that he might be describing? I don't think so, and it would be interesting to do an empirical study to examine these claims. I can't help suggesting at this juncture, although it smacks of ad hominem, that Gross's own position as an assistant professor at Harvard (at the time of his book's publication) may be coloring how he views academic life. There is certainly considerable attention paid to prestige among those whose academic lives are centered around research departments. But some folks choose other paths, and it is not because they have failed to attain the holy grail of Big Name research. For example, involvement with the latter can at times produce an intellectual conservatism, which some people shun. Also, some people prefer teaching. (Of course, Gross is aware that philosophers take different paths. However, in places he seems to forget or sidestep the multiplicity of reasons for these paths.)

6. There are times that Gross will just use the term "philosopher" or "intellectual," but it's clear from other passages that he has in mind those who work in universities and colleges.

7. See Mead, *Mind, Self, and Society*; and "The Social Self," in *Selected Writings*.

8. Gross states, "I take it as axiomatic that all social actors have self-concepts. . . . I also assume, borrowing from that strain of social-psychological work on the self that attempts to tie together self-processes and theories of social roles, that people have different self-concepts for different domains of social activity" (267).

9. Gross quotes Morris Rosenberg, *Conceiving the Self*, 57.

10. Gross has little to say here regarding how processual symbolic interactionists might explain the mechanisms in question. His account does little more than gesture to features of the ways in which symbolic interactionists could address

aspects of this issue, for example, variations in self-concept. He does not explain how they would account for the mechanisms through which self-concepts are sustained. Gross invokes Mead's notion of the "me," which could be of some assistance, without discussing it.

11. One might say that this is not an issue for Gross since he is talking about academia in America, and his reference to "output" can be seen purely in terms of American society. Yet, when one uses a phrase like "overall drive for ego coherence," one surely doesn't mean to confine this notion to at most 150 years of American academic history. Gross's theoretical aspirations appear to be in tension with his caveats regarding the scope of his theory. So it is reasonable to raise questions about the place of "output" in his model. Implicit and explicit in his book is the claim to be developing a theory that may have implications for those outside academia in America.

12. Marcuse, *One-Dimensional Man*.

13. Although Gross will utilize and criticize Bourdieu's views on the strategic, Nietzsche is only mentioned once in the book, and this is in reference to a letter Rorty wrote to the Guggenheim Foundation in support of Alexander Nehamas's work on Nietzsche.

14. In making this claim, Gross refers to "Christian Smith's 'subcultural identity' model of the growth of religious denominations" (281).

15. Bourdieu declares, "*Illusio* is the very opposite of ataraxy: it is to be invested, taken in and by the game. . . . Each field calls forth and gives life to a specific form of interest, a specific *illusio*, as tacit recognition of the value of the stakes of the game as practical mastery of its rules" (*Invitation*, 116–177).

16. Bourdieu tends to see the strategic as transhistorical and inescapable, in spite of his alleged sensitivity to the historical and institutional. And his linking of the idea of struggle and conflict to fields only reinforces this conclusion. Notice the way that Bourdieu speaks of struggle and fields in the following passage.

> The school system, the state, the church, political parties, or unions are not apparatuses but fields. In a field, agents and institutions constantly struggle, according to the regularities and the rules constitutive of this space of play (and, in given conjunctures, over those rules themselves), with various degrees of strength and therefore diverse probabilities of success, to appropriate the specific products at stake in the game. Those who dominate in a given field are in a position to make it function to their advantage but they must always contend with the resistance, the claims, the contention, "political" or otherwise, of the dominated. . . . There is history only as long as people revolt, resist, act. Total institutions—asylums, prisons, concentration camps—or dictatorial states are attempts to institute an end to history. Thus apparatuses represent a limiting case, what we may consider to be a pathological state of fields. But it is a limit that is never actually reached, even under the most repressive "totalitarian" regimes. (Bourdieu and Wacquant, *Invitation*, 102)

I don't know how to read a passage of this sort without coming to the conclusion that fields, and their inherent modes of conflict, are a fundamental feature of the human condition. Institutions or regimes that seek to totally undermine fields are, we are told, pathological and can't fully succeed. Is making assertions about "struggle," and the strategic that is inevitably bound to conflict, in this manner *a difference that makes a difference* when compared with the claim that "struggle" is transhistorical and even natural? I find myself at a loss to say that it does.

17. I would argue that Habermas tends to downplay other ways of thinking about freedom. In my view, he too closely associates freedom with a Kantian notion of autonomy.

18. Habermas, *Between Naturalism and Religion*, 155–157. Habermas is arguing against interpreting the results of Benjamin Libet's experiments as proof of determinism. In one experiment subjects were instructed to move their arms in a spontaneous fashion. The conscious decision, or the experience of a decision, to move their arms occurred after unconscious processes in the cerebral cortex, leading some to conclude that freedom or free will is an illusion. Habermas argues, "The Libet experiments can hardly bear the entire burden of proof ascribed to them in defending the thesis of determinism" (154). The comments quoted on pages 155–157 regarding deliberation are part of his critique.

19. One can give a good sociological account for contexts that foster the emergence of creativity, insofar as it entails processes of anticipation and reflection, for example, by building on Dewey's and Mead's work.

20. It is certainly true for Gross that one's self-concept can include the notion of oneself as a source of original ideas (272). But a self-concept that involves originality tells us very little about whether the individual is actually creative. She may or may not be. I don't believe that Gross would want to conflate the two. (And to take this from the opposite angle, according to Dewey, Mead had very little sense of himself as an original thinker, one who generated novel ideas. One can be original without having a conception of oneself as original.)

Chapter 7

1. Marcuse has his own concerns about the ultimate efficacy of a maternal libidinal morality.

> However, *even if* a maternal libidinal morality is traceable in the instinctual structure, and *even if* a sensuous rationality could make the Eros freely susceptible to order, one innermost obstacle seems to defy all project [*sic*] of a non-repressive development—namely, the bond that binds Eros to the death instinct. The brute fact of death denies once and for all the reality of a non-repressive existence. For death is the final negativity of time, but "joy wants eternity." (231, emphasis added)

2. Marcuse then quotes Hegel, "'Something has its Determinate Being only in Limit' and the 'Limits are the principle of that which they limit'" (*RR*, 136). And he continues, "Hegel summarizes the result of this new interpretation by saying that the existence of things is 'the unrest of Something in its Limit; it is immanent in the Limit to be the contradiction which sends Something on beyond itself'" (136).

3. Perhaps a more obvious way to address negation is by linking it with Thanatos. Negation would then be viewed as the work of Thanatos, while the negation of the negation could be viewed, paradoxically, as Thanatos overcoming itself, that is, succumbing to a process of unification, which would transform it into a form of Eros. But this would be an Eros that "contained" negation or Thanatos.

4. Marcuse's language of self-determination and alienation here suggests that he is thinking of Eros *not* only in terms of barriers and negation but as a type of subject or as related in a specific way to a subject. One reason that this is a plausible hypothesis follows from Marcuse's own concerns about a dialectic of nature, that is, a dialectic that does not relate to humanity and to human history but deals merely with nature. This sort of dialectic lends support to a crude mechanistic Marxism.

Chapter 8

1. I use the phrase "the biological or physiological dimension of emotions" in order to bypass the complex question of the relationship between emotions and biology. For the arguments of this chapter, it is only necessary to acknowledge that emotions and feelings have a physiological component, which I take to be a noncontroversial claim. Certainly there is also a social dimension.

2. Hegel, *Phenomenology of Spirit*. "Self-consciousness is faced by another self-consciousness; it has come *out of itself.* This has a twofold significance: first, it has lost itself, for it finds itself as an *other* being; secondly, in doing so it has superseded the other, for it does not see the other as an essential being, but in the other sees its own self" (111).

3. Many years ago I published an article that addressed the relationship between men and women in light of Hegel's dialectic. See "From Domination to Recognition," in Gould, *Beyond Domination*, 175–185.

4. We, the observers of the dialectic, know that knowledge entails mediation, but self-consciousness, the I = I, at this juncture does not comprehend the point that in order to be aware of oneself as a self-consciousness, there must be a distance from self, a moment of negativity, a moment of mediation. Without such a moment consciousness would be an undivided whole and, therefore, incapable of self-consciousness. For Hegel, the self-conscious unity of the subject

is achieved, not given. It is the result of alienation and development, and it exists in ideality, as a unity of differences.

5. "In this sphere, self-consciousness exhibits itself as the movement in which this antithesis [between the awareness of the objects of sense certainty and self-consciousness itself] is removed, and the identity of itself with itself becomes explicit for it" (105). But this identity is fraught because of the presence of "otherness."

6. Hegel now speaks of how that which appears to self-consciousness, what we have been referring to as the sensuous world, returns into itself, just as self-consciousness returns into itself on its side. As such the sensuous world becomes Life. Self-consciousness "is the unity *for which* the infinite unity of the differences is; [life], however, is only this unity itself, so that it is not at the same time *for itself*" (106).

7. The first chapters of the *Phenomenology* show just how unsophisticated it is to believe that objects are simple givens, as if consciousness is not involved in the experience of them. Hegel is a post-Kantian philosopher, after all.

8. Notice that this is not a purely conceptual realization. Self-consciousness doesn't simply understand that objects have their own life. It must sweat, so to speak, their reality, their material reality, if you will. Hegel is a peculiar idealist. The development of the dialectic cannot escape elements of material conditions. He tells us, "Desire and the self-certainty obtained in its gratification, are conditioned by the object, for self-certainty comes from superseding this other; in order that this supersession can take place, there must be this other" (109).

9. Natural objects cannot achieve the independence and self-determination of spirit. They cannot remain themselves while being different from themselves. Human beings can achieve this in communities of mutual recognition. Natural objects lose their determinate being, that is, they are destroyed or die, when they are forced to become other than themselves. This is what it means to be intrinsically finite and limited.

10. "The differentiated, merely *living*, shape does indeed also supersede its independence in the process of Life, but it ceases with its distinctive difference to be what it is. The object of self-consciousness, however, is equally independent in this negativity of itself; and thus is *for itself* a genus, a universal fluid element in the peculiarity of its own separate being; it is a living self-consciousness" (110).

11. "It is aware that it at once is, and is not, another consciousness, and equally that this other is *for itself* only when it supersedes itself as being for itself, and is for itself only in the being-for-self of the other. Each is for the other the middle term, through which each mediates itself with itself and unites with itself; and each is for itself, and for the other, an immediate being on its own account, which at the same time is such only through this mediation. They *recognize* themselves as *mutually recognizing* one another" (112).

12. Hyppolite, *Genesis and Structure of Hegel's "Phenomenology of Spirit."* Here is Hyppolite's reading of this section of Hegel's text: "Unlike animals, men desire not only to persevere in their being, to exist the way things exist; they also imperiously desire to be recognized as self-consciousnesses, as something raised above purely animal life. . . . It is a fight—in which the spiritual vocation of man is manifested—to prove to others as well as to oneself that one is an autonomous self-consciousness" (169).

13. Hegel, *Philosophy of Right*, 114, paragraph 166 (emphasis added).

14. Beauvoir, *The Second Sex*, 75; also see xix–xxxvi, 66–81, 716–732. On pp. xxxiv–xxxv, she writes, "Our perspective is that of existentialist ethics. Every subject plays his part as such specifically through exploits or projects that serve as a mode of transcendence; he achieves liberty only through a continual reaching out toward other liberties. There is no justification for present existence other than its expansion into an indefinitely open future. Every time transcendence falls back into immanence, stagnation, there is a degradation of existence into the '*en-soi*'—the brutish life of subjection to given conditions—and of liberty into constraint and contingence."

15. Hegel tells us, "They speak of the existence of *external* objects, which can be more precisely defined as *actual*, absolutely *singular, wholly personal, individual* things. . . . If they actually wanted to *say* 'this' bit of paper which they mean, if they wanted to *say* it, then this is impossible, because the sensuous This that is meant *cannot be reached* by language, which belongs to consciousness, i.e. to that which is inherently universal. In the actual attempt to say it, it would therefore crumble away; those who started to describe it would not be able to complete the description" (66). My point here is not that this mode of consciousness always speaks. My point is that it can speak. It possesses language. (In speaking, for Hegel, it happens to undermine its own claims about sense-certainty.)

16. Ibid. One could try to get Hegel off the hook here by claiming that it is "we" the readers of the *Phenomenology* who are aware of the importance of language. This will not work because the consciousness described in "sense-certainty" is already a language bearing consciousness.

17. A qualification is necessary. There is a sense in which one is "self-conscious" when one is aware of significant symbols, that is, when one is aware of their meanings. And this can happen before or after there is a self. For Mead, however, self-consciousness properly understood is related to a self, which requires a generalized other.

18. One might argue that the "I" is always prereflective in the early chapters of the *Phenomenology*. But besides the fact that this position can't hold up because of the presence of reflection in certain kinds of consciousness—for example, in "The Understanding"—in general the Hegelian position on mediation would make it difficult to draw a distinction between the prereflective and reflective.

One might say that the former is continually transcended by the latter. This is one way of thinking about the relationship of the implicit to the explicit in Hegel.

19. There is, of course, a sense in which the first sort of recognition that one receives is not fully mutual, ontogenetically speaking, because an adult can recognize others in ways that a child cannot, for example, in terms of respect or dignity. However, mutual respect or reciprocal relations between adults should not be the sole criterion for mutual or reciprocal recognition. The adult and child can recognize each other in terms of specific attitudes, which then reinforce each other, and that's all we need for the kind of mutual or reciprocal recognition being addressed. If you ask why an adult or parent needs "recognition" from a child, the answer is straightforward: as confirmation that the parent or adult is being understood. This sets the stage for more complex interactions eventually involving generalized others. See Chapter 3 for a discussion of Mead on the genesis of the self.

20. Interestingly, in a certain sense Mead falls between Habermas and Hegel here. For Habermas, communication for the purpose of understanding precedes strategic communication, at least logically. And this form of communication assumes a degree of mutuality. For Hegel, the dialectic calls for an agonistic moment (actually many) before we can proceed to mutual recognition. For Mead, the strategic and communicative are more intertwined than in Habermas's account of communicative action in *The Theory of Communicative Action*, but he certainly doesn't assume that the sort of agon that Hegel suggests is necessary for the development of self-consciousness. This is in part because Mead doesn't see mutual recognition as a telos in the way that Hegel does. It's present from the outset in human interactions, although more sophisticated and morally praiseworthy versions become possible as children mature.

21. Miller, *Toward a New Psychology of Women*. Miller's work is informed by psychoanalysis and object relations theory, and she cites figures such as Heinz Kohut, Harry S. Sullivan, and Karen Horney. She also draws on her experience as a clinician in this work.

22. After noting this point, she discusses the objectives of what she refers to as the movement's more radical spokeswomen: physical frankness, sexual frankness, emotional frankness, human development, protesting against objectification, private and public equality, and personal creativity (24–25).

23. Not accepting the "rightness of weakness" does not translate into the conviction that one must always try to transcend vulnerability and fragility. "That women are better able than men to consciously admit to feelings of weakness or vulnerability may be obvious, but we have not recognized the importance of this ability. That women are truly much more able to tolerate these feelings—which life in general, and particularly in our society, gener-

ates in everybody—is a positive strength" (31). I think it important to bear in mind that Miller's book was originally published in 1976. It's an interesting question how much of this language might change if Miller were to write this book today. I doubt that she would think that the basic dynamic has changed, although there has been more talk of "male vulnerability" in the United States since the book was published.

24. Hegel, *Phenomenology*, 117.

25. Hegel appears to argue that the extent to which the slave is aware of the master's dependence on him is limited, at least at first. However, even if the slave became aware of this dependence, he might not or would not have the power or self-assurance to overthrow the master. It's no accident that the section that follows the master-slave dialectic is on Stoicism.

26. See Aboulafia, *The Cosmopolitan Self*, 7–27.

27. Hegel makes a fundamental distinction between the Understanding and Reason. One of the characteristics of the Understanding is that it avoids contradictions by placing opposing sides in different frames of reference, as opposed to dealing with conflict and overcoming it. This "trick" of the Understanding has its counterpart in the dominant/subordinate, male/female relationships when the partners obscure conflicts by too readily viewing their partners' interests as their own, avoiding basic inequities because it serves to keep the peace, so to speak.

28. Miller does not explicitly focus on the "instincts" in her book. But the importance of the body and "instinct" can be inferred from the way in which she discusses emotional and social life, in particular, sexuality. For example, "When one is an object, not a subject, all of one's own physical and sexual impulses and interests are presumed not to exist independently. . . . Any stirrings of physicality and sexuality in herself would only confirm for a girl or woman her evil state" (60). Notice that Miller uses the term "impulse" here. See note 33 in Chapter 4 for Mead's view on the distinction between "impulse" and "instinct."

29. Marcuse, *One-Dimensional Man*, 56–74.

30. In Chapter 4 I quoted Mead on his preference for the term "impulse" over "instinct." His statement reminds us that acknowledgment of the "instinctual," when it is understood in terms of modifiable impulses, need not lead us to the position that physiology or genetics is destiny.

31. Mead, "National-Mindedness and International-Mindedness," in *Selected Writings*, 358–359.

32. Mead, "Philanthropy from the Point of View of Ethics," in *Selected Writings*, 392.

33. Ibid.

34. Hegel, *Philosophy of Right*, 114, paragraph 166 (emphasis added).

35. On how the biological plays a role in Mead's work that it does not in Bourdieu's, see Chapter 3.

36. Mead, "National-Mindedness and International-Mindedness," in *Selected Writings*, 358.

37. For example, see Dewey's remarks in Chapter 2 on how preferences are organic. They should not be confused with conscious choices and judgments.

38. Quoted in Cook, *George Herbert Mead*, 33.

Bibliography

Aboulafia, Mitchell. *The Cosmopolitan Self: George Herbert Mead and Continental Philosophy*. Urbana: University of Illinois Press, 2001.

———. "From Domination to Recognition." In *Beyond Domination: New Perspectives on Women and Philosophy*, edited by Carol C. Gould, 175–185. Totowa, N.J.: Rowman and Littlefield, 1983.

———. *The Mediating Self: Mead, Sartre, and Self-Determination*. New Haven, Conn.: Yale University Press, 1986.

Arendt, Hannah. "The Crisis in Culture: Its Social and Its Political Significance." In *Between Past and Future, Eight Exercises in Political Thought*, 197–226. New York: Viking Press, 1968.

———. *Lectures on Kant's Political Philosophy*. Edited by Ronald Beiner. Chicago: University of Chicago Press, 1982.

Asoka. *The Edicts of Asoka*. Edited and translated by N. A. Nikam and Richard McKeon. Chicago: University of Chicago Press, 1959.

Batson, C. Daniel, Karen Sager, Eric Garst, Misook Kang, Kostia Rubchinsky, and Karen Dawson. "Is Empathy-Induced Helping due to Self-Other Merging?" *Journal of Personality & Social Psychology* 73, no. 3 (September 1997): 495–509.

Beauvoir, Simone de. *The Second Sex*. Translated by H. M. Parshley. New York: Vintage Books, 1989.

Bourdieu, Pierre. *In Other Words: Essays Towards a Reflexive Sociology*. Translated by Matthew Adamson. Stanford: Stanford University Press, 1990.

———. "A Lecture on the Lecture." In *In Other Words: Essays Towards a Reflexive Sociology*, translated by Matthew Adamson, 177–198. Stanford: Stanford University Press, 1990.

———. *The Logic of Practice*. Translated by Richard Nice. Stanford: Stanford University Press, 1990.

———. "A Reply to Some Objections." In *In Other Words: Essays Towards a Reflexive Sociology*, translated by Matthew Adamson, 106–119. Stanford: Stanford University Press, 1990.

Bourdieu, Pierre, and Loïc J. D. Wacquant. *An Invitation to Reflexive Sociology*. Chicago: University of Chicago Press, 1992.

Caspary, William R. "Dewey and Sartre on Ethical Decisions: Dramatic Rehearsal Versus Radical Choice." *Transactions of the Charles S. Peirce Society* 42, no. 3 (2006): 367–393.

Cialdini, Robert B., Stephanie L. Brown, Brian P. Lewis, Carol Luce, and Steven L. Neuberg. "Reinterpreting the Empathy-Altruism Relationship: When One into One Equals Oneness." *Journal of Personality & Social Psychology* 73, no. 3 (September 1997): 481–494.

Cohen-Solal, Annie. "Introduction." In Jean-Paul Sartre, *Existentialism Is a Humanism*, translated by Carol Macomber. New Haven, Conn.: Yale University Press, 2007.

Cook, Gary A. *George Herbert Mead: The Making of a Social Pragmatist*. Urbana: University of Illinois Press, 1993.

Darwin, Charles. *The Descent of Man, and Selection in Relation to Sex*. 2d ed., rev. London: John Murray, 1882. First published 1871.

Detmer, David. *Freedom as a Value: A Critique of the Ethical Theory of Jean-Paul Sartre*. Chicago: Open Court, 1988.

Dewey, John. *The Correspondence of John Dewey*. Vol. 1, *1871–1918, Past Masters*. Electronic edition, Copyright © 1997 InteLex Corporation. [Manuscript notation omitted].

———. *The Correspondence of John Dewey*. Vol. 3, *1940–1952, Past Masters*. Electronic edition, copyright © 1997 InteLex Corporation.

———. *Experience and Nature*. The Later Works, vol. 1, 1925, edited by Jo Ann Boydston. Carbondale: Southern Illinois University Press, 1981.

———. *Logic: The Theory of Inquiry*. The Later Works, vol. 12, 1938, edited by Jo Ann Boydston. Carbondale: Southern Illinois University Press, 1991.

———. "The Need for a Recovery of Philosophy." The Middle Works, vol. 10, 1916–1917, edited by Jo Ann Boydston, 3–48. Carbondale: Southern Illinois University Press, 2008.

———. *Psychology*. The Early Works, vol. 2, 1887, edited by Jo Ann Boydston. Carbondale: Southern Illinois University Press, 1967.

———. "The Reflex Arc Concept in Psychology." In Early Works, vol. 5, 1895–1898, edited by Jo Ann Boydston, 96–109. Carbondale: Southern Illinois University Press, 1972.

Dewey, John, and James Hayden Tufts. *Ethics*. Rev. ed. The Later Works, vol. 7, 1932, edited by Jo Ann Boydston. Carbondale: Southern Illinois University Press, 1989.

Du Bois, W. E. B. "The Conservation of the Races." *American Negro Academy Occasional Papers #2*, 1897. In *The Oxford W. E. B. Du Bois Reader*, edited by Eric J. Sundquist, 38–47. Oxford: Oxford University Press, 1996.

———. *Dusk of Dawn: An Essay Toward an Autobiography of a Race Concept*. New Brunswick, N.J.: Transaction Publishers, 2002. First published 1940.

———. "The First Universal Races Congress." *The Independent* 70, August 24, 1911. In *The Oxford W. E. B. Du Bois Reader*, edited by Eric J. Sundquist, 55–59. Oxford: Oxford University Press, 1996.

———. "On *The Souls of Black Folk*." *The Independent*, November 17, 1904. In *The Oxford W. E. B. Du Bois Reader*, edited by Eric J. Sundquist, 304–305. Oxford: Oxford University Press, 1996.

———. *The Philadelphia Negro: A Social Study*. New York: Schocken, 1967. First published 1899.

———. *The Souls of Black Folk*. New York: Penguin Books, 1989. First published 1903.

———. "The Strivings of the Negro People." *Atlantic Monthly* 80 (1897): 194–198.

Good, James A. *A Search for Unity in Diversity: The "Permanent Hegelian Deposit" in the Philosophy of John Dewey*. Lanham, Md.: Lexington Books, 2006.

Gould, Carol C., ed. *Beyond Domination: New Perspectives on Women and Philosophy*. Totowa, N.J.: Rowman and Littlefield, 1983.

Gross, Neil. *Richard Rorty: The Making of an American Philosopher*. Chicago: University of Chicago Press, 2008.

Habermas, Jürgen. *Between Naturalism and Religion: Philosophical Essays*. Translated by Ciaran Cronin. Cambridge: Polity Press, 2008.

———. "Individuation Through Socialization: On George Herbert Mead's Theory of Subjectivity." In *Postmetaphysical Thinking: Philosophical Essays*, translated by William Mark Hohengarten, 149–204. Cambridge, Mass.: MIT Press, 1992.

———. *The Theory of Communicative Action*. Vol. 2, *Lifeworld and System: A Critique of Functionalist Reason*. Translated by Thomas McCarthy. Boston: Beacon Press, 1987.

Hall, David L. *Richard Rorty: Prophet and Poet of the New Pragmatism*. Albany: SUNY Press, 1994.

Hegel, G. W. F. *Hegel's Science of Logic*. Translated by A. V. Miller. London: George Allen and Unwin, 1969.

———. *Phenomenology of Spirit*. Translated by A. V. Miller. Oxford: Oxford University Press, 1977. First published 1807.

———. *Philosophy of Right*. Translated by T. M. Knox. Oxford: Oxford University Press, 1967. First published 1821.

———. *Reason in History: A General Introduction to the Philosophy of History.* Translated and edited by Robert S. Hartman. Upper Saddle River, N.J.: Prentice-Hall, 1997.

Herder, Johann Gottfried von. *Reflections on the Philosophy of the History of Mankind.* Abridged with an introduction by Frank E. Manuel. Chicago: University of Chicago Press, 1968.

Horkheimer, Max, and Theodor W. Adorno. *Dialectic of Enlightenment.* Translated by John Cumming. New York: Herder and Herder, 1972.

Hyppolite, Jean. *Genesis and Structure of Hegel's "Phenomenology of Spirit."* Translated by Samuel Cherniak and John Heckman. Evanston, Ill.: Northwestern University Press, 1974.

James, William. "Does 'Consciousness' Exist?" In *The Writings of William James*, edited by John J. McDermott, 169–183. New York: Random House, 1968. First published 1904.

———. "The Notion of Consciousness." In *The Writings of William James*, edited by John J. McDermott, 184–194. New York: Random House, 1968. First published 1905.

———. *The Principles of Psychology.* Vol. 1. New York: Dover Publications, 1950. First published 1890.

———. *Psychology: The Briefer Course.* Edited by Gordon Allport. New York: Harper and Row, 1961. First published 1892.

Kant, Immanuel. "Idea for a Universal History from a Cosmopolitan Point of View." Translated by Lewis White Beck. In *On History*, edited by Lewis White Beck, 11–26. Indianapolis: Bobbs-Merrill, 1963.

Kestenbaum, Victor. *The Phenomenological Sense of John Dewey: Habit and Meaning.* Atlantic Highlands, N.J.: Humanities Press, 1977.

Lear, Jonathan. *Radical Hope: Ethics in the Face of Cultural Devastation.* Cambridge, Mass.: Harvard University Press, 2006.

Lemke, Sieglinde. "Berlin and Boundaries: *Sollen* Versus *Geschehen.*" *boundary 2* 27, no. 3 (2000): 45–78.

Manuel, Frank E. "Editor's Introduction." In *Reflections on the Philosophy of the History of Mankind*, ix–xxv. Chicago: University of Chicago Press, 1968.

Marcuse, Herbert. *Eros and Civilization: A Philosophical Inquiry into Freud.* 2d ed. Boston: Beacon Press, 1966.

———. *One-Dimensional Man: Studies in the Ideology of Advanced Industrial Society.* 2d ed. Boston: Beacon Press, 1991.

———. *Reason and Revolution: Hegel and the Rise of Social Theory.* 2d ed. Boston: Beacon Press, 1960.

Marx, Karl. "Economic and Philosophical Manuscripts of 1844." In *Karl Marx and Frederick Engels: Collected Works, Marx and Engels 1843–1844*, 229–346. New York: International Publishers, 1976.

Mead, George Herbert. "A Behavioristic Account of the Significant Symbol." In *Selected Writings: George Herbert Mead*, edited by Andrew J. Reck, 240–247. Chicago: University of Chicago Press, 1964. First published 1922.

———. *Mind, Self, and Society: From the Standpoint of a Social Behaviorist*. Edited with an introduction by Charles W. Morris. Chicago: University of Chicago Press, 1974. First published 1934.

———. *Movements of Thought in the Nineteenth Century*. Edited with an introduction by Merritt H. Moore. Chicago: University of Chicago Press, 1972. First published 1936.

———. "National-Mindedness and International-Mindedness." In *Selected Writings: George Herbert Mead*, edited by Andrew J. Reck, 355–370. Chicago: University of Chicago Press, 1964. First published 1929.

———. "Philanthropy from the Point of View of Ethics." In *Selected Writings: George Herbert Mead*, edited by Andrew J. Reck, 392–407. Chicago: University of Chicago Press, 1964. First published 1930.

———. *The Philosophy of the Present*. Edited with an introduction by Arthur E. Murphy. Chicago: University of Chicago Press, 1980. First published 1932.

———. "Scientific Method and the Moral Sciences." In *Selected Writings: George Herbert Mead*, edited by Andrew J. Reck, 248–266. Chicago: University of Chicago Press, 1964. First published 1923.

———. "The Social Self." In *Selected Writings: George Herbert Mead*, edited by Andrew J. Reck, 142–149. Chicago: University of Chicago Press, 1964. First published 1913.

Miller, Jean Baker. *Toward a New Psychology of Women*. 2d ed. Boston: Beacon Press, 1986. First published 1976.

Nietzsche, Friedrich. *Twilight of the Idols*. In *The Portable Nietzsche*, translated by Walter Kaufmann, 463–563. New York: Viking Penguin, 1968.

Nussbaum, Martha. *Upheavals of Thought: The Intelligence of the Emotions*. Cambridge: Cambridge University Press, 2001.

Ostrow, James M. *Social Sensitivity: A Study of Habit and Experience*. Albany: SUNY Press, 1990.

Reed, Adolph L., Jr. *W. E. B. Du Bois and American Political Thought: Fabianism and the Color Line*. Oxford: Oxford University Press, 1997.

Rorty, Richard. *Philosophy and the Mirror of Nature*. Princeton: Princeton University Press, 1979.

Rosenberg, Morris. *Conceiving the Self*. New York: Basic Books, 1979.

Rosenthal, Sandra B., and Patrick L. Bourgeois. *Mead and Merleau-Ponty: Toward a Common Vision*. Albany: SUNY Press, 1991.

Said, Edward. *Representations of the Intellectual*. New York: Pantheon, 1994.

Sartre, Jean-Paul. *Being and Nothingness: An Essay on Phenomenological Ontology.* Translated by Hazel E. Barnes. New York: Philosophical Library, 1956. First published 1943.

———. *Existentialism Is a Humanism.* Translated by Carol Macomber. New Haven, Conn.: Yale University Press, 2007. First published 1946.

———. *The Philosophy of Jean-Paul Sartre.* Edited by Robert Denoon Cummings. New York: Vintage Books, 1965.

———. "Post-Lecture Discussion." In *Existentialism Is a Humanism,* translated by Carol Macomber, 54–72. New Haven, Conn.: Yale University Press, 2007.

———. *Search for a Method.* Translated by Hazel Barnes. New York: Vintage Books, 1968.

———. *The Transcendence of the Ego: An Existentialist Theory of Consciousness.* Translated by Forrest Williams and Robert Kirkpatrick. New York: Noonday Press, 1957. First published 1936–1937.

Sartwell, Crispin. "Rorty: In Memoriam." Society for the Advancement of American Philosophy, Newsbriefs. 2007. *http://american-philosophy.org/communication/SAAPNewsbriefs.htm.*

Smith, Adam. *The Theory of Moral Sentiments.* Edited by D. D. Raphael and A. L. MacFie. Indianapolis: Liberty Classics, 1982.

Sundquist, Eric J., ed. *The Oxford W. E. B. Du Bois Reader.* Oxford: Oxford University Press, 1996.

Taylor, Charles. *Sources of the Self: The Making of Modern Identity.* Cambridge, Mass.: Harvard University Press, 1989.

Zamir, Shamoon. *Dark Voices, W. E. B. Du Bois and American Thought, 1888–1903.* Chicago: University of Chicago Press, 1995.

Index

Adorno, Theodor: *Dialectic of the Enlightenment*, 131
anticipatory experience: Bourdieu on, 65; Dewey on, 29, 36–38, 39, 46, 63–64, 180*n*19; Mead on, 63–64, 65, 122, 145–46, 180*n*19; and reflection, 117–18. *See also* choice
Arendt, Hannah: on communication, 75; on fears of philosophers, 13; on judgment, 72, 170*n*3; on Kant, 72, 75; and Mead, 75
Aristotle: on habit, 53
Asoka, 157*n*4

Batson, C. Daniel, 171*n*19
Beauvoir, Simone de: on freedom, 183*n*14; on gendered relationships, 137, 143, 144; and Hegel, 137, 138, 143, 144, 149, 152; and Miller, 149, 152; *The Second Sex*, 137, 138, 143, 144, 149, 183*n*14
Blumer, Herbert, 112
Boas, Franz, 92
Bourdieu, Pierre: on determinism, 50–52, 54, 61, 62; and Dewey, 49, 166*n*3, 167*n*12, 169*n*46; on dualisms, 49, 51, 64–65, 166*n*3; on fields, 49, 51, 54, 58–59, 60, 61, 62, 67, 115, 166*nn*1,4, 168*n*26, 177*n*3; 179*nn*15,16; on freedom, 49, 50–52, 54, 61, 62–63; on gestures, 54–55, 56; Gross on, 107–8, 110, 114–16, 166*n*5, 177*nn*2,3, 179*n*13; on the habitus, 51, 52–53, 58, 61–63, 65, 110, 135, 166*n*3, 168*nn*28,37, 177*n*3; on the impartial spectator, 169*n*49; on interest/*illusio*, 66–68, 115, 179*n*15; and James, 51–52; "A Lecture on the Lecture," 51; *The Logic of Practice*, 50–51; and Mead, 48, 49–68, 167*n*12, 168*n*26, 186*n*35; and Nietzsche, 53–54, 64–65, 168*n*43, 179*n*13; on novelty, 62–63, 65–66; on practice, 55–56, 64; on reasonableness, 55–56; on reflection, 52–53, 55–56, 57, 64–65; on science, 55, 57, 64; on self-consciousness, 59–60; on significant symbols, 56–57; on strategic considerations, 107–8, 114–16, 179*nn*13,16; on subjectivism vs. mechanism, 50–52, 54, 61; on theories, 166*n*4
Bourgeois, Patrick L.: on Mead, 169*n*46
Buber, Martin, 66, 73

Caspary, William R.: "Dewey and Sartre on Ethical Decisions," 162*n*8
Castle, Henry, 154

choice: and deliberation, 5, 8, 9, 19, 33–35, 43–46, 48, 63–64, 107, 116–18, 163*n*20, 180*n*18; Dewey on, 30, 31–32, 34–35, 42, 43–44, 63–64, 185*n*37; and given circumstances, 2, 5, 8, 32–33, 42, 116–18, 119, 134, 135; Marcuse on determinate choice, 10, 125, 126, 132, 133–35; Rorty on, 13, 21–15, 160*n*11; Sartre on, 13, 21–22, 23, 25, 33–34, 43, 44–48, 162*n*8, 163*nn*19,20, 165*n*42. *See also* anticipatory experience; freedom

Cialdini, Robert B., 171*n*19

Collins, Randall: Gross on, 107–8, 115–16, 177*n*2

compassion. *See* sympathy

consciousness: Hegel on, 144–45, 161*n*6, 182*n*7, 183*nn*15,16,18; James on, 28–29, 52, 120, 161*n*6, 174*n*15; preflective vs. reflective, 3, 29, 33–37, 41–42, 43, 60–61, 64–65, 160*n*9, 163*n*20, 164*nn*23,28, 168*n*31, 169*n*46, 183*n*18; Sartre on, 6–7, 9, 13, 14, 20, 23, 25, 28, 29, 33–34, 35–36, 37, 41–42, 44–45, 61, 161*n*7, 163*n*21, 164*nn*22,28, 168*n*31; spontaneity of, 6–7, 23, 32, 33–34, 35, 41–42, 44, 45, 160*n*9, 163*n*20, 168*n*31. *See also* self-consciousness

Cook, Gary, 57

cosmopolitanism: and cultural pluralism, 2, 3, 4–5, 8, 9; and Du Bois, 9, 89, 90, 95; in "The Edicts of Asoka," 157*n*4; and Mead, 2–3, 9, 50, 68, 72, 74–75, 76, 83, 85, 86–88, 96, 154, 158*n*12; and moral obligation, 71–72, 76–79; relationship to cultural self-determination, 2, 3–4, 4–5, 8–9; relationship to individual self-determination, 2, 3–4, 5–6, 8–9; and respect for other cultures/peoples, 2, 8, 73, 90–91, 157*n*4, 159*nn*17,18; and sympathy, 71–72, 83, 86–87, 95, 154; and undeserved suffering, 72, 86–87, 170*n*1

creativity, 139, 180*n*19; Bourdieu on, 62; Dewey on, 1; relationship to self-concepts, 114, 116–18, 119; Rorty on the strong poet and, 17, 160*n*5. *See also* Mead, George Herbert, on novelty

cultural/national self-determination, 3–6, 8, 72, 88, 157*n*3, 158*n*5; Herder on self-determination of peoples, 1, 2, 4–5, 6, 96–97, 100, 157*n*1, 158*n*11; vs. individual self-determination, 3–4, 5–6, 9, 158*n*11; relationship to expression of cultures, 3–5, 6

cultural pluralism, 2, 3, 4–5, 8, 9, 158*n*5

Cumings, Robert Denoon, 164*n*22

Daniels, Robert, 27

Darwin, Charles: *The Descent of Man*, 71; and Dewey, 25, 138, 161*n*7; and Mead, 25, 138, 144, 152; on sympathy, 71

deliberation, 29, 55; and choice, 5, 8, 9, 19, 33–35, 43–46, 48, 63–64, 107, 116–18, 163*n*20, 180*n*18; Dewey on, 43–44, 45, 164*n*23; relationship to self-concepts, 116–18; Sartre on, 44–46. *See also* anticipatory experience; reflection

determinate choice, 10, 125, 132, 133–35

determinate negation, 125, 126, 132–35

determinism: Bourdieu on, 50–52, 54, 61, 62; Dewey on, 38, 40–41; of Freud, 126, 139; and Gross, 107, 115, 116; James on, 51–52; and Libet experiments, 180*n*18; Marcuse on, 124, 134–35; Rorty on physicalism, 22, 23–25; Sartre on, 14, 22, 38, 39, 40; sociological determinism, 9–10

Detmer, David: *Freedom as a Value*, 32; on ontological vs. practical freedom, 32–33; on Sartre, 31, 32–33, 43; on subjectivity of values, 43

Dewey, John: on action, 30, 39–43, 165*n*44; on anticipatory experience, 29, 36–38, 39, 46, 63–64, 180*n*19;

and Bourdieu, 49, 166*n*3, 167*n*12, 169*n*46; on choice, 30, 31–32, 34–35, 42, 43–44, 63–64, 185*n*37; on communication, 30; and Darwin, 25, 138, 161*n*7; on deliberation, 43–44, 45, 164*n*23; on determinism, 38, 40–41; on dramatic rehearsal, 162*n*8; *Ethics*, 30, 34–35, 40, 42–43, 44, 164*n*23, 172*n*21; on existentialism, 27, 28; *Experience and Nature*, 25; on freedom, 33, 34–35, 37–39, 40–41, 42–43; on habit, 37, 38, 41, 42, 43–44, 165*n*47; on Hegel, 28, 31–32, 34, 161*nn*2,6, 164*n*28; on impartiality, 172*nn*21,29; on intelligence, 1, 36–37, 38; and James, 18, 23, 25, 28–29, 51–52; *Logic: The Theory of Inquiry*, 36, 37; and Mead, 18, 23, 49–50, 63–64, 154, 172*nn*26,29; on mediation, 29, 31–32, 34; "The Need for a Recovery of Philosophy," 1, 36, 38; on past-future relationship, 33, 36–39, 41, 42–43; on popular and high culture, 167*n*12; on pragmatic intelligence, 1; on preferences, 43–44, 185*n*37; *Psychology*, 29; on reflection, 32, 34–35, 37, 164*n*23, 180*n*19; "The Reflex Arc in Psychology," 37; on responsibility, 30, 46, 47–48; Rorty on, 16, 25, 110; and Sartre, 9, 26, 27–48, 154, 161*n*7, 162*nn*8,15; on science, 39, 165*n*44; on the self, 29, 34, 40–41, 42–43, 47, 100, 138, 161*nn*6,7, 162*n*8; on self-consciousness, 161*n*7; on sympathy, 172*n*21; on systems, 58–59, 168*n*26; on values, 43, 44, 165*n*47

Dilthey, Wilhelm, 57, 175*n*16

Du Bois, W. E. B.: on asymmetrical relationships, 99–100; "Conservation of the Races," 175*n*18; and cosmopolitanism, 9, 89, 90, 95; on culture, 9, 90–91, 92, 101; on double-consciousness, 9, 90, 92, 93, 97–99, 100, 147, 176*n*26; *Dusk of Dawn*, 101; on economic exploitation, 101; experience as African American, 89–90, 91, 100, 174*n*6; "The First Universal Races Congress," 175*n*18; and Hegel, 9, 92, 97–98, 100, 101, 176*n*47; and Herder, 96–97, 100, 101, 175*nn*16,20, 176*n*27; on humanity, 96–97; on impartiality, 92, 95, 97, 99; and James, 90, 92, 93, 95–96, 97, 98, 100, 175*n*16, 176*n*24; and Marxism, 90, 101; and Mead, 88, 99, 100, 101; on mutuality, 98, 99, 100; *The Philadelphia Negro*, 89; on race, 9, 89–90, 92, 96–97, 99–100, 101, 175*nn*18,20; on reason, 91–92, 97; on recognition, 90, 93, 100; and Santayana, 98; *The Souls of Black Folk*, 89–92, 95, 97–101, 173*n*2, 175*n*18; "The Strivings of the Negro People," 176*n*26; on sympathy, 89, 90, 91–92, 95–96, 99–100

emotions: biological/physiological dimension of, 136, 138, 151–52, 153, 181*n*1

empathy: Mead on role-taking, 9, 50, 54, 56–59, 72–74, 75–76, 78–80, 81, 82, 84–85, 86, 87, 99, 145–46, 169*n*49, 170*nn*4,7, 171*n*20; Nussbaum on, 170*n*4; vs. sympathy, 75–76, 78, 83, 95, 170*n*4, 172*n*21

Enlightenment, the, 80, 87

Epictetus, 137

Erikson, Erik: on individual identity, 112–13

Eros: Freud on, 125, 127–28; Marcuse on, 124–35, 151–52

evolution, biological, 25, 63, 86

existentialism, 3, 4; authenticity in, 65; Dewey on, 27, 28; and Marcuse, 124, 125, 126, 135; vs. pragmatism, 9; Rorty on, 18, 20–21, 25–26, 119, 154. *See also* Heidegger, Martin; Kierkegaard, Søren; Sartre, Jean-Paul expression: of essential natures, 4–5; relationship to cultural/national self-determination, 3–5, 6; relationship to individual self-determination, 3–4, 6

freedom: Bourdieu on, 49, 50–52, 54, 61, 62–63; Dewey on, 33, 34–35, 37–39, 40–41, 42–43; Habermas on, 117, 180nn17,18; James on, 51–52; practical vs. ontological, 30–35, 45–48, 163n20; Rorty on, 21–25, 160n11, 161n13; Sartre on, 6–7, 9, 14, 20, 21–22, 23, 25, 27, 31, 32, 35–36, 37–39, 40, 44, 45–46, 48, 107, 118, 122, 163nn19,20. *See also* choice; spontaneity

Freud, Sigmund: *Civilization and Its Discontents*, 83; determinism of, 126, 139; on Eros, 125, 127–28; and Marcuse, 124, 126, 127–28; Miller on, 148; Rorty on, 160n6; on Thanatos, 83

Gadamer, Hans-Georg, 14, 18, 20; relationship with Rorty, 15, 16; *Truth and Method*, 15

gendered relationships, 9; Beauvoir on, 137, 143, 144; and Hegel's master-slave dialectic, 136–39, 142–44, 147–50, 181n3; inequities related to, 10, 185n27; Miller on, 137–39, 148–51

generalized other. *See* Mead, George Herbert

given circumstances, 3, 13–14, 39, 66, 124; and freedom of choice, 2, 5, 6–7, 8, 32–33, 42, 116–18, 119, 134, 135

globalization, 2, 88

Good, James A., 29

Gross, Neil: and American academic philosophers, 106, 108–10, 177n4, 178n5, 179n11; on Bourdieu, 107–8, 110, 114–16, 166n5, 177nn2,3, 179n13; on Collins, 107–8, 115–16, 177n2; definition of a philosopher, 109, 110; on drive to achieve moral superiority, 115, 179n14; on Erikson, 112–13; and James, 110; and Mead, 110–11, 119–23; on predictability, 115–18, 120–23; on processual symbolic interactionism, 112, 120, 178n10; on public vs. academic intellectuals, 109–10; and Rorty, 9–10, 105, 106–7, 108, 110, 114, 118–19, 121–23, 159n4, 177n4, 179n13; on self-concepts, 106, 107, 108–9, 110–18, 120, 121–23, 149, 177n4, 178n8,10, 180n20; on sociology of ideas, 9–10, 105–6, 107–14, 124, 166n5; on strategic considerations, 107–9, 114–16, 122, 177n4, 179n13; on structural interactionism, 112

Habermas, Jürgen: on communication, 58, 80, 184n20; on freedom, 117, 180nn17,18; on impartiality, 53; and Mead, 53, 80, 184n20; on philosophies of consciousness, 13; on philosophies of language, 13; on reflection, 117; relationship with Rorty, 16; *The Theory of Communicative Action*, 184n20; on universal pragmatics, 21

habit, 8, 35; Aristotle on, 53; Dewey on, 37, 38, 41, 42, 43–44, 165n47; James on, 52; Mead on, 52, 65, 79

Hall, David L.: *Richard Rorty*, 177n1

Hartshorne, Charles, 106

Hegel, G. W. F.: and Beauvoir, 137, 138, 143, 144, 149, 152; on biological life, 142, 143, 146, 147, 148, 149, 151, 152–53, 154; on conflict and contradictions, 151; on consciousness, 144–45, 161n6, 182n7, 183nn15,16,18; and "cultural transcendence," 136; Dewey on, 28, 31–32, 34, 161nn2,6, 164n28; dialectic of limit, 10, 125–26, 129–30, 132–33; and Du Bois, 9, 92, 97–98, 100, 101, 176n47; on the family, 153; and gender, 136–39, 140, 142–44, 147–51, 152–53, 181n3; and Herder, 6; on language, 145, 183nn14,16; *Lectures on the Philosophy of History*, 176n24; and Marcuse, 124, 125–26, 129–30, 132–33, 134, 135, 136; master-slave dialectic, 5, 10, 98, 100, 135–38, 139–44, 146, 147–51, 175n24, 181n3, 185n25; and Mead, 5–6, 10, 25, 76, 122, 123, 135, 136, 139, 144–46, 152–53, 154, 184n20; on mediation, 31–32, 34, 41, 139, 141, 143, 181n4, 183n18; and Miller, 135, 137–39, 144, 146, 147–54; on natural objects, 141, 182nn7–9; *Phenomenology of Spirit*, 5, 16, 97–98, 136–38, 139–45, 181n2, 182n7, 183n18; *Philosophy of Right*, 142–43, 153; on recognition, 5, 10, 90, 98, 100, 136, 141, 143–44, 146, 150, 176n24, 182nn9,11, 184nn19,20; and Rorty, 16; and Sartre, 136, 164n28; *Science of Logic*, 129; on self-consciousness, 90, 97–99, 136, 137, 139–46, 148, 153, 176nn24,26, 181nn2,4, 182nn6,8,10,11, 183n12, 184n20; on sense knowledge, 145; and Smith, 176n24; on Stoicism, 137; on Understanding vs. Reason, 185n27

Heidegger, Martin, 14, 17, 18, 20, 49, 65, 119

Herder, Gottfried von: on cultural and racial differences, 90; and Du Bois, 96–97, 100, 101, 175nn16,20, 176n27; and Hegel, 6; on humanity (*Menschheit/Humanität*), 97, 100; and Mead, 73, 171n9; on race vs. *Volk*, 175n16; *Reflections on the Philosophy of the History of Mankind*, 96–97, 175n16; on self-determination of peoples, 1, 2, 4–5, 6, 96–97, 100, 157n1, 158n11; and Taylor, 4–5

Horkheimer, Max: *Dialectic of the Enlightenment*, 131

Horney, Karen, 184n21

Hussein, Saddam: American beliefs regarding, 86

Husserl, Edmund, 57, 65

Hyppolite, Jean: on Hegel, 183n12

"I," the. *See* Mead, George Herbert
impartiality: Du Bois on, 92, 95, 97, 99; James on, 90, 92, 94, 97, 98, 99; Mead on, 66, 79–81, 99, 154, 169n49, 172n29; Smith on, 53, 95, 169n49

Indian Ocean tsunami, 81–82, 173n32
instinct, 9, 10, 123, 136, 138; vs. impulse, 173n33, 185nn28,30; Marcuse on, 10, 124–35, 139, 151–52, 153; Miller on, 138, 151–52, 153, 185n28. *See also* Mead, George Herbert, on biological impulses

James, William: and Bourdieu, 51–52; on consciousness, 28–29, 52, 120, 161n6, 174n15; and Dewey, 18, 23, 25, 28–29, 51–52; and Du Bois, 90, 92, 93, 95–96, 97, 98, 100, 175n16, 176n24; on freedom vs. determinism, 51–52; on God, 94; on habit, 52; on the impartial spectator, 90, 92, 94, 97, 98, 99; on the material, social, and spiritual selves, 92–96, 174nn12,14,15; and Mead, 18, 23, 25, 29, 51–52, 67, 68, 120, 174n13; *Principles of Psychology*, 23, 28–29, 92–96; on property and labor, 93; on pure ego, 92; on recognition, 94–95, 174n13; on reflection, 174n15; and Sartre, 28–29, 39; and Smith, 92, 95; on stream of consciousness, 52, 120, 174n15; on sympathy, 90, 92, 95–96, 97; on transcendental ego, 29, 161nn6,7, 174n14

Judaism, 66

Kant, Immanuel: Arendt on, 72, 75; on autonomy, 180n17; *Critique of Judgement*, 72; on enlarged mentality, 68, 72; on feelings and morality, 82; Rorty on, 26, 119, 122; on transcendental self, 26, 119; on war, 83

Kierkegaard, Søren, 17, 23, 119, 158*n*10, 159*n*15; *Either/Or*, 75
Kohut, Heinz, 184*n*21
Kuhn, Thomas: on normal vs. revolutionary science, 17, 119, 122

language: Hegel on, 145, 183*nn*14,16; Mead on, 6, 50, 54, 56–57, 64, 72, 73, 83, 86, 120, 145, 154, 171*n*20, 183*n*17; Nietzsche on, 16–17; Rorty on, 9, 13, 16, 20–21, 24–25, 119, 122
League of Nations, 85
Lear, Jonathan: on Crow culture, 7–8, 158*n*14, 159*n*15; on cultural ideals, 7–8, 19*n*15, 158*n*14; *Radical Hope*, 7–8, 158*n*14, 159*n*15; on socialization, 7–8, 158*n*14, 159*n*15
Leibniz, Gottfried Wilhelm, 42
Lemke, Siegland, 96
Levinas, Emmanuel, 82
Libet, Benjamin, 180*n*18
Locke, John: on labor and property, 93

Manuel, Frank E., 97, 157*n*1, 158*n*11, 175*n*20
Marcus Aurelius, 137
Marcuse, Herbert: on alienation, 131–32; on death instinct, 125, 128, 180*n*1; on determinate choice, 10, 125, 126, 132, 133–35; on determinate negation, 125, 126, 132–35; on determinism, 124, 134–35; dialectical method of, 124, 125, 126, 129–35; on Eros, 124–35, 151–52, 180*n*1; *Eros and Civilization*, 125, 126–28, 130, 135; and existentialism, 124, 125, 126, 135; and Freud, 124, 126, 127–28; and Hegel, 124, 125–26, 129–30, 132–33, 134, 135, 136; on history, 133–34; on the instinctual, 10, 124–35, 139, 151–52, 153; and Marxism, 125, 134, 135; on maternal libidinal morality, 180*n*1; and Miller, 151–52; *One-Dimensional Man*, 124, 126, 133–35; on the performance principle, 113; on pleasure vs. satisfaction of want, 130–32; on potentialities and talifications, 129–30; on the project, 125, 126, 133–35; *Reason and Revolution*, 125–26, 129–30; on the status quo, 124; on the superego, 128
Marx, Karl: on alienation, 131; on history, 134; *Manuscripts of 1844*, 131; Rorty on, 160*n*6
Marxism, 30, 31; and Du Bois, 90, 101; and Marcuse, 125, 134, 135
McKeon, Richard, 106
"me," the. *See* Mead, George Herbert
Mead, George Herbert, 18, 23, 25, 107, 180*n*20; on abstract groups, 68, 169*n*51; on anticipatory experience, 63–64, 65, 122, 145–46, 180*n*19; and Arendt, 75; on biological impulses, 10, 53, 63, 76, 79, 83–84, 86, 138, 146, 152–54, 173*n*33, 185*nn*28,30, 186*n*35; on bodily dispositions, 51, 53; and Bourdieu, 48, 49–68, 167*n*12, 168*n*26, 186*n*35; and Christianity, 53, 66, 68, 169*n*48; and cosmopolitanism, 2–3, 9, 50, 68, 72, 74–75, 83, 85, 86–88, 96, 154, 158*n*12; and Darwin, 25, 138, 144, 152; on democracy, 53; and Dewey, 18, 23, 49–50, 63–64, 154, 172*nn*26,29; on dualisms, 49, 51; and Du Bois, 88, 99, 100, 101; on feelings, 153–54; on generalized others, 9, 50, 58–60, 79–81, 82, 86, 111, 145, 146, 170*n*4, 174*n*13, 183*n*17; on gestures, 54–55, 56–57, 59, 136, 167*n*19; and Gross, 110–11, 119–23; and Habermas, 53, 80, 184*n*20; on habit, 52, 65, 79; and Hegel, 5–6, 10, 25, 76, 122, 123, 135, 136, 139, 144–46, 152–53, 154, 184*n*20; and Herder, 73, 171*n*9; on the "I," 50, 54, 60–61, 66, 112, 119–20, 167*n*24; on impartiality, 66, 79–81, 99, 154, 169*n*49, 172*n*29; on individual interests vs. interests of others, 67, 68; on individuality and change, 66;

and James, 18, 23, 25, 29, 51–52, 67, 68, 120, 174*n*13; on language, 6, 50, 54, 56–57, 64, 72, 73, 83, 86, 120, 145, 154, 171*n*20, 183*n*17; on the "me," 50, 52, 54, 58–61, 110–11, 112, 119–20, 121, 167*n*24, 179*n*10; and Miller, 138, 146, 152, 153; on modernity, 75, 81, 83, 85, 169*n*51, 171*n*13, 172*n*28; on moral obligation, 72, 76–81, 152, 154; *Movements of Thought in the Nineteenth Century*, 73–74, 170*n*5; on mutuality, 53, 54, 66, 68; on nationalism, 84–88; on novelty, 2–3, 9, 25, 50, 54, 60, 61, 63, 65–66, 73, 76, 112, 119–21, 122–23, 160*n*8, 168*n*34; *Philosophy of the Present*, 160*n*8, 168*nn*34,40; as political progressive, 72; on reciprocity, 54, 58, 72, 86, 146, 184*n*19; on recognition, 146, 184*nn*19,20; on reflection, 52–53, 55, 56–57, 60, 63–64, 65, 77, 121–22, 123, 139, 144, 169*n*46, 180*n*19; on reflexivity, 56–57, 61, 72, 74, 81, 121; on rights, 77, 80, 172*n*23; on role-taking/perspective-taking, 9, 50, 54, 56–59, 72–74, 75–76, 78–80, 81, 82, 84–85, 86, 87, 99, 145–46, 169*n*49, 170*nn*4,7, 171*n*20; and romanticism, 73–74, 80, 87, 170*n*8, 171*nn*9,13; and Rorty, 23, 161*n*12; and Sartre, 61; on science, 53, 121, 154, 171*n*13; on the self, 2–3, 5–6, 9, 10, 29, 50, 52, 53, 54–56, 58–61, 66, 67, 68, 72, 73–75, 83, 86, 99, 100, 110–11, 112, 119–20, 121, 122, 123, 136, 139, 144–46, 154, 167*nn*13,24, 170*n*7, 171*nn*10,13, 179*n*10, 184*n*19; on self-consciousness, 54–56, 59–61, 72, 144–46, 152, 167*n*13, 183*n*17; on selfishness, 74–75; on significant symbols, 2, 56, 80, 120, 136, 167*n*19, 183*n*17; and Smith, 76; on sociality, 3, 9, 50, 63–64, 68, 121, 158*n*.7; "The Social Self," 29; on social unity, 84, 86, 87–88; on subject and object, 51; on sympathy, 66–67, 68, 75–83, 85–87, 152; on universality, 80, 81, 82, 172*nn*23,30; on war, 72, 83–87, 152; on women's roles, 150

Merleau-Ponty, Maurice, 49, 65, 169*n*46

Miller, Jean Baker: and Beauvoir, 149, 152; on conflict in gendered relationships, 150–51; on dominant vs. subordinate groups, 147; on emotion, 138, 151–52, 153; on feelings of weakness/vulnerability in men vs. women, 148–50, 184*n*23; on Freud, 148; on gendered relationships, 137–39, 148–51; and Hegel, 135, 137–39, 144, 146, 147–54; on instinct, 138, 151–52, 153, 185*n*28; and Marcuse, 151–52; and Mead, 138, 146, 152, 153; and Sartre, 138; *Toward a New Psychology of Women*, 137–38, 147, 184*n*21; on women's movement, 148, 184*n*22; on women's needs, 150–51

modernity: Mead on, 75, 81, 83, 85, 169*n*51, 171*n*13, 172*n*28; self-determination in, 1–2

moral obligation: and cosmopolitanism, 71–72, 76–79; Mead on, 72, 76–81, 152, 154; relationship to sympathy, 76–83, 87

nationalism, 72, 83, 84–88

Nazi Germany, 157*n*3

negation, 35, 37, 164*n*28, 176*n*24, 182*n*10; and Eros, 125, 126, 129, 130–35; and Hegel's dialectic of limit, 125–26, 129–30, 132–33; and self-consciousness, 136, 140–42, 146, 181*n*4, 182*n*5

Nehamas, Alexander, 179*n*13

Nietzsche, Friedrich, 66, 110, 119; and Bourdieu, 53–54, 64–65, 168*n*43, 179*n*13; on human condition, 114; on language and self-definition, 16–17; and Rorty, 16–17; on Socrates, 168*n*43

Nussbaum, Martha: on empathy, 170*n*4

Obama, Barack, 10

Peirce, Charles Sanders, 18, 25
Pietism, 1, 157*n*1
Plato, 37
Platonism, 21, 22, 166*n*3
pragmatism, 3, 5, 6, 50, 172*n*26; vs. existentialism, 9; and novelty, 18, 25. *See also* Dewey, John; James, William; Mead, George Herbert; Peirce, Charles Sanders; Rorty, Richard
Putnam, Hilary: relationship with Rorty, 16
Pythagoreans, 159*n*17

reciprocity, 58, 90, 97, 100, 125, 126, 128, 150; Mead on, 54, 58, 72, 86, 146, 184*n*19
recognition: Du Bois on, 90, 93, 100; Hegel on, 5, 10, 90, 98, 100, 136, 141, 143–44, 146, 150, 176*n*24, 182*nn*9,11, 184*nn*19,20; James on, 94–95, 174*n*13; Mead on, 146, 184*nn*19,20
Reed, Adolph L., Jr., 90
reflection: Bourdieu on, 52–53, 55–56, 57, 64–65; Dewey on, 32, 34–35, 37, 164*n*23, 180*n*19; Habermas on, 117; James on, 174*n*15; Mead on, 52–53, 55, 56–57, 60, 63–64, 65, 77, 121–22, 123, 139, 144, 169*n*46, 180*n*19; Sartre on, 33–34, 37, 44–46, 160*n*9, 163*nn*20,21, 168*n*31. *See also* anticipatory experience; deliberation; reflexivity; self-consciousness
reflexivity, 117, 131–32, 133, 171*n*13; Mead on, 56–57, 61, 72, 74, 81, 121. *See also* reflection; self-consciousness
respect for other cultures/peoples, 2, 8, 73, 90–91, 157*n*4, 159*nn*17,18
responsibility: Dewey on, 30, 46, 47–48; Rorty on, 19, 22–23; Sartre on, 19, 22–23, 46–48
romanticism, 73–74, 80, 87, 170*n*8, 171*nn*9,13

Rorty, Richard: on abnormal vs. normal philosophy, 14, 17–19, 20–22, 23, 26; and analytic philosophy, 106, 159*n*4, 160*n*5; on choice, 13, 21–15, 160*n*11; on Dewey, 16, 25, 110; on edifying vs. systematic philosophy, 14, 17–18, 19, 23, 118–19, 160*n*6; on existentialism, 18, 20–21, 25–26, 119, 154; on freedom, 21–25, 160*n*11, 161*n*13; and Gross, 9–10, 105, 106–7, 108, 110, 114, 118–19, 121–23, 159*n*4, 177*n*4, 179*n*13; and Hegel, 16; as historian of philosophy, 106, 159*n*4, 160*n*5; on Kant, 26, 119, 122; and Kuhn, 119; on language, 9, 13, 16, 20–21, 24–25, 119, 122; on Marx, 160*n*6; and Mead, 23, 161*n*12; on the Mirror of Nature, 13; and Nietzsche, 16–17; *Philosophy and the Mirror of Nature*, 13, 14–15, 17–26, 118–19; on philosophy as conversation, 14, 15–16, 19, 20–21, 105; on philosophy as inquiry, 19; on physicalism, 22, 23–25; and pragmatism, 18, 23, 25, 106; relationship with other philosophers, 15–16; on responsibility and discourse, 19; on responsibility and objective knowledge, 22–23; and Sartre, 9, 13–26, 118–19, 160*nn*6,11; Sartwell on, 15, 159*n*2; on self-transformation through redescription, 16; on the strong poet, 17, 160*n*5; on truth, 20–21, 22; on types of discourse, 14, 16, 17–18
Rosenberg, Morris: on self-concept, 110
Rosenthal, Sandra B.: on Mead, 169*n*46
Rousseau, Jean-Jacques, 97

Said, Edward: *Representation of the Intellectual*, 109
Santayana, George, 98
Sartre, Jean-Paul: on action, 39–43; on behaviorism, 39–40; *Being and Nothingness*, 20, 23, 28, 29, 30, 32, 33,

34, 36, 38, 39–40, 41–42, 44–45, 47, 48, 61, 158*n*13, 162*n*15, 163*n*20; on choice, 13, 21–22, 23, 25, 33–34, 43, 44–48, 162*n*8, 163*nn*19,20, 165*n*42; on circumscription of the self by the other, 14, 15–16; on commitment to engagement, 30–31, 46–47; on consciousness, 6–7, 9, 13, 14, 20, 23, 25, 28, 29, 33–34, 35–36, 37, 41–42, 44–45, 61, 161*n*7, 163*n*21, 164*nn*22,28, 168*n*31; on deliberation, 44–46; on determinism, 14, 22, 38, 39, 40; and Dewey, 9, 26, 27–48, 154, 161*n*7, 162*nn*8,15; on the *en-soi* (in-itself), 6, 14, 15, 18–21, 23, 25, 26, 35, 38, 41–42, 119, 159*n*3; on existence preceding essence, 14, 20, 21, 30–31, 42, 160*n*11; "Existentialism Is a Humanism," 21, 29–31, 33, 42, 44, 46–48, 160*n*10, 163*nn*15,20; on existential psychoanalysis, 165*n*56; on freedom, 6–7, 9, 14, 20, 21–22, 23, 25, 27, 31, 32, 35–36, 37–39, 40, 44, 45–46, 48, 107, 118, 122, 163*nn*19,20; on God, 13, 21, 22, 45, 160*n*10; and Hegel, 136, 164*n*28; and James, 28–29, 39; and Mead, 61; and Miller, 138; on morality, 31; on past-future relationship, 33, 35–39, 42, 44, 45–46, 47–48; on popularization, 30–31; on the *pour-soi* (for-itself), 6–7, 14, 15, 18–21, 23, 25, 26, 35–36, 37, 42, 45, 119, 158*n*13, 160*n*9, 162*n*15, 163*n*21; on practical vs. ontological freedom, 32–33, 34, 37–38, 48; on projects, 6–7, 10, 14, 22–23, 32, 37–39, 42, 44–46, 47, 50, 118, 163*n*19, 165*n*42, 168*n*31; on questioning, 38; on reflection, 33–34, 37, 44–46, 160*n*9, 163*nn*20,21, 168*n*31; on responsibility, 19, 22–23, 46–48; and Rorty, 9, 13–26, 118–19, 160*nn*6,11; on the self, 29, 39–43, 158*n*13, 168*n*31; *The Transcendence of the Ego*, 6–7, 28, 29, 30, 33, 34, 158*n*13; on values, 19–20,

43, 45; on the will, 7, 33–34, 43, 45, 163*n*20, 164*n*22

Sartwell, Crispin: on Rorty, 15, 159*n*2

science: Bourdieu on, 55, 57, 64; Dewey on, 39, 165*n*44; Kuhn on, 17, 119, 122; Mead on, 53, 121, 154, 171*n*13

Scottish philosophy: impartiality in, 90, 95, 159*n*49; influence on Hegel, 176*n*24; influence on James, 23, 90, 92, 94, 95, 176*n*24; influence on Mead, 9, 53, 76, 153, 176*n*24; theories of sentiment in, 3, 53, 76, 90, 92, 153, 176*n*24

self. *See* Dewey, John; Gross on self-concepts; James on material, social, and spiritual selves; Mead, George Herbert; Sartre, Jean-Paul; self-consciousness

self-consciousness: Bourdieu on, 59–60; Du Bois on double-consciousness, 9, 90, 92, 93, 97–99, 100, 147, 176*n*26; Hegel on, 90, 97–99, 136, 137, 139–46, 148, 153, 176*nn*24,26, 181*nn*2,4, 182*nn*6,8,10,11, 183*n*12, 184*n*20; Mead on, 59–61, 72, 144–46, 152, 167*n*13, 183*n*17; and negation, 136, 140–42, 146, 181*n*4, 182*n*5

self-determination. *See* anticipatory experience; choice; cultural/national self-determination; deliberation; freedom; reflection; self-consciousness

Smith, Adam: and Hegel, 176*n*24; on imagination and distress, 78; on the impartial spectator, 53, 95, 169*n*49; and Mead, 76; on moral sentiments, 76, 92, 169*n*49; social interactionism of, 176*n*24

Smith, Christian, 179*n*14

sociology of ideas: and academic success, 105–6, 107–8, 110; Gross on, 9–10, 105–6, 107–14, 124, 166*n*5

Socrates, 168*n*43

Sophists, 159*n*17

Spinoza, Benedict de, 24; on *conatus*, 62

spontaneity, 29, 118; of consciousness, 6–7, 23, 32, 33–34, 35, 41–42, 44, 45, 160*n*9, 163*n*20, 168*n*31; Mead on, 60, 61, 120–21, 122. *See also* freedom; Mead, George Herbert, on novelty
Stoics, 67, 137, 158*n*4, 159*n*17, 169*n*49, 185*n*25
structuralism, 50
Sullivan, Harry S., 184*n*21
sympathy: as compassion, 75–76, 171*n*20; and cosmopolitanism, 71–72, 83, 86–87, 95, 154; Darwin on, 71; Du Bois on, 89, 90, 91–92, 95–96, 99–100; vs. empathy, 75–76, 78, 83, 95, 170*n*4, 172*n*21; and Indian Ocean tsunami, 81–82, 173*n*32; James on, 90, 92, 95–96, 97; Mead on, 66–67, 68, 75–83, 85–87, 152; relationship to moral obligation, 76–83, 87; sources of, 78, 171*n*19

Taylor, Charles: on expression and self-determination, 3–4; on Hegel as expressivist, 5; and Herder, 4–5
Thanatos, 83, 125, 128, 181*n*3
Tufts, James, 30

values: Dewey on, 43, 44, 165*n*47; vs. facts, 19–20; freedom as a value, 31, 32; Sartre on, 19–20, 43, 45

Weber, Max: on rationalization, 8; on traditional cultures, 8
Wittgenstein, Ludwig, 17, 49, 118, 119
Wundt, Wilhelm, 54

Yudhoyono, Susilo Bambang, 173*n*32

Zamir, Shamoon: *Dark Voices*, 92, 97–98, 174*n*12

The authorized representative in the EU for product safety and compliance is:
Mare Nostrum Group
B.V Doelen 72
4831 GR Breda
The Netherlands

www.ingramcontent.com/pod-product-compliance
Lightning Source LLC
Chambersburg PA
CBHW021726220426
43662CB00008B/726